TRANSCENDING
THE LEVELS OF
CONSCIOUSNESS

ALSO BY DAVID R. HAWKINS, M.D., PH.D.

Dissolving the Ego, Realizing the Self

Along the Path to Enlightenment

Letting Go

Healing and Recovery

Reality, Spirituality, and Modern Man

Discovery of the Presence of God: Devotional Nonduality

Truth vs. Falsehood: How to Tell the Difference

I: Reality and Subjectivity

The Eye of the I: From Which Nothing Is Hidden

Power vs. Force:
The Hidden Determinants of Human Behavior

Dialogues on Consciousness and Spirituality

Qualitative and Quantitative Analysis and Calibration
of the Levels of Human Consciousness

Orthomolecular Psychiatry (with Linus Pauling)

Please visit:

Hay House USA: www.hayhouse.com®
Hay House Australia: www.hayhouse.com.au
Hay House UK: www.hayhouse.co.uk
Hay House India: www.hayhouse.co.in

TRANSCENDING
THE LEVELS OF
CONSCIOUSNESS

THE
STAIRWAY TO
ENLIGHTENMENT

David R. Hawkins, M.D., Ph.D.

HAY HOUSE, INC.
Carlsbad, California • New York City
London • Sydney • New Delhi

Previously published by Veritas Publishing (ISBN 978-097150075-4)

Grateful acknowledgment is made for permission to reprint the following previously published material:

"Moral Relativism," an article that originally appeared in the Philadelphia Trumpet, June, 2005 Copyright © 2005. Used by permission.
Library of Congress Control Number: 2013947044

Tradepaper ISBN: 978-1-4019-4505-3

24 23 22 21 20 19 18 17 16 15
1st Hay House edition, March 2015

Printed in the United States of America

SUSTAINABLE FORESTRY INITIATIVE

Certified Chain of Custody
Promoting Sustainable Forestry

www.sfiprogram.org
SFI-01268

SFI label applies to the text stock

Straight and narrow is the path ...
Waste no time.
Gloria in Excelsis Deo!

DEDICATION

This work is dedicated to
the liberation of the human spirit
from the bondage of adversity
and limitation that besets mankind
from both within and without.

TABLE OF CONTENTS

TABLES AND CHARTS

FOREWORD

The purpose of prior works was to explore and explain a new research technique based on consciousness and its application to all areas of life, including subjective spiritual experiences and realizations. The development of a pragmatic clinical science of truth emerged that could be used as a compass to guide man's endless quest for truth. As described in previous studies, by virtue of its very structure, the human mind is incapable of discerning truth from falsehood, a fact of which mankind is painfully aware. The price of this ignorance and limitation has been enormous. Not only individuals but also whole civilizations have gone through staggering amounts of agony, suffering, and death.

The levels of consciousness will be examined specifically for the sake of the spiritual student, devotee, and integrous person interested in self-improvement for its own sake. By analyzing the various obstacles and levels to be transcended, certain principles that support spiritual evolution are self-revealing.

This work is therefore a practical manual rather than a comprehensive analysis, which has been presented in prior books (e.g., Section 1 of *Truth vs. Falsehood*, 2005). Although it alludes to prior work, the basic principles will again be covered. Material is also provided for the frustrated seeker who has 'read everything, been everywhere', attended all kinds of workshops, and yet seems to be 'stuck'. ("My mind is like a sponge: It has absorbed all the information, but I'm still in the same place!")

Because the lower levels of consciousness are the most painful and difficult to endure, it seemed best to start up the ladder of consciousness from the very bottom levels, which are the most agonizing. Just because they are the most painful does not mean they are the most difficult to transcend. On the contrary, the very pain of such lower levels urges one forward to seek relief.

In transcending the levels of consciousness, the importance of the human 'will' is emphasized because it is the most critical of all functions in spiritual work. Relatively little attention has been paid to the will in proportion to its extreme importance, for the will is the invitation to Divine intervention.

PREFACE

The basic research on the nature and levels of consciousness has been described in previous works. The first was published in the form of a dissertation (*Qualitative and Quantitative Analysis and Calibration of the Levels of Human Consciousness*, 1995.) Next came *Power vs. Force* (also 1995), which included explanations and elaborations. The following two books were devoted to spiritual truth and enlightenment: *The Eye of the I* (2001), and *I: Reality and Subjectivity* (2003).

While the last two books were devoted to personal enlightenment, *Truth vs. Falsehood* (2005) investigated the distribution and evolution of levels of consciousness in public life and society, as well as in the individual. The thrust of that study was to denote a roadway to peace and integrity and hopefully lessen the likelihood of war by providing an accessible, pragmatic, clinical science of truth.

This book returns to focusing on the individual and studying the experiential subjective blocks to the advancement of consciousness that leads to progressive spiritual awareness and on to higher levels of consciousness preparatory to advanced states such as Enlightenment itself. The material is drawn from multiple sources, including fifty years of psychiatric practice; psychoanalysis; twenty-five years of research into the nature of consciousness; and transformative, subjective spiritual experiences that have been described elsewhere.

In this book, as in previous ones, the calibrated levels of major statements are included.

Note that due to more recent discoveries in the evolving field of consciousness research, the instructions for doing the muscle test have been revised and updated (see Appendix B).

INTRODUCTION

The all-pervasive universal energy field called consciousness is of infinite power and dimension beyond time and is compositionally nonlinear. It is the 'light of the world' as it emanates from the Unmanifest to the Manifest, from the nonlinear, infinite potentiality to its linear expression as the unfolding of Creation (the circumscribed, perceived physical domain).

The power of the infinite field of consciousness and its infinite potentiality manifests as matter. Later, the interface of the Light of Divinity as the field of consciousness in its encounter with matter results in the emergence of the unique quality and energy of life itself. Although matter has enormous potentiality, it lacks the innate quality or power to evolve to the field of existence termed 'life'. Matter plus evolution results in the dimension of 'time'. Then, matter plus time is expressed as 'space', subsequent to which the existence of time, space, and matter is discernible by intelligence, an aspect of Divinity expressed as Life. That life emanates solely as a consequence of Divinity is confirmable at consciousness level 1,000, the level of the Absolute.

Creation is capable of being known solely by virtue of the presence of consciousness, which is the very matrix of existence itself. Thus, consciousness is the irreducible a priori reality by which the linear is perceived by the subjective awareness of the nonlinear.

Consciousness then evolves through progressive levels of power that can be calibrated as to relative strength, much as is done with a light meter or any other measurement of energy waves, whether kinetic, radio, or magnetic components of the well-known stratifications called the electromagnetic spectrum.

In the 1970s, a clinical science emerged based on the use of life energy and its interaction with the infinite field of consciousness itself. This resulted in the calibrated levels of the Map of Consciousness that has subsequently become well known worldwide as a consequence of its presentation in a series of books in many languages and numerous lectures in the United States, Canada, Asia, and Europe.

The designated levels were stratified in accordance with their numerical, calibrated levels of power according to a logarithmic scale from '1' (indicating existence) to the highest level at '1,000', which is the highest energy field possible in the human domain and reached by only the few throughout history who have traditionally been referred to as the Great Avatars (the founders of the world's great religions, such as Jesus Christ, Buddha, Zoroaster, and Krishna), and who were enlightened by the Divine Presence that replaced the linear, limited, ordinary human mind with the nonlinear Reality. The Self, indicative of the presence of the Divine as immanent, is sometimes referred to in classical literature as Universal Mind. By transcendence, the ego-self is replaced by the non-ego Self (see Hawkins, 1995, 2001, 2003). This phenomenon has been traditionally termed 'Enlightenment'.

The emergence of a clinical science of truth has been described in previous works. One important statement about the infinite field of consciousness is that it represents the Absolute by which all else can be calibrated as to degrees of being relative to it. The mechanism is the living clinical science of muscle testing, which uses the human nervous system and the energy of life as expressed through the acupuncture energy system as the requisite sensitive biological measuring instrument. (The technique cannot be duplicated by nonliving scientific instruments.) In the presence of Truth, the body's musculature goes 'strong'. In contrast, it goes 'weak' when confronted with falsehood (which is the absence of truth, not its opposite). This is a rapid and transitory response that quickly reveals the degree of truth of the presented stimulus.

The infinitely powerful, all-present timeless field of consciousness is comparable to an electrostatic field that is motionless unless triggered by the challenge of a presenting electrical charge that then activates the electrostatic field, which responds with an equal and opposite charge to precisely the same degree. The electrostatic field, in and of itself, does not 'do' anything but merely responds and records.

Unlike the electrostatic field, the timeless field of consciousness is permanent and thereby records all that has occurred or existed from within time/space/evolution. The field itself stands beyond time, space, or any known dimension and instead includes all dimensions, without being altered by them. The infinite field is omnipresent, omnipotent, omniscient, and uniquely identifiable as the Absolute by which all expressions of evolution or existence can be compared.

Everything in the universe, including even a passing thought, is recorded forever in the timeless field of consciousness, which is everywhere equally present. All that has ever occurred, either physically or by thought, is equally available because the field is beyond time and space. There is no 'here' or 'there'; there is no 'now' or 'then'. The totality is equally and permanently present everywhere.

The Map of Consciousness is therefore a very practical and pragmatic guide to understanding the evolutionary levels of consciousness to be transcended in pursuit of spiritual advancement, enlightenment, or self-improvement. It also provides a pragmatic map of the obstacles to overcome in order to achieve more optimal levels of consciousness. Calibrations do not establish truth but merely confirm it and lend additional corroboration.

MAP OF THE SCALE OF CONSCIOUSNESS®

God-view	Life-view	Level		Log	Emotion	Process
Self	Is	Enlightenment	⇧	700-1000	Ineffable	Pure Consciousness
All-Being	Perfect	Peace	⇧	600	Bliss	Illumination
One	Complete	Joy	⇧	540	Serenity	Transfiguration
Loving	Benign	Love	⇧	500	Reverence	Revelation
Wise	Meaningful	Reason	⇧	400	Understanding	Abstraction
Merciful	Harmonious	Acceptance	⇧	350	Forgiveness	Transcendence
Inspiring	Hopeful	Willingness	⇧	310	Optimism	Intention
Enabling	Satisfactory	Neutrality	⇧	250	Trust	Release
Permitting	Feasible	Courage	⇕	200	Affirmation	Empowerment
Indifferent	Demanding	Pride	⇩	175	Scorn	Inflation
Vengeful	Antagonistic	Anger	⇩	150	Hate	Aggression
Denying	Disappointing	Desire	⇩	125	Craving	Enslavement
Punitive	Frightening	Fear	⇩	100	Anxiety	Withdrawal
Disdainful	Tragic	Grief	⇩	75	Regret	Despondency
Condemning	Hopeless	Apathy	⇩	50	Despair	Abdication
Vindictive	Evil	Guilt	⇩	30	Blame	Destruction
Despising	Miserable	Shame	⇩	20	Humiliation	Elimination

Section One

Calibration Levels Below 200
The Ego

Section One – Overview

The Evolution of Consciousness

To understand the calibrated levels of consciousness, it is helpful to recapitulate the emergence of consciousness on the planet and its evolution through the animal kingdom into its expression as humankind. The initial focus of interest is the evolution of the ego, with its innate limitations. The term 'ego' has a different meaning in spiritual work than it has in psychology, psychoanalysis, and the theories of Carl Jung or Sigmund Freud. The differences will be clarified later.

The ego is not overcome by seeing it as an enemy. It is one's biological inheritance, and without it, nobody would be alive to lament its limitations. By understanding its origin and intrinsic importance to survival, the ego can be seen as being of great benefit but prone to becoming unruly and causing emotional, psychological, and spiritual problems if not resolved or transcended.

From the Unmanifest to the Manifest, the energy of consciousness itself interacted with matter, and as an expression of Divinity, by that interaction life arose. In its earliest forms, the animal expressions of life were very primitive and did not have an innate, inner source of energy. Survival therefore depended on acquiring energy externally. This was not a problem in the plant kingdom where chlorophyll automatically transforms solar energy into necessary chemical processes. Animal life had to acquire what was needed from its environment, and that principle then established the main core of the ego, which is still primarily involved in self-interest, acquisition, conquering, and rivalry with other organisms for survival. Importantly, however, it also had the characteristics of curiosity, searching, and, therefore, learning.

As evolution progressed, the survival mechanisms became more elaborate as the quality of intelligence, by which information is acquired, stored, processed, compared, integrated, correlated, and stratified. This observation is the basis for the theory of 'Intelligent Design', which does not require any presumption of Divinity or a Creator. It confirms that an innate quality of the energy of life is that through experience, it acquires information and is capable of processing it in a progressive integration and in stratifications of increasing complexity.

Life then evolved into progressively higher life forms, and if this is charted over great evolutionary epics of time, its expression in the animal kingdom becomes apparent. (Reprinted here from *Truth vs. Falsehood* for convenience.)

CONSCIOUSNESS LEVELS OF ARCHAELOGICAL ERAS

TIME PERIODS ROCK SYSTEMS	APPROXIMATE DURATION MILLION YEARS	LIFE FORMS	CALIBRATED LEVEL OF LIFE
Quaternary	1	Rise and dominance of man	212
Upper Tertiary		Modern animals and plants	212
Lower Tertiary	60	Rapid development of modern mammals insects and plants	112
Upper Cretaceous	60	Primitive mammals; last dinosaurs	84
Lower Cretaceous		Rise of flowering plants First birds, first mammals.	
Jurassic	35	Diversification of reptiles; coniferous trees.	68
Triassic	35	Rise of dinosaurs; cycad-like plants; bony fishes	62
Permian	25	Rise of reptiles. Modern insects. Last of many plant and animal groups	45
Pennsylvanian (Carboniferous)	85	First reptiles, amphibians, primitive insects; seed ferns; primitive conifers	35
Mississippian (Carboniferous)		Climax of shell-crushing sharks.	33
Devonian	50	First amphibians, first land snails. Primitive land plants. Climax of brachiopods First traces of land life.	27
Silurian	40	Scorpions, First lungfishes Widespread coral reefs.	17
Ordovician	90	First fish. Climax of trilo-bites. First appearance of many marine invertebrates.	12
Cambrian	70	First marine invertebrates	8
Proterozic Archeozoic	Over 1300	Protozoa	2
(Precambrian)		Algae, Lichens, Bacteria	1

Age of oldest dated rocks is about 1,850,000,000 years

Source: Adapted from Britannica World Language Dictionary. New York: Funk & Wagnalls Co.

It is noticeable that at consciousness levels below 200 (with the exception of most birds), life could be described as rapacious. It acquires its energy at the expense of others, and because survival is based on acquisition, it sees others as rivals, competitors, and enemies. Life up to consciousness level 200 is therefore strongly rivalrous and self-interested. Because it sees others as potential enemies, in modern languaging it would be called possessive, competitive, hostile, and, in extreme expressions, aggressive and savage.

At consciousness level 200, there is a shift to the more benign, that is, in addition to the carnivore, there emerges the herbivore. From consciousness level 200 up, the nature of life becomes more harmonious. Maternal caring appears, along with concern for others, pack loyalty, identification with others, and the beginning of what is later expressed in human nature as relatedness, socializing, play, family and pair bonding, and group cooperation for shared goals, such as survival via community activities.

Animal Kingdom

Bacteria	1	Snakes	45
Protozoa	2	Alligators	45
Crustaceans	3	Dinosaurs	60
Insects	6	Whales	85
Arachnids	7	Dolphins	95
Amphibians	17	Migratory birds	105
Fish	20	Birds of prey	105
Octopus	20	Rodents	105
Sharks	24	Rhinoceros	105
Vipers	35	Baboons	105
Komodo dragon	40	Song birds	125
Reptiles	40	Doves	145
Predatory mammals		Polar bear	160
(hyena, lion, tiger)	40	Grizzly bear	160

Water buffalo	175	Farm horse	240
Black bear	180	Cats	240
Jackal, foxes	185	Parrot, African gray	240
Wolves	190	Family cat	245
Hippopotamus	190	Race horse	245
Javelina	195	Dogs	245
Grazers		Family pig	250
(zebra, gazelle, giraffe)	200	Black crow	250
Deer	205	Gorilla	275
Bison	205	Chimpanzees	305
Domestic pig	205	Exceptions:	
Elk	210	Alex, trained African gray	401
Dairy cow	210	Koko (trained gorilla)	405
Sheep	210	Song bird's song	500
Range cattle	210	Cat's purr	500
Elephants	210	Dog's wagging tail	500
Monkeys	210		

With the advancement of evolution, the bipeds appeared with two limbs that they did not need for locomotion so, standing upright, the two free limbs developed manual dexterity and, as a consequence of the development of the thumb, were enabled to develop tool-making crafts.

The increased complexity was facilitated by the emergence of the forebrain and the prefrontal cortex as the anatomical seat of human intelligence. However, because of the predominance of animal instincts, intelligence initially served primitive instincts. Thus, the prefrontal cortex became subservient to animal-survival motivations. As is apparent from even casual observation, evolution represents Creation, and the basic quality of Creation is evolution because they are one and the same thing.

Primitive man appeared as sprouts of the evolutionary tree, starting presumably with "Lucy" three million years ago, and then much later as Neanderthal, Cro-Magnon, Homo erectus, and others, all of whom calibrated at approximately 80 to 85. Most recently, perhaps 600,000 years ago, there appeared in Africa the probable predecessor of modern man, *Homo sapiens idelta*, with consciousness level also at 80 to 85.

The persistence of the primitive ego in man is referred to as the narcissistic core of 'egotism', which, at calibration levels below 200, indicates the persistence of the primitiveness of self-interest, disregard for the rights of others, and seeing others as enemies and competitors rather than as allies. For safety's sake, humans coalesced into groups and discovered the benefit of mutuality and cooperation, which again was a corollary to the animal world of group, pack, and family formation in the mammalian and bird kingdoms.

The calibrated consciousness level of humans evolved slowly. At the time of the birth of the Buddha, the collective consciousness of all of mankind calibrated at 90. It then rose to 100 by the time of the birth of Jesus Christ and slowly evolved over the last two millennia to 190, where it stayed for many centuries, until the late 1980s. Then, at about the time of the Harmonic Convergence in the late 1980s, it suddenly jumped from 190 to 204-205, where it stayed until November 2003, when again, it suddenly jumped from 205 to its current level of 207. At the present time, approximately seventy-eight percent of all humanity calibrates below consciousness level 200, although that figure is only forty-nine percent in America. The significance is that the consciousness level of close to eighty percent of the world's population is still below 200 and therefore dominated by primitive animal instincts, motivations, and behaviors (as reflected in the nightly news).

Of major significance on the calibrated Scale of Consciousness (see below) is that the critical level of 200 differentiates truth from falsehood. Therefore, levels over 200, which progress logarithmically, indicate levels of power, and those below 200 indicate reliance on force, whether emotional, physical, social, or by whatever expression. This differentiation is denoted by the dictum that the pen (ideology) is mightier than the sword (force).

Of major significance is that the brain's physiology also changes dramatically at consciousness level 200, which is the level where the quality of life changes, not only in man but also in the animal kingdom, from predatory to benign. This is expressed by the emergence of concern for the welfare, survival, and happiness of others rather than just for the personal self. The benefits of the evolution of caringness and spiritual growth are clearly shown in the following chart.

Correlation of Levels of Consciousness
and the Rate of Happiness

LEVEL	LOG	PERCENT
Enlightenment	700-1,000	100
Peace	600	100
Joy	570	99
Unconditional Love	540	96
Love	500	89
Reason	400	79
Acceptance	350	71
Willingness	310	68
Neutrality	250	60
Courage	200	55

▲
▼

Pride	175	22
Anger	150	12
Desire	125	10
Fear	100	10
Grief	75	9
Apathy, hatred	50	5
Guilt	30	4
Shame	20	1

The dynamics of the ego will be investigated in each of the following chapters as they apply to a specific level, thereby clarifying the subject in greater detail.

CHAPTER 1

Shame: Despair

(Calibration Levels 20 and Below)

Introduction

This level is perilously proximate to death, which may be chosen as conscious suicide or more subtly elected by failure to take steps to prolong life. Death by neglect, indifference, carelessness, or accident is common at this level. Everyone is aware of the pain of 'losing face', becoming discredited, or of seeming to be a 'non-person.' In Shame, people hang their heads and slink away, wishing they were invisible. Banishment is a traditional accompaniment of shame, and in the primitive societies from which humankind originates, banishment is equivalent to death. It is the basis of the fear of disapproval, rejection, or failure.

Early life experiences such as neglect or physical, emotional, or sexual abuse lead to shame and warp the personality for a lifetime unless these issues are later resolved. Shame, as Freud determined, produces neurosis. It is destructive to emotional and psychological health and, as a consequence of low self-esteem, makes one prone to the development of physical illness. The shame-based personality is shy, withdrawn, introverted, and self-deprecating.

Shame is used as a tool of cruelty, and its victims often become cruel. Shamed children are cruel to animals and cruel to each other. The behavior of people whose consciousness is only in the 20s is dangerous. They are prone to hallucinations of an accusatory nature, as well as paranoia, and some become psychotic or commit bizarre crimes.

Some shame-based individuals compensate by perfectionism and rigidity, becoming driven and intolerant. Notorious examples of this are the moral extremists who form vigilante groups, projecting their own unconscious shame onto others whom they then feel justified in righteously attacking. Serial killers have often acted out of shame, hate, and sexual moralism with the justification of punishing 'bad' women. Because it pulls down the whole level of personality, Shame results in a vulnerability to the other negative emotions, therefore often producing false pride, anger, and guilt.

Clinical

Severe depression is a serious level of consciousness that can be immobilizing and life threatening. It occurs not only in individuals but also in most of the large groups of people who die of apathy or even suicide.

Despair is characterized by helplessness and hopelessness and is therefore described as a dispirited state and hellish to endure. The will to live is lost, but in the deepest depths, even the act of suicide is not possible due to lack of energy. Passive suicide occurs through the failure to eat or provide for physical necessities. Paradoxically, as the person comes out of the severe apathy of depression and gains more energy, they then become capable of the act of suicide, which explains the misunderstood clinical paradox that, supposedly, antidepressants 'cause' suicide, especially in children and teenagers. This phenomenon was well known clinically over great periods of time long before antidepressants became available. When the apathetic depressive begins to improve, the phase of agitated depression emerges in which the energy to carry out suicide exists. Many years ago, before antidepressants, patients were placed on close watch during the periods when they had 'improved' from apathy to the agitated state (Hawkins, 2005).

Shame is also reflective of self-hatred that, when turned outward, can result in severe, even homicidal aggression. It is notable that a sizeable percent of senseless classmate killers were reportedly on antidepressants.

Depression is accompanied by major changes in brain physiology and low levels of critical neurotransmitters, such as norepinephrine and serotonin. The propensity to depression includes strong genetic and karmic factors and is often familial. It is also correlated with vulnerability to alcoholism. It is estimated that at least one-third of adults will have a serious or moderately severe degree of depression at sometime in their lives.

Clinically, depression usually necessitates professional help. To complicate it further, it is also difficult to differentiate true suicidality from the relatively more frequent suicidal gestures or threats that arise from a different problem, usually involving interpersonal relationships and resentments.

Depressions of a serious degree can be worked through under appropriate conditions, but they are really indicative of the need for psychiatric or other professional clinical help, as well as protection and support. The loss of hope and the will to live, along with the accompanying depression, frequently occur in lonely isolated persons, the elderly, and in ordinary people who have gone through the psychological depletion of severe stress, such as divorce, financial disaster, loss of loved ones, and the process of grieving itself. Suicide is a leading cause of death in adolescents.

Like other illnesses, major emotional problems are comprised of physical, mental, and emotional components. There may also be additional interpersonal and social factors as well as karmic influences. Recovery may require addressing any or all of the factors. Even a seemingly simple physical problem such as undiagnosed functional hypoglycemia may be a major contributor. (Many depressives have recovered simply by avoiding sugar.) Failure to seek or accept appropriate help is frequently due to pride (spiritual), denial (psychological), or simply ignorance (karmic). The mood fluctuations then affect interpersonal relations and even employment (e.g., workplace homicides and rages). With humility, all the contributing factors can be examined, and recovery from even very serious, near-fatal conditions can be achieved, as is seen in spiritually-based recovery groups.

The Attraction of Death

Although there is the common presumption that everyone fears death and has an aversion to it, paradoxically, death is also, under appropriate conditions, seen as an attraction (the end of suffering) or as a final act of revenge, heroic sacrifice, or an extreme acting out of self-pity. There is also 'the romance of death' by which it is celebrated for its intrinsic drama (legends, opera, and fiction, such as *Romeo and Juliet*).

The thrill of death pervades the Roman Coliseum, dueling, the racetrack, and acts of war. To 'flirt with death' is also an attraction of high risk-taking (e.g., as represented by motorcyclists' jackets and tattoos with skull and crossbones).

Death can also be ceremonial (hari-kari) and is solemnly celebrated via funerals with the casket drawn slowly by horses in State funeral processions.

Freud postulated an intrinsic death instinct termed 'Thanatos' (in contrast to 'eros', the life instinct) that is buried deep in the primitive unconscious where it exerts a potential influence that can be strengthened by indoctrination (kamikaze pilots, Islamic suicide bombers, cult mass suicide). Currently there is a long waiting list of zealous volunteers among Islamic extremists ("We worship death, not life," said bin Laden.) There is therefore the 'Cult of Death,' which is glamorized to impressionable, naïve youth who are induced to commit not only suicide but also simultaneous mass murder of the innocent. There were numerous kamikaze volunteers during World War II. Thus, a dramatic exit has a unique attraction and the glamour of drama. Most commonly, suicide is an act of despair and desperation consequent to the loss of faith or hope.

Spiritual: The Dark Night of the Soul

The state of feeling abandoned by God and being hopeless results in a global feeling of depression and may include an alteration of the experience of time comparable to the experiential lower levels of Hell as described by Dante: "Abandon hope all ye who enter here." This state may also be a transitory phase as a consequence of intense inner spiritual work, especially in a devotee who throws all caution to the wind and explores the deepest levels of consciousness, at which depth the devotee intuitively senses that it is necessary to relinquish the ego and remove all doubt. Thus, this state may represent the need to reach inner validation of spiritual truth before total abandonment of the ego itself. Oddly, this can be the very route taken by the devoted atheist who is proving whether actual Godlessness is true or even survivable. Severe spiritual depression can represent the last toehold of the ego as it fights for survival. The ego's basic illusion is that it is God and that without it, death will occur. Thus, what is described as 'the dark night of the soul' is actually the dark night for the ego.

Confrontation with the core of the ego may be unexpected and the consequence of letting go of attachments, along with the ego's illusions and cherished false spiritual/religious beliefs and fantasies about God, e.g., God will respond to intense entreaty or bargaining ('rattling the gates of Heaven'): "O God, look how I suffer for thee."

Paradoxically, the dark night of the soul is often a sign of significant spiritual progress for it is not really the soul (higher Self) but the ego that is in the dark. Some comfort can be obtained by recalling the spiritual dictum that one can only go as high as they have been low, or that Jesus Christ sweat blood in Gethsemane, or that the Buddha reported that he felt as though his bones were being broken and he was being attacked by demons.

In the pits of spiritual despair and black hopelessness, the necessary Knowingness to be followed is that, spiritually, all fear is illusion. The reason it is safe to let go completely of all that one holds dear, along with the belief that the inner core of the ego is the very source of life itself, is because it is *not* the source, no matter how intensely the experience may seem. The last barrier to relinquish and turn over to God is the seeming irreducible substrate of the core of existence itself. The reason it is safe do so is because that is not true.

With the surrender of what seems to be the very source, irreducible core, and essence of one's life, the door swings open when karmically appropriate, and the Presence shines forth with the Radiance of Divinity. The personal 'I', along with the mind, dissolves into the Infinite 'I' of the Eternal, with its profound peace and state of Oneness beyond all time. This state is not a consequence of the mind or the ego but rather the replacement when they cease to function. The final steps take courage, conviction, and surrender at great depth. It is here where Truth in the form of the vibration and the aura of a true teacher is of maximal assistance (the historical 'grace of the guru'), as is the calling upon one's chosen master, Savior, or ultimate spiritual reality, be it Buddha, Christ, Krishna, or God directly.

Another form of the dark night of the soul arises as a consequence of experientially falling from a high state (such as devotional joy or ecstasy), as has been well described in the lives of the Christian saints. It is as though one has been 'deserted by the Beloved'. (See *Butler's Lives of the Saints*.) This may arise because one has 'used up their good karma', subsequent to which the remainder of karmic attachments and proclivities surface to be processed out and surrendered to God. Some of these are deep, such as self-hatred, resentments of God, and cherished beliefs that are often attached to beliefs about suffering itself (e.g., that it will leverage God's favor, etc.).

In the dark night of the soul, faith in certain beliefs is pitted against the actual Reality. All beliefs about God are second-hand information derived from others and handed down, and thus, even these have to be surrendered. The reason for this can be found by examining the analogy of the fact that only a cat truly knows what it is to be a cat by virtue of being a cat. It does not know 'about' being a cat and has no belief systems. Therefore, all erroneous beliefs about God are extraneous to the experiential Reality. The door to Enlightenment is through the deep honesty of unknowingness.

The experience of Divinity within as Self, or God Immanent, is quite different from belief in God Transcendent. It is for this reason that the Buddha counseled against all depictions or nominalizations of God because Enlightenment is a condition or state in which the Self-knowing is that of Identity. In this condition or state, there is no 'this', such as self, with which to describe the Self. The condition or state is best described as Self-effulgent, and in that state the Knowingness is its own Reality. (The subject is revisited in later chapters.)

Although the term 'karma' is not used specifically in Western religions, it is nevertheless a basic reality as it is spiritual accountability that determines the fate of the soul after death. The term also includes the spiritual problems that are inherent to being a human being, including the fact that humankind is characterized by limited spiritual understanding ('ignorance'). Thus, the purpose of human life is to overcome and transcend these inherited limitations via spiritual truth as revealed by the great religious and spiritual teachers.

'Karma' is often confused in the Western mind with rebirth, reincarnation, or multiple human lifetimes.

Generically, karma merely refers to the fact that the soul is evolutionary in both origin and fate and accountable for its decisions.

Everyone already has a specific calibrated level of consciousness at birth. Pragmatically, how the condition came about could be viewed as irrelevant. The various religions, as well as consciousness research, offer different explanations. Whatever the reasons may be, each individual has to proceed from wherever they find themselves in the evolutionary process. Without an understanding of karma, however, individual circumstances would seem to be accidental or capricious and thus not in accord with the findings of consciousness research that demonstrate that all Creation is a reflection of Divine Harmony, Justice, and Balance.

Karmic Despair

Karmic despair is often experienced via major tragic events or catastrophes. There is also the collective human group karma that is merely the consequence of being human. It may also be expressed as group conditions that may be ethnic, religious, geographic, or aligned in other ways due to acts or agreements in the past. Karma is linear, propagates via the soul, and is inherited as the consequence of significant acts of the will. The likelihood of such seemingly negative consequences can readily be deduced from human history, which frequently and recurrently involved useless slaughter of the innocent as well as willful and wanton acts of desecration (i.e., negative karma).

Inclusion in what seems to be negative karmic consequences occurs as a result of prior concurrence and/or participation. Thus, the cheers at the death of a gladiator are karmically significant as is taking grim satisfaction from pain and suffering or the death of others. To cheer on the implementation of the guillotine is to join with its karmic consequences. To take justice into one's own hands is done at karmic risk for "Justice is mine, sayeth the Lord." Faith that Divinity guarantees absolute justice is difficult to accept in a world of seeming injustices. It is better to trust in the absolute justice of God and "judge not, lest ye be judged," for it is well to remember that "Let he who is without sin cast the first stone."

A useful analogy to Divine Justice (Laws of Karma) is the realization that the infinite omnipresent and omniscient field of consciousness is itself the Radiance of Divinity in which all passing events, no matter how seemingly trivial, are recorded. At birth, one is automatically aligned with the overall karmic field as a consequence of the quality of that linear field in the infinite field of consciousness itself. Thus, only by acts of the will can an entity bring about its own fate. One's consciousness calibration is affected for better or worse by inner decision and act of the will, and as a consequence, the individual entity is drawn to its own appropriate level of consciousness, which is dominated by an 'attractor field' (see *Power vs. Force*, 1995). Thus, one's level of consciousness represents karmic inheritance.

From an overall understanding of the nature of consciousness, it can be seen that justice (karma) is automatic as a consequence of the interaction of the vibration of the soul within the overall infinite field of consciousness. The science of truth and consciousness calibration research confirm the scriptural passage, "Every hair on one's head is counted" (numbered). All is known by the infinite field of Divinity by which justice therefore automatically prevails. Mankind's fantasies are projections from the unconscious of an anthropomorphic god who is vengeful, jealous, wrathful, and the alleged 'cause' of disasters. However, it is obvious that natural disasters of greater proportion than have happened during the history of mankind occurred before man even existed and are, in fact, presumed to have been the condition that brought about the termination of the age of the dinosaur.

To summarize, as is commonly known, karma (spiritual fate) is the consequence of decisions of the will and determines spiritual destiny after physical death (the celestial levels, hells, purgatory, or the so-called inner astral planes *[bardos]*). Included also is the option of reincarnation in the human physical domain, which, by consciousness calibration research, can only be done by agreement with the individual will. Thus, all humans have, by agreement, chosen this pathway. In addition, consciousness research confirms that all persons are born under the most optimal conditions for spiritual evolution, no matter what the appearance seems to be.

Karma really means accountability, and, as cited in previous spiritual research, every entity is answerable to the universe. It is also well known that positive karma (good works, prayer, selfless service, benevolent acts, etc.) can compensate for and undo negative ('bad') karma. In this process, 'merit' accrues, which at times can even be drawn against in confronting vicissitudes. Spiritual progress ensues automatically from choosing good will, forgiveness, and lovingness as a way of being in the world at large rather than viewing it as a gain-seeking transaction.

Working through one's 'karma' includes not only this lifetime but historical, long-forgotten evolutionary aspects as well. Spiritual work may bring up repressed attitudes, thoughts, or beliefs from the personal unconscious, as well as aspects of the collective human unconscious that are energetically aligned analogously to the chakra system of the Jungian archetypes (e.g., the heart of the child, the spleen of the warrior, the naïveté of the adolescent, etc.). Due to the nature of human development, even a mature, intelligent, fully-grown adult still has repressed or forgotten, but still functional, infantile and childish drives that operate out of awareness. One of the most common is the out-of-awareness balance between the 'good me' and the 'bad me.' (This is the area of the split and compartmentalized Jekyll-and-Hyde personality disorders.) The good/bad dichotomy may be the source of multiple psychological difficulties, of which projecting the 'bad me' onto others is the most common.

Group: Catastrophe, Regional, and Situational

Severe poverty, deprivations, and starvation are geographically endemic to whole regions, cultures, and major areas of the world, as described and graphed in a prior work (*Truth vs. Falsehood*, Chapter 14). They are characterized by high birth and infant mortality rates, short life spans, high rates of disease, civil disorders, tribal-type warfare, cruelty, and mass slaughter.

Consciousness research confirms that regional endemic poverty is of group karmic origin and expresses itself in correlation with genetic transmission.

Early forms of hominids (calibration level 85-90) have come and gone, and Homo sapiens, from an evolutionary viewpoint, is only a very recent emergence from the evolutionary tree. At this time, in fact, the majority of the human population (seventy-eight percent) calibrates below 200, which therefore initiates and attracts experiences in accord with that level.

Each calibrated level of consciousness indicates progress beyond the levels below it and may also represent the level to which those who were once higher have fallen as a consequence of volitional choices. This descending level is well documented in the cases of very famous political leaders who started out as integrous and idealistic, calibrating in the 400s, and who later, as a consequence of the development of megalomania, crashed to very low numbers (Napoleon, Hitler, et al.). The same phenomenon occurs in ordinary individuals as well as in groups, such as Easter Island and other societies that have come and gone.

What is commonly known as negative karma is sometimes referred to as 'debt', e.g., "Forgive us our debts as we forgive our debtors." Although decisions of the will have karmic consequences, they are recoverable with appropriate spiritual alignment and dedication.

As people evolve spiritually, each ascended level has its corollary tests or temptations into which the unwary may fall. Of these, the best known, of course, are wealth, power, and prestige (pride goeth before the fall; power corrupts and absolute power corrupts absolutely, etc.). This is clinically described as the 'Lucerific Temptation' of power for its own sake or power over others. The source of the error is ascribing the source of power to the ego 'I' instead of to Divinity. Similar falls are exhibited in the secular world where corporate CEOs seem to lose all sense of reality and succumb to the greed of unlimited power. Shame is also the consequence of the abuse of spiritual/religious status and influence as seen in the catastrophes of fallen gurus who once had worldwide acclaim and vast wealth.

Much of the world's literature includes fables, such as those of the old Greek and Germanic gods, as well as those of the Old Testament and other religions that were later superseded by the development of monotheism. That spiritual work can be arduous is attested to by the recorded histories of Christian saints. Many of them are aptly described, as in the Temptation of St. Anthony and the Confessions of St. Augustine. The Buddha also described how he was attacked by illusions and the negative 'demon' energies of *Mara* (illusion).

From previous studies, it was learned that everyone is born under optimal conditions for karmic opportunities; therefore, it is wise to judge not, for what appears as misery or catastrophe may be the doorway to liberation for those who have negative karma to undo. Thus, seemingly catastrophic events may be the very essential and necessary elements for the evolution of the soul.

Transcendence

At the bottom of despair, there is the exhaustion of energy and of even the will to survive. It is often only in the very pits of Hell and absolute despair that the ego can be surrendered, even right up to the point of imminent physical death. In extreme, timeless agony, the soul may entreat, "If there is a God, I ask him for help," and a great transformation occurs. This confirms the truth of the Zen teaching, "Heaven and hell are only one-tenth of an inch apart." Bizarrely, the ego may reach this point as an attempt to make God wrong, including even one's physical death (the ego will grasp at any straw), and thus, even in the last moment, the ego struggles to prove that death is a reality and that God is not.

The Dualities of Shame

Shame is a consequence of the negation of the realities of both self and Self. It is transitory in normal life but denotes a very major obstacle to spiritual evolution as a prevailing level of consciousness, and when severe, even threatens physical survival.

THE DUALITIES OF SHAME

Attraction	Aversion
Self-punitive	Self-forgiveness
Depression	Choose life
Judgmental	Surrender to God's Mercy
Negativity	Let go of position
Shrink, hide	Be visible
Self as worthless	Affirm gift of life
Rigid self-view	Correctable, flexible
Condemn	Forgive
Mortification	Choose self-worth
Denigrate	Honor self
Self-hatred	Self-forgiveness
Severe	Benign
Imbalanced	See both sides
Blame self	Blame ego's ignorance
Exaggerate faults	Transcend limitations
Partial selective view	Balanced overall view
Self as loser	Self as corrected
End of the road	Beginning of the new
Unlovable	Worth as child of God
Error unforgivable	Error as lesson
Narcissistic orientation	Concern for others
Serve self	Serve life
Indulgent self-evaluation	Let go of egoistic position
Self as center of life	Self as participant in life
Focus on self	Focus on others
'Should have'	Was not able then

CHAPTER 2

Guilt and Vindictive Hate

(Calibration Level 30)

Introduction

Guilt, so commonly used in the form of blame by our society to manipulate and punish, manifests itself in a variety of expressions, such as remorse, self-recrimination, masochism, and the whole gamut of symptoms of victimhood. Unconscious guilt results in psychosomatic disease, accident proneness, and suicidal behaviors. Many people struggle with guilt their entire lives, while others desperately attempt to escape it by amorally denying guilt altogether.

Guilt domination results in preoccupation with 'sin', an unforgiving emotional attitude frequently exploited by religious demagogues who use it for coercion and control. Such 'sin and salvation' merchants, obsessed with punishment, are likely either acting out their own guilt or projecting it onto others.

Subcultures displaying the aberration of self-flagellation often manifest other endemic forms of cruelty, such as the public ritual killing of animals. Guilt provokes rage, and killing is frequently its expression. Capital punishment is an example of how killing gratifies an angry and guilt-ridden populace, but it has never been demonstrated to have any deterrent or corrective value. Instead, it satisfies the emotional need for 'just' retribution.

Clinical

This is the level of serious guilt and self-condemnation as being bad, evil, and seeing God as being punitive as well as vindictive. Guilt is a learned behavior with major psychological components. There is input from society, parents, and religion, as well as negative programming by social programs. Thus, shame may predominate, with consequential self-judgment as being unworthy, undeserving, unlovable, and a worthless worm that is hated by God and undeserving of salvation, much less forgiveness. This is the level of self-judgment of being unforgivable and beyond hope or redemption.

Guilt takes the form of penance, self-hatred, psychological and physical self-punishment, suicide, self-abnegation, and self-propagating addiction. "Oh look, God, how I suffer" becomes a subtle attempt to manipulate God.

One way the ego mechanism handles guilt is by projection, so that one's motives and emotions are disowned and seen as being 'out there' and therefore an object for justified hate and vindictiveness. A spiritual paradox is represented by the religious teaching of 'hating sin', which merely expresses the very thing it deplores. This pitfall can be bypassed with compassion, forgiveness, and the realization that mankind and individuals are limited, ignorant, and really do not know or understand why or what they do.

Ignorance is an automatic byproduct of the ego's inherited internal mental mechanisms, which were examined and clarified from an evolutionary viewpoint in *Truth vs. Falsehood* (Section I). Guilt can also be ameliorated by recognizing the truth of Socrates' statement that 'all men seek only what they perceive as the good', but unfortunately, due to the limitations of perception, truth cannot be discerned from falsehood, nor the truly good from that which is perceived as desirable (wealth, success, possession, power over others, etc.).

Guilt is the consequence of the memory of regretted past actions as they are recalled. These can be transcended only by recontextualization. Mistakes are the natural, impersonal consequence of learning and development and therefore unavoidable.

As evolution progressed, the capacity of learning, called 'intelligence', arose as a consequence of trial and error, which is a process that is operationally required for survival. The process of trial and error then accumulates as data and memory. This accrues as the long and experiential time continuum that sorts events into 'then' and 'now'. The present self 'is', and the former self 'was', and, in truth, that which 'was' is not identical with that which 'is'. Regret and guilt result from equating the present self that 'is' with the former self that 'was' but actually is no more; they are not the same.

Guilt can be an educative emotion that arises as a warning not to repeat the same mistake. The past cannot be rewritten, but it can be recontextualized so as to be a source of constructive learning. Regret over past events or decisions can be ameliorated by realizing that they 'seemed like a good idea at the time'.

Inasmuch as the human mind is defective and not omniscient, guilt and regret are sourced by ignorance and limitation and represent evolutionary stages. Past errors are due to limitation and belong to a certain point in the timeline of evolution, not only personally but also collectively. What was acceptable in the past is no longer acceptable. Ignorance is due to fallacy of perception or interpretation. Therefore, whatever the content of regret may be, it is actually the same identical defect but merely appearing under different circumstances. The literal, absolute definition of the word 'sin' is 'error'. This later becomes compounded with religious dictums, elaborations, and rankings according to alleged degrees of seriousness and culpability.

Operationally, there is just one single recurrent 'sin', which is that of error, ignorance, misperception, mistake, or miscalculation. It is a consequence of a limitation of human consciousness. Self-forgiveness is facilitated by humility and acceptance of this limitation. Realistically, what is usually appropriate is a 'decent regret', as was cited by Bill W., the famous founder of Alcoholics Anonymous. Excessive guilt and remorse are a disguised form of egotism in which the self becomes blown up, exaggerated, and the hero of the tragedy, the negativity of which feeds the ego. Therefore, release from guilt requires surrender of this basic egotism because the ego reenergizes itself through the negativity.

Another egoist position is 'I should have known better', which brings in the hypothetical, which is always fallacious. (All hypothetical positions calibrate as false.) Wallowing in guilt is feeding the ego and is an indulgence. Therefore, there has to be the willingness to surrender it.

In psychological terms, the source of guilt, as termed by psychoanalysis, is the so-called superego, so named by Freud. This is the part of the mind comprised of introjected judgments, points of view, and learned content. A hypertrophied superego can be the source of excessive guilt or scrupulosity, or it can be projected onto others, which justifies vindictiveness in extreme forms as revenge against the 'evil' enemy. This rationalizes killing others as their being 'deserving' of death, which is further supported by culturally distributed propaganda and cult-style brainwashing by authority figures (e.g., religious terrorists). Severely low levels of consciousness are reached by those persons who fall victim to a combination of the Luciferic error (pride, distortion of truth) and the Satanic error (cruelty, savagery). Thus, the worst ravages of humanity have often been done in the name of God (the classic Luciferic inversion of good and evil). From a developmental viewpoint that reveals the limitations of the ego, it can be seen that the perpetrators of savagery are themselves the victims of rudimentary levels of consciousness.

From an analysis of its origins and dynamics, it can be summarized that guilt is but another form of egotism in which error is inflated instead of being relinquished to a higher power. God is not a sadist, so self-degradation or self-punishment serves neither God nor one's fellowman.

The 'Gothic' side of historic Christianity tended to glorify sackcloth, ashes, and suffering as penance. With greater understanding of the ego and its mechanism, it can be seen that this mechanism is subtly self-serving and may lead to extremes of asceticism or persecution (e.g., the Inquisition).

In psychology, one process of relieving guilt is called 'undoing', which has to do with bringing up the punitive superego (conscience) into a more realistic view of life and compensating for error so it becomes more benign and less judgmental and punitive.

In an ideal childhood development, the introjected (identified with) parental figures are not harsh but supportive and loving as teachers. The punitive superego may also be projected outward as an aggressive, judgmental, extreme political positionality that propagates by the 'juice' of political hatred. Another expression of this error is the socially pervasive model of perpetrator/victim that can be superimposed onto any social situation. In psychoanalysis, such a device is called 'projection' in order to keep the conflict repressed instead of becoming conscious and responsible for it.

In classical Freudian terminology, the 'ego' is understood and contextualized quite differently than it is in spiritual terminology. The Freudian ego is that aspect of the mind that has to deal with external reality, as well as balance and resolve the inner conflicts between the 'Id' (primitive drives) and conscience. Thus, psychological health is equated with having a healthy, realistic, and balanced personality.

When the malignant superego is ameliorated and becomes benign, it then sees authority as protective and its role as that of teaching. Thus, it does not need to be projected onto the external world or turned against oneself.

Guilt and Memory

As has been described, the dualistic structure of the ego results in perception (edited linear program) being mistaken for reality. (For example, the reported percentage of error in eyewitness testimony in courts is fifty percent.) Memory and recall are not of reality but of one's perceptions at the time. (See Section I, *Truth vs. Falsehood*, for more information.) Although literal historical facts may be recalled correctly, their meaning is not understood because, if guilt remains, then the events were not truly understood from the context of a greater Reality.

Transformation

While the psychological/sociological explanations are helpful, they do not explain the true healing that occurs when these lower levels of consciousness are transcended. By spiritual alignment, the past circumstances underlying the guilt are recontextualized under the influence of spiritual energy. This process is occasioned by an exercise of the spiritual will, which, by its intention, invocation, prayer, and declaration, initiates a process that is not of the ego but of the nonlinear Self. This process is extensively described in *A Course in Miracles* (cal. 600), and the experience is subjectively miraculous, transformational, and results in a feeling of peace and healing. This phenomenon is facilitated by participation in spiritual groups where the personal spiritual energy is augmented by the group's intention, support, and spiritual field (e.g., AA calibrates at 540, the level of Unconditional Love).

As attested to by many thousands of people, negative perceptions and guilt can thereby be replaced by a positive understanding and a shift in comprehension and memory. This is the basis for the statement commonly used in such groups, "I see things differently now." Via this transformation, formerly hated persons can be forgiven, the formerly frightening can be seen as peaceful, and hatred is replaced by compassion for human frailty. Although the transformation is invited by the personal self, it is occasioned by the invocation of the power of the spiritual will by which the seemingly impossible becomes not only possible but an experiential actuality.

Understanding the Ego's Mechanisms of Dominance

Illusion is the secondary, automatic consequence of

positionality. What happens in a miraculous transformation is that the positionality dissolves, allowing for a greater contextualization, outside of time and place, by which the linear content is replaced with the nonlinear (context). The primary underpinning of the persistence of negativity is the ego's secret pay-off from negativity ('juice'). This secret pay-off is the ego's only source of energy, so it sees forgiveness, as well as compassion, as the 'enemy'. (In totalitarian armed forces, no expressions of benevolence, sympathy, or compassion are allowed as they are considered signs of weakness and are strictly prohibited.)

In the spiritual world, the basic dictum is, "There are no justified resentments." This statement is abhorred by the ego. "Oh yeah," it says, "but what about so-and-so?" It then goes through its laundry list and litany of horrors, violations of 'rights', injustices, presumptive arguments of 'ethics', 'morality', etc. Every counselor, sponsor, or professional is familiar with such recitations. To recover, the question one has to face is whether one wishes to cling to it (and thereby get the 'juice') or give it up. This is the point of decision, without which healing cannot occur.

The decision made at this turning point has actual consequences in the brain's physiology and its capacity to even comprehend the wisdom of choosing forgiveness instead of hate. (See Brain Physiology diagram, Chapter 9.)

To help with acceptance of this necessary step, a strong example can be useful and supportive. Probably the largest and most striking example is that of the veterans of World War II in which the experience of groups as well as individual combatants was horrific to the maximal degree. After the end of the war, the majority of former enemy combatants very quickly forgave each other, even formally saluting each other, and celebrated the end of the conflict. They shook hands in renewed mutual respect. There were the kamikaze pilots who had strafed one's ship, killed one's comrades, and left many wounded and crippled casualties. On the other side, Americans were the ones who dropped the atomic bombs that killed thousands of civilians. Subsequent to the cessation of hostilities, there was a strange, almost blanket-like acceptance that it was all over and that it had all 'just been about war'. Former combatants even became close personal friends and periodically visited each other's families. To this day, the survivors still commemorate great battles together.

Reluctance to forgive is a consequence not only of unwillingness to let go of the ego juice of perceived injustice but also the illusion that others do not 'deserve' it. In reality, it is the forgiver and not the forgiven who benefits the most. The purpose of the example is to demonstrate that even the most severe conditions can be transcended, but only by an act of the will and the willingness to surrender the nursing of hatred and revenge.

One might ask how could such a saintly transformation even be possible, given the horrific circumstances on both sides, including imprisonment in POW camps, starvation, personal torture, gross cruelty, and carnage. In actuality, and psychologically, it really could not be done by the ego/mind at all because it lacks the necessary power when it is caught up in the energy field of hate, which calibrates at only 30. Therefore, the transformative source of power cannot originate from the mind or the personality called the personal 'I'. The neces-

sary power resides in the nonlinear quality of consciousness termed the 'Will', which alone can open the gates to
the power necessary to dissolve the ego's positionality.

By invitation, the Holy Spirit transforms comprehension by virtue of the presence of the healing power
of Grace. What the ego cannot lift with all its might is
like a feather to the Grace of God. As a consequence of
the process of transformation, not only are the views of
others transformed from hateful to benign, but the
view of self is also transformed.

Guilt-ridden cultures commonly have a negative
view of God as being judgmental, vindictive, angry, and
punitive via natural disasters, which are contextualized
as punishments for wickedness that stem from God.
Personal judgment is based on perception that is reinforced by belief and prior programming, all of which
are held in place by the pay-off of the negative energies
of the ego. The ego just 'loves' suffering a 'wrong', being
the martyr, being misunderstood, and being the endless
victim of life's vicissitudes. It thereby gets an enormous
pay-off, not only from the positionality itself but also
from sympathy, self-pity, entitlements, importance, or
being 'center stage' in which the self is the hero or
heroine of the melodrama. The ego hoards 'slights' and
injuries, nurses 'hurt feelings', and stockpiles grievances in this inner melodrama of injustice collecting. To
this end, the collective ego milks 'rights', which can be
summoned up and rationalized for any positionality or
extremist viewpoint. The battle over 'rights' is the main-
stream of the media and contentious social strife
termed 'politics', for which truth is willingly sacrificed
for gain and for which millions die.

Inner examination and self-honesty reveal the

secret delights the ego gets from the nurturance of these justifications and protestations. The ego's illusion is that this process is self-nurturing, whereas, in actuality, it has exactly the opposite effect.

In releasing this vicious cycle, it is well to view the totality of human suffering and recontextualize the events from the level of compassion. As the Buddha pointed out, being mortal automatically entails suffering, which is why he taught to seek Enlightenment in order to preclude that karmically determined recurrence. When one willingly lets a hated perpetrator 'off the hook' by forgiveness, it is not that person who is taken off the hook but oneself. As the Buddha also said, there is no necessity to punish or get even with others because they will bring themselves down by their own hand.

The public often expresses concern that the guilty might go unpunished. Anyone familiar with the reality of consciousness and spiritual truth realizes that no such thing is possible. Everyone is accountable to the universe and is subject to Divine Justice by the very dynamics of the universe itself. Like a cork in the sea, each soul floats to the level of its own buoyancy, which is not due to some arbitrary act by the sea. There is no hand on the tiller but one's own, which is the total freedom accorded to life by God. No man falls but by his own hand. Even the supposed 'accidental' occurrence is merely a perception. There are no accidents in the universe, nor are they even a possibility. What it really means is that they are unpredictable or incomprehensible to the linear ego and its limitation to the Newtonian paradigm of cause and effect (cal. level 450).

In the headlines twenty years ago was the example

of an airplane flying at a high altitude when part of the fuselage flew off and just one person out of the hundreds of passengers on board was sucked out. People congregate in groups because they are aligned with the same attractor field. When fish at the bottom of the sea swoop about in schools or birds fly in flocks, each one is where they are, not as a result of their alignment with the others but because they are all attuned to exactly the same attractor field. Each one, individually, is following a powerful magnetic-like field that in turn is subject to the next higher attractor field, and so on up to Divinity. (The above passage calibrates at 995.)

The Politics of the Ego/Hate

The dualistically structured ego propagates itself by a positionality that tends to see everything in terms of perpetrator/victim (the classic relativistic Karl Marx error). By virtue of an arbitrary positionality, it splits events into opposites, and the consequent blame that occurs may be directed inwardly as guilt or projected outwardly as hate and paranoia. Thus, the ego is judgmental and unwittingly becomes its own victim. If it hates, it feels unconsciously guilty for violating truth and may repress the accumulated guilt, which adds more energy to the projected hatred. As will be discussed in a later chapter, this also contributes to the level of fear, for what the ego projects out, it unconsciously expects to return.

Despite its devices, the ego cannot escape consequences, whether it turns the attack within or without. The inherent fallacy of ego position is that it is not actually the real person who feels guilt or hate, but only the ego itself. The real Self is unaffected because truth is immune to falsity. Thus the hate/guilt game is operationally just internal politics in which different voices seek to dominate and win over one's allegiance.

The ego is envious of that which it intuits as being superior to its limitations and thus readily hates and denounces what it cannot understand. It has a vested interest in making wrong or denigrating what it cannot comprehend. Thus, the skeptic subtly hates spiritual truth or higher consciousness and its values (love, truth, Divinity, beauty). Hatred for purity or aesthetics is expressed by obscenity and gross vulgarity, as well as by desecration (destroy the *Pieta*, defile femininity, insult erudition, defame integrity, etc.).

Much purported criticism (masquerading as 'free speech') is thinly-disguised, envious hatred accompanied by rationalized justification in order to diminish guilt. Ideological hatred fuels public debate on almost every topic or issue in current society, from which the ego derives what it perceives as gain in the form of attention. Hatred often takes the form of projecting guilt via blame.

Analogously, the politics of the ego have their counterpart in society, which is very preoccupied with blame. While individuals do play a part, unfortunate events will often represent a failure of the underlying social process itself due to policies that are innately fallacious. While punishing the guilty culprits satisfies the public, it usually shortchanges society because the resolution is discovered by examining the underlying process itself.

Guilt that stems from some past poor judgment is overcome by the devices of reparation, confession, and moral rededication, as well as by compensation from good works (the process of 'undoing'). Humility helps recovery with the admission that a portion of the guilt stems from pride, e.g., "I shouldn't have made that mistake."

There is an error in the word 'should', which represents the hypothetical. The hypothetical is never reality and is actually an idealized abstraction. The hypothetical therefore represents a fantasy.

Personal past history represents the best that one could actually do then under given circumstances, which included one's perceptions and emotional mental states at the time. Mistakes can have a positive effect because they serve the maintenance of a realistic humility. The ego is a defective compass that often gives wrong directions. When one considers the degree of its limitations, it is a wonder that anyone survives long enough to even make mistakes.

A study of the history of civilization quickly reveals that not only individuals but also great multitudes have fallen and died as a direct consequence of the human mind's inability to discern truth from falsehood. Millions of people, whole countries, and even generations of citizens are repeatedly devastated by false beliefs, illusions, delusions, and the failure to recognize nonintegrous leaders. Thus, Mackay's famous *Extraordinary Popular Delusions and the Madness of Crowds* has been in constant print since 1841.

Because the evolution of consciousness, both individually and collectively, is progressive, the past, by selection, appears to compare unfavorably with the present. Lessons can be learned only by the unfolding of experience over a time continuum; thus, there is always more that hypothetically could be known. In reality, one cannot know at age twenty-five the information that is accrued by age fifty. Everyone thinks, "If I had only known that, I would have done it differently." Thus, with humility, it can be seen that every given moment includes limitation. What we were is not what we are now. Mistakes are intrinsic to the learning process, which is the fate of the human condition itself. Because the mind's awareness is limited, it compensates by substituting presumptions (an educated guess) and therefore, operationally, choices and decisions are based on the seemingly best option, as stated by Socrates' dictum.

Spiritual guilt is the consequence of morality, ethics, and religious belief systems, which, although they contribute to guilt, also include time-honored processes for the alleviation of and recovery from guilt, such as confession, forgiveness, penance, and the renewal and rededication to spiritual principles, as well as good works, selfless service, and humanitarian efforts. Guilt can be put to good use as a motivator for change for the better. Reasonable guilt is also evidence that one does have a conscience, and therefore, one is correctible. The psychopath lacks such an asset and therefore blindly goes on, making the same mistakes over and over, thereby sinking lower and lower. The spiritually-oriented person can therefore be thankful to have standards to live by that can serve as realistic inner guides to behavior.

'The Ego-Ideal'
Another structure of the psychological ego was

termed by Freud as 'the Ego-Ideal' (in contrast to the Id of repressed animal instincts and the superego, or conscience). This mental mechanism is composed of admired, hoped-for and wished-for idealized standards, goals, and identity. It is what one plans and hopes to become. Idealized figures become introjected as models and therefore inspirationally subserve ambitions and life planning.

Achievement of these ideals brings increased self-esteem and satisfaction, but alternately, failure to live up to expectations can also result in guilt. Unrealistic self-expectations thus have to be periodically revised so that they do not become oppressive. Holding a goal in mind is inspirational and is actually helpful to its accomplishment, because what is held in mind tends to actualize. However, it is a mistake to attack oneself with guilt for failing to achieve the ideal. Upon examination, it will be frequently discovered that it was not really the goal that was desired but the satisfaction that was associated with it.

Every moment simultaneously includes both options and limitations. These encompass the overall consequences of karmic factors collectively expressed as the totality of the circumstances of one's life inheritance and situation. The ego/self is linear and therefore subject to limitation and hindrance. Recognition of this human dilemma can result in choosing spiritual rather than material goals. ("You can't take a U-Haul to Heaven.") The dictum, "Store up treasures in Heaven rather than on Earth" is helpful to remember. In the long run, the consequences of merely being kind to others and all of life have far greater positive consequences than worldly success, which is temporary and eventually lost. It is beneficial to periodically reassess goals and ask whether they are really important or just the consequence of egotism. Success in any venture is simply the automatic consequence of being the best that one can be as a lifestyle, without looking for gain. In recovery from guilt, prayer and rededication to spiritual values are extremely helpful as is the compassionate realization that the human condition is difficult at best for everyone despite appearances.

The Problems of Working Through Guilt or Moral Defects

Guilt is a function of the normal superego, or conscience, and is a mechanism of restraint to counterbalance the animal instincts and impulses of what Freud termed the 'Id', which is composed of very primitive repressed instincts, including even the killer impulses.

While an excess of guilt calls for correction, its total absence is more serious and is generally a consequence of a congenital pathological condition that leads to various forms of criminality and psychopathology, as are seen in serial killers, psychopathic personalities, or in politics as malignant messianic narcissism.

In normal people, there are normal mechanisms of guilt that act as deterrents to selfishness, cruelty, or predatory impulses. The useful aspects of guilt include regret, restraint, and corrective self-criticism, which are all components of responsible morality and ethics. These aspects of the conscience counterbalance the extremes of egotism that are exhibited by the criminal/psychopathic personalities. Without restraint, the normally repressed, very primitive impulses of hatred are let loose on society as the killer, the rapist, the pedophile, the serial killer, and the mass murderer. All these conditions calibrate at consciousness levels of approximately 30, or even lower. Because of the bizarreness of the expressed behaviors, such persons have been classically referred to as 'possessed' (i.e., by evil). They are thus dominated by levels of consciousness that have been characterized as 'lower astral'.

These disorders are often diagnosable as early as age three by the characteristic inability to delay gratification, to learn from experience, or to anticipate consequences. These disorders thus far have proven to be incurable, and their clinical course is one of recidivism and chronic criminality as a lifestyle. If the disorder is also accompanied by an adequate intellect, it may take the form of corporate fraud or even pathological distortions of religion that are then used as camouflage for predation. This is seen in bizarre cults or aberrant distortions of traditional religions that become cults by nature and even lead to individual as well as group suicide or the killing of innocents in the name of Divinity.

Another variant is seen in the compartmentalized split personality in which the normal side is presented to society, and the concealed predator side acts out as a double agent, espionage agent, or traitorous informer. In its major political expressions, the disorder is also seen as messianic narcissistic megalomania that, when severely threatened, calls for the killing of even large numbers of countrymen (Nero, Hitler, Hussein, Stalin, et al.)

The Balance of Guilt

As is obvious from the foregoing, the absence of guilt is a condition more severe than its opposite of excessive guilt. Its absence leads to a form of mental disorder that, a century ago, was termed 'moral imbecility'. In contrast, the hypertrophic conscience is associated with scrupulosity or obsessive-compulsive disorder in which the person lives in fear of guilt over even minor trivia, such as making just a normal mistake.

In spiritual evolution, guilt is recontextualized so that it results in benefit. It needs to be reframed as caution and seen as a safeguard against being dominated by destructive impulses. It is later represented as the wisdom of maturity and is the ethical balance to self-centeredness. Thus, guilt is transcended when it has been recontextualized, harmonized, and balanced with responsibility and conscientious, internalized morality. Guilt can then be accepted when it is recontextualized as being protective, a safeguard, and a mechanism of learning.

Guilt is unpleasant because it is associated with loss of love and disapproval of internalized parental figures, along with loss of self-esteem. It is often used as a tool to control others ('guilt mongers'). It is also symbolic of rejection, disgrace, and loss of status. From religion, it becomes closely associated with sin and fear of the God who threw Adam and Eve out of the Garden of Eden, which marked the onset of the historic origins of the karma of simply being a human and thus prone to error and defiance of Divine authority. Upon examination, the error appears to be one of uncontrolled infantile curiosity, so the serpent was successful in tempting the curious inner child who is gullible and naïve.

A useful interpretation and use for guilt is respect for parameters and boundaries. Thereby, guilt and fear are matured into caution and wisdom. This results in respect for moral precepts and boundaries that replace guilt and eventuate as character traits that support survival, success, and happiness.

The ego also hates those who make it feel guilty, which contributes to immature hatred of all authority that is then misperceived as being arbitrary, authoritarian, and repressive instead of benignly protective. Because guilt is viewed as painful, another mechanism to avoid it is by denial and projection of responsibility onto others via blame, which ameliorates the pain of the conscience and, in addition, justifies externalized hatred that otherwise might have been used to attack the self. Society is therefore eager to accuse and affix blame, and it searches endlessly for guilty culprits upon whom blame and hatred can be guiltlessly projected (e.g., the paradox of 'hating sin').

Unconscious Guilt

In normal persons, deviation from truth and honesty results in the accumulation of guilt that is then repressed because of its unpleasant, painful nature. Thus, over time, a sizeable reservoir of guilt accumulates, which escapes attention or awareness unless discovered by periodic, fearless inventories. This is a very common condition that contributes to social discord and contention. Moral/ethical lapses are often excused by rationalization, but the unconscious mind is not fooled by deception and innately knows when it is being lied to by self or others.

A common social source stems from the current proclivity for persuasive politicalization of all aspects of society that then requires rationalized justifications. This results in distorting evidence that would weaken the positionality. An example would be the arguments against any reference to religion or Divinity in public. The arguments 'against' cite the constitutional "make no law respecting an establishment of a religion," but then purposely do not finish the cited sentence that goes on to say "or prohibiting the free exercise thereof." The Constitution is Deistic but not theistic, a major differentiation.

The presentation of half-truths in order to win a position is rationalized and the guilt suppressed. Examples abound regarding opposition to social programs that opponents purposely fail to report are strictly voluntary, or the support of perpetrators' rights that ignore the rights of victims. Accumulation of social guilt eventuates as overt projected accusations or vilifications that then require further justification reinforced by further subtle distortions and elaborate rhetoric.

Guilt and hatred are ameliorated by the acceptance of the limitations of the ego/mind with its inherent structure and operational defects. Instead of hatred, it becomes sad to see people destroying their own lives as well as the lives of others. It is also quite apparent that there is no profit in hating them. The capacity for forgiveness arises from accepting with honest humility the limitations inherent in the human condition itself, which is, after all, merely on a learning curve of the evolution of consciousness. It was only in the last twenty years that the overall consciousness level of mankind even crossed over the level of Truth at 200, and seventy-eight percent of the world's population still calibrates below 200, (forty-nine percent in America).

Guilt and the Process of Spiritual Evolution

Spiritual aspirants often ask where to begin the inner work and how to proceed. First, there is usually a period of acquisition of spiritual knowledge through study, by visiting spiritual groups, or attending lectures, meetings, or retreats. Then begins the focus on the inner journey of self-exploration that, to be successful, should have some overall direction rather than proceeding in sporadic fits and starts that all too often result in discouragement or abandonment of the project altogether.

Very importantly, before taking an inner moral inventory, it is essential to become knowledgeable about one's own conscience and how it operates. It is important for it to become benign and be utilized constructively, for if not recontextualized, it ends up with self-blame or an increase of guilt, shame, or the loss of self-esteem. It must be clearly seen that all defects are intrinsic to the ego structure itself, which is naïve and unable to discern appearance from essence. It actually does not have the capacity to know truth from falsehood about either the world or the personal self.

It is best to speak to the inner conscience and commit it to becoming a useful ally and teacher rather than a sadistic self-perpetrator. It is important to decisively bind its purpose to be educative. One must make a decision that a mature conscience is a useful tool and a helpful guide with which one is in accord by the choice of one's own will. By exercise of the will, the conscience can then be prohibited from becoming just another self-indulgent, wallowing-in-guilt, paradoxically egoistic perpetrator.

It is good to be aware that wearing sackcloth and

ashes may be melodramatic, but it is useless to the world or spiritual integrity and is actually a sly self-indulgence. Guilt can be replaced with just a decent regret as an inherited human limitation, in contrast to which perfection is an equally unrealistic idealization. Guilt is alleviated by acceptance of limitation that, in turn, is a positive consequence of humility. Thereby, guilt can be rejected as merely another form of self-indulgence.

Self-honesty requires courage, humility, patience, and compassion for the immature aspects of the conscience, which, after all, arose originally as a product of childhood. Therefore, it has a tendency toward exaggeration, or alternately, to being dismissed if it stands in the way of impulsiveness. The task is to honestly acknowledge inner defects or faults of character without triggering guilt attacks of self-hatred, anger, or resentment of self or others.

The ego/mind is a learned set of behaviors, and the ultimate goal is to transcend its programming and functioning by virtue of the power of the Radiance of the Self, which recontextualizes life benignly. The Presence of the Self is experienced as compassion for all of life in all its expressions, including its evolution as one's personal self. As a consequence, forgiveness replaces condemnation, which is a sign that it is now safe to proceed deeper into serious inner inventory without undue stress.

The above process represents the collective wisdom of the totality of the very successful twelve-step self-help groups, as well as others. It also represents the basic premise that is followed in in-depth analysis, such as psychoanalysis, where the basic rule is to always approach the exploration of intrapsychic conflicts first from the side of the superego. It is also helpful to remember that the world benefits from wisdom and not from hatred, blame, or guilt. On the road of inner discovery, one comes across memories and events that are deserving of regret and simply result in the decision to do better.

Another very useful tool in spiritual and therapeutic work is a sense of humor to offset the downside of the worldly theater of the absurd and its outrageous slings and arrows. Humor is the consequence of seeing through the illusions of paradox.

While the great teachers taught that the basic human defect is ignorance, it is even more helpful to see human limitation as naïveté, which is primarily a shortcoming. With adequate preparation, inner work and rigorous self-honesty can be taken on safely without falling into shame, despair, hopelessness, self-condemnation, depression, or loss of self-esteem. As the crook remarked when caught red-handed, "Well, nobody's perfect, are they?"

While world religions have formal periods of penance and self-examination, these tend to become compartmentalized and also viewed as unpleasantly somber. Mature spiritual work results in rewarding growth and education that lead to greater happiness and joy. Penance tends to be episodic; spiritual growth is permanent.

Theology and Guilt

Humankind is a progressively evolutionary species whose origins were very primitive and ignorant of reality. The theological beliefs of ancient civilizations were therefore birthed out of the myths of uneducated imagination that included a preponderance of negativity in accord with the prevailing low levels of consciousness. The allegory of 'Adam and Eve' calibrates at 70, and the idea that man was 'born in sin' calibrates at a level of truth of only 30. Divinity was perceived as oppressive and frightening.

An alternate view that stems from consciousness research is that humans emerged as basically innocent but ignorant, which calibrates at 200. In contrast, there is the view of man as expressed by Socrates that all men are intrinsically innocent because they can only choose to do what they perceive as the good, but they are unable to discern the true good from the false illusions of the world. (Socrates' statement calibrates at 700.) Extensive research, as well as clinical and spiritual experience, history, and investigation, corroborate the truth of Socrates.

Because man lacked the capacity to discern truth from falsehood, the system of good and bad was instituted, which was pragmatic and of social value for children and for the large segment of the populous that calibrates below 200. Because the nonevolved or immature lack a sense of spiritual/ethical/moral standards, they are guided by 'rules' of 'good and bad'. Below consciousness level 200, there is no concern for others, and therefore, 'good and bad' dictums substitute for the lack of awareness. What is tempting to the non-integrous would not even be thinkable as an option to people who are more evolved (e.g., to murder someone for their money, etc.). Crime is related directly to the personal level of consciousness (inmates in prison calibrate at an average of 50). Thus, guilt serves as a valuable function collectively where it is appropriate as a social counterbalance to the acting out of primitive instincts.

There is a similar value to good/bad guilt in children who also lack a sense of reality (e.g., it is 'bad' to squeeze a newborn kitten). In this case, guilt has its positive aspect as an inhibiting counterbalance to unrestrained, primitive instinctual drives of the nonevolved 'uncivilized' ego.

In more mature persons, instinctual primitive drives may unexpectedly break through defenses in the form of impulsivity that is later regretted or seen as a foolish mistake and therefore a helpful warning to be more aware of a trend that results in mistakes in judgment. Maturation is a life-long process, and, as the old saying goes, "The gray hairs of age have been earned." Some degree of remorse and regret over past errors is inevitable, contributing to the development of compassion for self and others. To make allowance for human error is indicative of a more benign, realistic conscience.

The Dualities of Guilt and Hate

Because the consequences to self and others can be extensive, guilt and hatred, whether directed within or projected onto others, necessitate serious attention. In return, the rewards from experiencing increased degrees of happiness are gratifying and experientially well worth the effort. The relinquishment of guilt and hatred is a major benefit at all levels of life as these ego positions are corrosive to self and others. Resistance stems from the secret pleasure the ego derives from negativity.

The Dualities of Guilt and Hate

Attraction	Aversion
Make judgment	Surrender judgment to God
Punish self or others	Forgive self or others
Refuse mercy	Accept mercy and compassion
Justify negativity	Surrender secret pleasure
Project feelings	Take responsibility
Choose perception	Choose essence
Rigid, narrow view	Flexible, see both sides
Penance, self-indulgence	Service to others
Cling to position	Ask God for miracles
Justify	Relent, choose options
Act out	Transcend
Enjoy meanness	Enjoy being gracious to self/others
Act against self and others	Act to help self and others
Choose the negative	Choose the positive
Be 'right'	Be wrong
Helpless, stuck	Flexible, grow
Reinforce	Transcend
Stuck in past	Live in the now
Malignant, cruel	Benign, merciful
Stingy	Benevolent
Project responsibility	Choose to be author
Vengeful	Merciful
Be small	Choose 'bigger than that'
Grasping	Benevolent

CHAPTER 3

Apathy
(Calibration Level 50)

Introduction
The level of Apathy is characterized by neglect, indifference, poverty, and in more severe degrees, by despair and hopelessness. The world and the future look bleak, and pathos is the theme of life. It is a state of helplessness, and its victims, needy in every way, lack not only resources but also the energy to take advantage of what may be available. Unless external energy is supplied by caregivers, death through passive suicide can result. Without the will to live, the hopeless stare blankly, unresponsive to stimuli. The eyes stop tracking, and there is insufficient energy left to even swallow proffered food.

This is the level of the homeless and the derelicts of society. It is also the fate of many of the aged and others who become isolated by chronic or progressive diseases. The apathetic are dependent; they are 'heavy' and feel like a burden to those around them. They represent the human expression of the tamas of the classic Hindu *gunas* (qualities) of the trilogy of *tamas* (inertia, resistance), *rajas* (high energy), and *sattva* (peace) that are innate to the world.

Society often lacks sufficient motivation to be of any real help to cultures or individuals at this level and sees them as drains of resources. This is the level of the streets of Calcutta, where only the saintly, such as Mother Teresa and her followers, dared to tread. It is the level of the abandonment of hope, and few have the courage to really look into its face.

Clinical

Unrecognized apathy in the form of inertia is at the core of many social, as well as personal, problems. The failure of bureaucratic/government agencies to 'take care' and assume responsibility can also result in mass catastrophes. Examples abound of failure to act or function, such as unpreparedness prior to Pearl Harbor, being 'blindsided' in the Korean War, warnings prior to 9/11 and other al-Qaeda attacks, lack of action after the USS Cole bombing, unpreparedness of the military for the Iraqi war, belated response to hurricane Katrina, and others.

Apathy indicates very low availability of energy and interest. This can be endemic in cultures and regions, including metropolitan and poverty areas. Laxity or indifference may be culturally carried by even subtle means. "What's the use?" is an infectious attitude.

Sloth is included as one of the seven deadly sins because it is a rejection of God's gift of life and is self-indulgence without love. In this state, there is no concern for the welfare of others or even appropriate concern for the quality of one's own life. The same attitude is then projected onto God who is seen as rejecting, unavailable, and uncaring. The waste of one's life results in a concept of God as indifferent, condemning, and unavailable. This leads to hopelessness and pessimism.

Apathy is often the basis for passivity and self-condemnation, resulting in low self-esteem and self-image. The feeling of worthlessness reinforces negative social attitudes and behaviors that result in poverty and low quality of life. Hopelessness leads to further decline, which is then used as a face-saving rationalization. The core is that responsibility is rejected and replaced by a chronic victim mentality that seeks to avoid the real issues by projecting the supposed source to the external world, which is then comfortably blamed as being the 'cause'. The dualistic split of victim/perpetrator is further reinforced by current 'post-modern', relativistic social theories that perpetuate the illusion.

Poor parenting is relatively influential in establishing early-life behavioral patterns in which there are a lack of love and ordinary motivating behavioral factors. This results in an inadequate inner reward system and low self-esteem, and discouragement compounds the problem. Although the 'ego-ideal' may develop and heroic figures may be admired, the inner conviction is that the idealized is not obtainable due to hopelessness and skepticism. The normal person receives some recognition for effort in trying, even if they fail. The hopeless person sees no point in even attempting a higher level of functioning.

The energy attractor field of apathy draws to it other expressions in the same low energy field (the well-known 'broken window' principle), which results in an overall depressing social milieu that breeds crime and poverty.

The apathetic condition indicates impairment that results in resorting to face-saving excuses. It may also result in hypochondriasis, chronic invalidism, and a self-centered personality that is passive, nonfunctional, and seeks dependent relationships. The comfort of drugs may also provide escape from the inner barrenness. When the temporary drug-induced euphoria subsides, the return of the downside becomes intolerable, so the drug dependence is not just an addiction but also a lifestyle. The self-perpetuating downward spiral may result in desperate attempts to survive, including clinging to abusive relationships. Self-condemnation is projected onto God and society which are therefore blamed for the condition.

The core of the disorder is identifiable as the inability or refusal to take personal responsibility, which results in guilt, shame, and low energy that may end up as homelessness, vagrancy, and social dependence. Lack of life skills leads to periodic descents into severe depression, which may result in suicide.

Transcending Apathy

Apathetic moments or even periods of time may occur temporarily in almost anyone's life in which there are times of 'downs' and feelings of discouragement. The lifestyle itself becomes a denial of the value of life and of Divinity as its source.

The only way out of this impasse is via the Will, which alone has the potential power to compensate for the lack of intrapsychic energy. The Will, which is spiritual in nature and origin, is not to be confused with 'will power', which is only mental and psychological. In an apathetic state, the personal will is weak and ineffectual. This can be transcended only by the invocation of Divine Will, which calibrates at 850 and has the power of regeneration. While the ego/self routinely takes credit for survival, its true source is the presence of Divinity as Self. It is only because of the Self that the ego is capable of being self-sustaining. It is only a recipient of life energy and not its origin, as it believes.

Divine entreaty may or may not result in a desired outcome because, to the Self, adversity, or even physical death, may be the only way to defeat the ego. To the Self, surrender of the personal world or the physical body may be the requisite for the transformation of the soul. Thus, in this seeming paradox, defeat to the ego/mind/body entity is, in actuality, the sacrifice of the temporary for the permanent (evolution of the soul) and therefore a karmic gain.

While the personal will only calibrates at the same level as does the person (extremely weak in the state of apathy, at approximately 30), the Will calibrates at a very powerful level. These are the conditions that illustrate the dynamic forces behind the truth that 'man's calamity is God's opportunity'.

The invitation to Divinity, for example, is well demonstrated by the twelve-step groups in which the initial steps (paraphrased) are, "We admitted we were powerless over our lives, and only God could relieve us of our insanity." By the admission of personal powerlessness and turning away from the ego, the decision is made to turn one's life over to God. This is followed by a fearless moral inventory and then seeking guidance through prayer and the establishment of a daily spiritual life pattern (*Twelve Steps and Twelve Traditions*, 1996).

The above process has been proven to bring about recovery from a whole gamut of very difficult, hopeless human problems in millions of people worldwide for many decades. The transformations that result are often described as miraculous because of their degree. This simple program originally began in Oxford, England, and was brought to the United States by Rowland, the hopeless patient of the famous Swiss psychoanalyst, Carl Jung, whose own honesty helped Rowland hit bottom when he said to him, "Alas, neither I nor my art can help you, and your only hope is to throw yourself wholeheartedly into a spiritual program, for it is recorded in history that, although rare, recoveries have occurred under those circumstances." Eventually Rowland's dramatic recovery set the paradigm for what is now the worldwide Twelve-Step movement, as well as other faith-based programs, and has even been effective in thirty-five percent of cases of extremely hardened chronic criminals.

Apathy is at the core of many seemingly hopeless conditions that are beyond the capacity of the human will or society to resolve. Recovery from any of these apathetic conditions is strengthened by participation in spiritual groups because their overall energy calibrates at 540, the level of Unconditional Love, which is rare in the overall population (0.4 percent).

Another nonspiritual but strong program devoted to recovering and improving one's life by strictly accepting responsibility was demonstrated by "est" (Erhard Seminars Training) at calibration level 400. The technique was one of constant confrontation with irresponsibility and the canceling of all excuses, rationalizations, and evasions of it.

In what is seen as apathy, there is actually a strong internal resistance as a subtly disguised pride and egotism described as "I can't" or "I don't want to." The persistence of the ego is so strong that it frequently takes a mass catastrophe, such as war or an earthquake, to confront it to the degree that it is willing to surrender. Thus, by collective karma, whole groups are drawn to specific situations that may appear as catastrophic yet hold unseen karmic benefits.

Accidents

The infinite field of consciousness is All Present, All Powerful, and includes All of Existence. Thus, nothing can possibly happen outside its infinite domain because it is the Source of Existence. Within this infinite field of power, there are decreasing levels of energy fields. As they are expressed progressively in form (linearity), their relative power decreases all the way down to the individual. The giant field could be compared to an immense electrostatic field in which the individual is like a charged particle that, because of the infinite power of the field, is automatically aligned within the field according to its individual 'charge'. The charge of the karmic spiritual body is set by intention, decision, and alignment by intention. It appears to naïve perception that what is not intellectually explicable seems to be 'accidental', especially when the event is unpredictable. Inasmuch as the infinite field of consciousness is unlimited in dimension, nothing can happen outside of it. All that occurs within it is under its influence, and therefore, nothing 'accidental' is possible in Reality.

Apathy in the Normal Individual

Periods of apathy are recurrent in almost everyone's life as a temporary and transitory phenomenon. To the spiritually oriented, the self-searching to the core of the phenomenon to understand its origins results in a positive outcome. Apathy in the normal individual usually applies to certain areas of life that have been neglected, resisted, or for which one has refused responsibility. These also express as aversions and attractions that, upon investigation, turn out to be based on illusions. Almost any resistance, aversion, or illusion can be dissolved by complete and total surrender and the willingness to relinquish illusory goals. Operationally, this can be described as surrendering the linear (the ego) to the nonlinear (Divinity).

Passive/Aggressive Dichotomy

Shame, apathy, and guilt are all forms of aggression against the self by attack with self-hatred, accusation, and negative judgmentalism. The alternate sides of these mechanisms are used in the defensive maneuver of projected, externalized hate and blame. Apathy is also a form of resistance to the maturation process and is a way of negation and refusal, i.e., concealed stubbornness.

With these mechanisms, personal responsibility is again denied, and otherwise seemingly normal individuals may periodically alternate with extreme aggression toward others. When the worm of self-hatred turns from attacking the self and is directed externally, it expresses as vituperation, malice, malevolence, slander, and even public vilifications that can be extreme.

Self-hatred directed externally calibrates very low because it is a denial of truth at a deep level and secondarily destructive to society and its standards. This externally directed aggression finds social approval and is therefore expressed in war, gang criminality, terrorism, environmental arson, crowd violence, the Ku Klux Klan, etc. These projections can only be possible if the conscience is either absent, such as with a psychopath, or assuaged by rationalization (liberationists justify revenge, 'holy' or political wars, etc.).

The need for justification is served by harboring grudges, distorted interpretations of society, and 'injustice' collecting. When this psychological mechanism operates in a charismatic leader, thousands or even millions of people periodically die. This syndrome is termed 'malignant messianic narcissism' and is described in detail in *Truth vs. Falsehood* (see Chapter 15). The extreme pathology of such leaders is obvious from the willing slaughter of their own countrymen who are hated and seen as 'dogs', cannon fodder, or 'deserving of death'. Such distorted personalities despise love (therefore, women), seeing it as weak and displaying internally feared vulnerability. When these projected mechanisms cannot be acted out, there are inner conflicts in consciousness, and the end of such messianic leaders is often by suicide.

These same mechanisms operate unconsciously, but to a more limited and attenuated degree, in publicity-seeking, hostile personalities who publicly make poisonous remarks and slander public figures through false accusations and distortions of events.

In psychoanalytical terms, intense negativity is disowned by projection in order to keep the illusion of the innocent 'good me', despite the transparency of the camouflage to the public. The consequence of dishonesty is often pomposity and seeing oneself as superior to others. The ego also incorporates spiritual images and concepts to bulwark its defenses that thereby become distorted into their exact opposites in order to justify the slaughter of infidels, nonbelievers, heretics, etc., who therefore 'deserve' to die. The projection of self-contempt for perceived inner weakness was dramatically acted out by the Japanese with American prisoners and in Manchuria and China when they summarily executed enemy soldiers who surrendered.

The very low energy fields may be rationalized by the intellect, which then sees pseudoreligious distortions as truth and bizarrely praises martyrdom and suicide. Hari-kari is a classic example of externalized acting out and dramatization of what would be repressed as internalized conflict in ordinary, healthy people.

Intrapsychic repression of unacceptable drives and conflicts depletes psychic energy that is unavailable for normal adaptational operations. This results in apathy expressed as exhaustion, feeling tired and below par, and the lack of pleasure in living (anhedonia).

Lack of pleasure through normal means may be artificially compensated through various addictions. When escapism is blocked or unobtainable, the inner depression returns, which may result in acting out and desperate measures of avoidance. Many actually choose to die rather than face the inner conflicts and own the responsibility for either the conflict itself or for seeking help and resolution.

The progressive downward spiral often eventually leads to a confrontational social crisis, such as arrest, divorce, losing one's job, bankruptcy, hospitalization, and homelessness. Therefore, confrontation is one of the positive consequences that arise from seeming calamities that are frequently lifesaving and rescues in disguise.

Statistically, the most successful resolutions to these types of recoveries from pathological life patterns are through faith-based groups, as self-honesty is a difficult, if not impossible, process for most people without strong prompting. Recovery requires strong support plus experienced know-how, and the example of recovered members tends to discourage denial as do the insistence on moral integrity and the admission of character defects without wallowing in guilt. In addition, helping others is beneficial and increases self-esteem.

Although strictly psychological measures may sometimes be temporarily beneficial, these disorders are usually chronic, and the recovery requires programs that are intrinsically spiritual in nature, as they address the core of the issue and see psychological and behavioral problems as secondary. The underlying and deep-seated self-hatred requires a therapy of a very high consciousness calibration level, such as that of Unconditional Love at 540. Psychological measures that calibrate in the 400s have insufficient power to actually bring about an inner healing. The healing process requires an advisor, sponsor, or counselor to provide guidance and serve as an example to identify with, love, and respect. In the decades-long experience of such groups, only a recovered member has the requisite authority that instills respect and therefore a therapeutic transference or identification. Through this mechanism, love returns in an acceptable form, and its acceptance is facilitated by realistic, spiritually integrous humility.

Spiritual humility should not be confused with its social interpretation as 'humiliation'. Paradoxically, the spiritually humble cannot be humiliated, and therefore, faults can be accepted without loss of self-esteem. Owning one's own inner flaws allows for nonjudgmental respect for others and opens the door to compassion for all humanity.

Apathy versus Motivation

Human behaviors can result from being instinctually driven or, alternately, from being attracted to or motivated by positive, idealized goals. The Freudian 'ego-ideal' is the internalization of admired qualities, achievements, or heroic figures that are inspirational and represent possibilities for growth and development. The admired figures are selected in accord with the individual's prevailing level of consciousness so that each level characteristically tends to have its commensurate inspirational leaders. Lack of such an internalized figure can stem from poor or absent parenting, or lack of self-esteem or sense of personal worth that leads to expectations of failure, pessimism, and the 'amotivational syndrome'.

The building of self-confidence is usually best done step-wise in small increments, aided by motivational encouragement. A negative self-image may be compounded by past failures or criticism by peers or parental figures, resulting in attitudes of "I can't" or "I'm not worth it."The old adage,"If at first you don't succeed, try, try again," falls on deaf ears as apathy is usually defended with many rationalized excuses and justifications in order to avoid shame. In some expressions, apathy may be consequent to clinical depression due to faulty brain chemistry that requires antidepressants to correct the imbalance, at least temporarily, in order to reorganize the psyche.

The classic counterbalances to apathy and negative self-image are 'faith, hope, and charity'. The benefit of helping others is very well demonstrated throughout society, whether it comes about through choice, inspiration, or even coercion. Often, for those who have fallen very low, even just caring for animals can serve as a very good start, as is demonstrated by the seeing-eye-dog training programs that have been very successful in populations of chronic recidivist prison inmates, some of whom even choose to stay on past their discharge date to complete their work with their assigned dogs. Apathetic geriatric patients perk up if the nursing home provides pet dogs. Current research indicates that the mere owning of a pet decreases the levels of depression and hypertension and has a positive effect on health overall. Therefore, caring for other living beings is therapeutic as is exhibited by hopeless alcoholics when they begin to help newcomers and dejected athletes recover from a defeatist attitude by the sheer act of encouraging other team members.

In spiritual work also, group participation remotivates as a consequence of the group's intrinsic spiritual energy. Thus, ministerial organizations serve a great purpose, as do mentors, trainers, motivational speakers, humanitarian organizations, the clergy, and inspirational teachers. The average person usually has some limited areas of apathy, at least for periods of time, that are areas of neglect due to economy of available time and energy or interest.

Spiritual apathy is also quite common as an expression of avoidance and reluctance to face inner conflicts that thereby become a deterrent to progress and growth. These delays can be expected and also traversed by prayer and the inspiration innate to active spiritual groups. Motivation is aided and augmented in almost any human endeavor by having a mentor, confidant, or trusted friend. Apathy is often the result of isolation and cured by involvement in and the activity of positive relationships that provide a source of caringness. Apathy is indicative of the absence of love, which is its most powerful antidote. This may be situational or the consequence of rejecting love due to egocentricity or very low self-esteem resulting from lack of love and nurturance in early life.

To choose love *for* God activates the love *of* God by prayer and worship. Therefore, despondency may be the very trigger that opens the door to the emergence of spiritual interest and progress. Many have found God only in the pits of hopelessness and despair. The ego is so strong that sometimes only severe 'hitting bottom' is a strong enough stimulus to activate the willingness to surrender allegiance to the ego's domination. When activated, the spirit within is renewed, and apathy is replaced by hope. To 'pray ceaselessly' may be the only option available to work through some severe or prolonged periods of karmic debt. It is sometimes referred to as a 'test of faith', which is best traversed by conviction that 'this too shall pass', and "They also serve who stand and wait."

Apathy, like any other obstacle on the evolutionary path, is resolved by acceptance rather than denial. Spiritual apathy can be helped by reexposure to basic spiritual truths, such as provided by scripture or spiritual literature. Reflection and meditation on verses, such as those in the Ninety-first Psalm or other favorite passages, often reactivate inspiration because of their innate high consciousness calibration. Reinspiration is also often consequent to repeating favorite prayers, hymns, or the playing of classical music in beautiful surroundings.

Music of high calibration presents an energy field directly that bypasses the intellect and negative mentation. Music that calibrates over 500 (listed in Chapter 9 of *Truth vs. Falsehood*) has an uplifting effect. It can vary all the way from the score of *Riverdance* to classical music, the stirring skirl of the bagpipes of the Scottish Black Watch, or even the irresistible music of the Bee Gees.

Transient apathy can indicate resistance to facing some inner personal defect, which is most rapidly overcome by direct admission and acceptance. This reactivates spiritual movement instead of being stultified. Even avoidance can be countered by accepting the fact that it is currently operative (avoiding the denial of denial). One can choose to avoid an issue consciously instead of being at the effect of it through avoidance. This alternative opens the option to just not deal with the issue currently and choose instead to take a vacation from it via what could be viewed as 'therapeutic escapism', such as going to the movies, taking a vacation, going on short trip, etc.

Acceptance by conscious choice has a different consequence from unconscious denial. Self-care is an integrous intention when done consciously. It is an exercise in developing self-love, especially if it is dedicated to God. It is sometimes necessary to rest and recuperate in order to become rejuvenated. This is one of the functions of play and recreation that serves retrenchment rather than just self-indulgence.

The Dualities of Apathy

As with other levels, positionalities express as dualities of attraction and aversion that have to be worked through, assisted by prayer and often the assistance of others.

The Dualities of Apathy

Attraction	Aversion
Blame, project 'cause'	Responsibility, own
"I can't"	"I won't"
See self as victim	See self as co-player
Indifference	Caring
Defeatist	Optimist
Justify, rationalize, excuse	Take action
See self as helpless	See self as able
Hopeless	Hope
Negate self-worth	Choose self-worth as gift from God
See self as weak	See self as potentially strong
Refuse solutions	Willing, accept
Self-sabotage	Self-endorsement
Indolence, sloth	Energy of action
Pessimism, cynical	Trust, faith, hope
See self as unworthy	Accept value of life
Future looks bleak	Future holds opportunity
See self as incapable	See self as willing to learn
Rigid, inflexible	Malleable, capable of growth
Passive	Active, put forth the effort
Reject help	Accept help
Self-pity	Compassion, then move on
Cling to position	Surrender positionality
Self-indulgence	Move on, 'get over it'
Excuse	Self-honesty
Sink lower	Evolve, move up
Succumb	Resist, refuse, reject

CHAPTER 4

Grief

(Calibration Level 75)

Introduction

This is the level of sadness, loss, and despondency. Most people have experienced it for periods of time, but those who remain at this level live a life of constant regret and depression. This is the level of mourning, bereavement, and remorse about the past. It is also the level of habitual losers and those chronic gamblers who accept failure as part of their lifestyle, often resulting in the loss of jobs, friends, family, and opportunity, as well as money and health.

Major losses in early life make one later vulnerable to passive acceptance of grief, as though sorrow were the price of life. In Grief, one sees sadness everywhere—the sadness of little children, of world conditions, and even the sadness of life itself. This level colors one's entire vision of existence. Part of the syndrome of loss is the sense of inability to replace what is lost or what it symbolized. There is a generalization from the particular, so that the loss of a loved one is equated with the loss of love itself. At this level, such emotional losses may trigger a serious depression or even death.

Though Grief is the cemetery of life, it still has more energy to it than does Apathy. Thus, when traumatized apathetic patients begin to cry, we know they are getting better, for once they start to cry, they will eat again.

Clinical

Grief is a universal human experience that is difficult to either view or go through because of its commonality and emotionality with which people are only too familiar. In minor degrees, it can be expressed as regret, but when major, it can be incapacitating and overwhelming.

The universality of the experience is due to the structure and nature of the ego, which misperceives the source of happiness as external or emotional and imbues it with specialness. In reality, the only source of happiness is from within, and its mechanism is intrapsychic and internal. When a desired object, situation, or relationship is obtained, the internal mechanism goes into operation with the satisfaction of that desire because the object, person, or condition has been imbued with special qualities. The value is in the eyes of the beholder or of the perceived and is not intrinsic to the desired object or person itself. Therefore, grief is linked to desire as well as ownership.

Society collectively assumes that certain conditions, objects, or qualities are valuable, and this agreement affects personal choice. The spiritually evolved person who has few wants or attachments is relatively immune to grief, as the experience of the source of happiness originates from within and is not dependent on externals. If the source of happiness is acquired through ego mechanisms, it is based on imagery, belief systems, and projected values rather than on Absolute Reality itself, which is invulnerable to loss. Objects, qualities, or relationships become overvalued by virtue of the mechanism of attachment and the ensuing projection of value. The more specialness projected onto the relationship with the desired object or person, the greater the potential for grief and loss. Fear of loss contributes to dependent attachments as well as materiality or social attributes, such as money and fame.

Happiness is the inner psychological reward for achievement of externalized goals as a self-reward system, and the error is to think that the source of happiness is due to the 'out there' instead of originating from within. The prototype is the set-up by the process of evolution itself. In that primordial, as well as later life, animal life forms were not self-energizing but depended on external sources of energy that could be found through search and trial and error. Thus, the biological mechanism was set up as need-search-trial and error-find-reward.

In humans, the same pattern persists at consciousness levels below 200 (see Brain Function chart in Chapter 9). Acquisition is basically animal-instinct survival, which depends upon the 'getting' of mate, food, territory, shelter, dominance, and control. Thus, to animal instincts, the source of happiness is programmed as coming from 'out there'. It is therefore 'gettable' and consequently subject to loss. With mating and animal bonding, this extends to mates and group members. Grief can be seen on the animal level in the reactions of wolf packs, elephant herds, and monkey, ape, and gorilla colonies that go through the grieving process.

The externalization of perceived sources of happiness leads to attachments and the emergence of control as a major survival mechanism, along with the desire for status and its symbols of security, and therefore, materialism.

Spiritual Orientation

Not uncommonly, major loss results in turning to religion and spirituality for help and answers. Emotionally, people find solace from sympathetic support, prayer, and returning to religious practices. Loss therefore provides an opportunity for increased intention to reevaluate spiritual principles and put them into actual practice rather than just intellectual appreciation.

A loss is at first an unwelcome event because it is disruptive and emotionally intrusive. The initial response may well be both shock and resentment, or even disbelief. Emotional storm demands energy and attention at a time when energy is low, resulting in anger. Processing the crisis is helped by focusing on certain inner realities and transcending their inherent limitations.

There are anger and resentment, as well as fear at loss of control when loss is involuntary and unexpected. Disruption of life by the unexpected also creates anxiety at the forced readjustment, which may require major decision making. It is well to know that spiritual research indicates that all suffering and emotional pain result from resistance. Its cure is via surrender and acceptance, which relieve the pain.

During the process, it will be noticed that the emotional pain of loss is not steady or continuous but comes in waves that can be diminished by consistent nonresistance and surrendering continuously to God. While the illusion that one is surrendering the loss of a seemingly essential person, object, desire, goal, or quality, one is actually processing the pain of disruption of the attachment; the 'what' one is surrendering is actually just the attachment itself. A basic truth to be realized in the process is that there is no possible, actual source of happiness outside one's self. Loss really brings long-standing illusions to the surface, along with opportunities to lessen its dominance in the psyche. The ego has a multitude of attachments to beliefs, slogans, objects, people, titles, money, conveniences, entertainment, furnishings, sentimental tokens, and memories of all the above. The ego/mind cherishes that which is temporary and transitory because it is valued as 'special' and therefore sees it as a 'source' of happiness.

Paradoxically, loss is simultaneously freedom and the opening of new options. Loss services inner adaptations and qualities that represent opportunities for growth. Simultaneously, the mind regrets and would like to undo change and return to the comfort of former circumstances, but evolutionary developmental growth is insistent. Therefore, the resentment is in having to change. Change may be a source of anticipatory pleasure if it is chosen and a source of resentment if it is resisted. Attachments are to the present and the anticipated future, as well as a clinging to the past. All these positions are illusory for there is never a time other than the present moment, and no one experiences either the past or the future, except in their imaginings and memories. The only source of happiness that is realistically based is in the present, and that which is in the present is not subject to loss.

All forms of loss are a confrontation to the ego and its survival mechanisms. All aspects of human life are transient; therefore, to cling to any aspect eventually brings grief and loss. Each incident, however, is an opportunity to search within for the source of life, which is ever present, unchanging, and not subject to loss or the ravages of time.

Grief or loss, like any stressful situation in life, can be seen as a valuable growth opportunity and a time for reassessment of values and goals. If this is followed, eventually it is possible to let go of all attachments, including belief systems, and experience the source of happiness that emanates from within.

Attachments

Attachment is the process whereby the suffering of loss occurs, irrespective of what the attachment is to or about, whether internal or external, whether object, relationship, social quality, or aspects of physical life. The ego perpetuates itself by its elaborate network of values, belief systems, and programs. Needs thus arise that gain more energy as they become embellished and elaborated, sometimes to the point of fixation. The source of pain is not the belief system itself but one's attachment to it and the inflation of its imaginary value. The inner processing of attachments is dependent on the exercise of the will, which alone has the power to undo the mechanism of attachment by the process of surrender. This may be subjectively experienced or contextualized as sacrifice, although it is actually a liberation. The emotional pain of loss arises from the attachment itself and not from the 'what' that has been lost.

It is difficult at first to surrender attachments and belief systems that have been reinforced socially by agreement, such as wealth, success, fame, beauty, and others. All these represent the same concept that some kind of an 'add-on' to what 'is' will bring greater happiness. Aside from the process of attachment, the other concomitant to the ego's mechanism is its belief in 'having'.

Consciousness research reveals that reported degrees of happiness are concordant with calibrated levels of consciousness rather than with externals. By consciousness level 540, reported levels of happiness are close to one-hundred percent.

The Illusion of Possession: 'Having' and 'Mine'

Grief has to do with loss, and loss implies prior ownership and a special relationship. The idea of 'mine' or 'my' denotes a unique contextualization and meaning that is a product of the ego's dualistic style of mentation by which a separate 'I' is magically bonded (in fantasy) to an 'it' or a 'you', and thereby to some quality, possession, or person. For example, a watch is merely just an object, but with claim of ownership, it is now imbued with a unique, special quality called 'mine'. What was just 'a' watch now becomes 'my' watch and thereby magically transformed. When this is emphasized, it becomes 'my *favorite* watch'. By this process, attachment, control, fear of loss, and sentiment are now added to the composition of the unique quality of specialness. One can really see that the stage is now set for tragedy, which occurs if a person thinks they have lost 'my' watch rather than just 'a' watch. It becomes obvious that the moment possession and the idea of 'mine' are introduced, bondage arises.

The emotional charge can be loosened by realizing that everything actually belongs only to God and that humans only exercise stewardship. In the world, ownership is a transitory specialness, and value and worth are only in perception, conceptualization, and legalities.

Accompanying possession are other attachments of the ego, such as pride, feelings of security, and sensory pleasure. The feeling of happiness is initiated by the satisfaction of an inner want that releases neurotransmitters in the brain, such as serotonin and endorphins, that are the consequence and concomitance but not the source of the experience of happiness itself. All sociological/psychological studies of happiness confirm that religious or spiritually-oriented people are generally happier all the time, no matter what the circumstances. (Wellas, 2005)

Processing out Negative Feelings
With loss, the spiritual process of nonresistance and surrendering is effective (however, it is not a suitable process for those emotional states that calibrate lower than 75, such as depression, guilt, and apathy).A spiritually-oriented person values all of life's experiences and sees each one as an opportunity to evolve spiritually. The technique of processing out involves very simple steps that all depend on willingness and the capacity to surrender.
1. Stay with the feeling and stay focused on it unswervingly. Realize that all pain is due to resistance. The suffering of loss stems from the attachment and specialness.
2. Be willing to become immersed in and surrender to the feelings without avoiding them. Notice that they come in waves and that surrendering to the most intense waves tends to decrease their emotional severity.
3. Ask God's help and surrender the personal will to God. (It is helpful to read the Ninety-first Psalm or other favorite spiritual passages.)

4. Be willing to endure and suffer out the process. If not resisted, it will process itself out and come to an end.

Although the suffering of loss is triggered by a specific event, the painful emotions of attachment have actually arisen from multiple sources over time, and there may be more of it below the surface than was first suspected. Thus, each loss actually represents all loss, for the experience is of loss itself and not just the specific event that brought it up to awareness.

A helpful source of strength during the processing out of painful emotions is to identify with all of humanity and realize that suffering is universal and innate to the phenomenon of being human and the evolution of the ego.

Nonattachment versus Detachment

This is an important distinction, and failure to understand it can lead to important spiritual error. 'Detachment' is an ongoing process that, unfortunately, can lead to apathy and emotional flatness, noninvolvement, and indifference. It can also result in passivity and loss of interest in life. There are misunderstandings of spirituality that teach that even love is an attachment, which is a misconception, for love is an aspect of God; possessiveness is an aspect of ego.

An incorrect understanding of the pathway of negation can result in the sterility of the 'Void' or 'Nothingness'. While the Void is an impressive spiritual experience (cal. 850), it is not the Ultimate State, which, correctly, is that of Allness. This arises from a misunderstanding of the teachings of the Buddha. 'Void' means nonlinear and the absence of 'thingness', or linearity. Beyond Voidness is the ultimate, all-inclusive nonlinear reality of Allness. The subjective experience of the Void, although very impressive, is considerably different from the Reality of the state of the Presence of God as Allness, including the very major quality of Infinite Love itself (see Chapter 18).

Resolution

The pain of processing out personal loss is lessened by an emotional/philosophical acceptance and realization of the overall reality of the human condition itself, which is shared by everyone:

1. Everything in the human domain is temporary, transitional, and evolutionary.
2. Nothing can really be 'owned' or 'mine'. All relationships are temporary and arbitrary. Legality affords only rights of control.
3. Everything belongs to God; consequently, all that is considered to be 'mine' and 'belonging to' me is a temporary condition, including the human body itself. Domination is only control; it is dominion that reigns.
4. See all ownerships and relationships as stewardships only. The obligation is to responsibility of alignment rather than attachment or involvement.
5. Cling to principles rather than people, objects, conditions, and transitory situations. The calibrated levels of consciousness are indicative of the principles that correlate with and determine that level and its overall attractor field of consciousness by which all is aligned and influenced.
6. Resolve to live with courage and dignity. This stance summons forth the unseen Power by which all life

survives. Accept that mourning is a normal process rather than resisting it.

7. Accept that all sentient beings live by faith. Despite naïve and pretentious claims to the contrary, all people live solely by the principle of faith—it is only a question of faith in 'what'. Faith can be placed in the illusory, the intellect, reason, science, progress, political and worldly power, ego satisfactions, pleasure, wealth, or hope (e.g., 'tomorrow').

These faiths are all based on presumptions that can be eclipsed at any moment because they are fragile beliefs. Even the hypothetical 'nonbeliever' or skeptic lives by faith in their own intellect, which, to that person, represents 'reality'. In the actual Presence of the Infinite Reality, all such pretensions evaporate, as do all positionalities of a 'this' (self) believing in a 'that' (proposition). Reality is self-affirming by virtue of being Identity, within which the dualistic nature of all beliefs falls away.

Disassembly of Grief (and also of Desire)

The value or worth of desires reflects what they represent symbolically or as a class. To see through the particulars to their perceived essence facilitates withdrawal of attachment and therefore diffuses both intensity of wantingness and importance of loss. Each 'thing', person, or item that is considered to be important is only valued by virtue of its representation of a more abstract quality. The grief at loss is thus not due to the particular but to an attractor field of consciousness of which it is a symbolic representation. Each 'thing' reflects abstract qualities that can be classified at progressive levels of abstraction:

Specific	Class	Abstract
'Old Rover'	'Dogginess'	Companionship
Money	Asset	Survival
Wealth	Means	Importance, prestige, comfort
Lover	Relationship	Sex, pride, security, companionship
Relative	Family, Tribal	Group identity
Auto	Possession	Practical transport, comfort, status
Title	Survival	Pride, status
House	Habitat	Convenience, survival, security
Luxuries	Possession	Comfort, pride, status
Job	Economic	Survival, status, skills
Youth	Opportunity, learn	Open future, vigor, attraction
Mate	Personal	Companion, help-mate, affection, love
Parent	Relationship	Family/group identity, the past
Child	Relationship	Love, future potential, parental role
Health	Physical/life	Survival as a body
'Valuables'	Possession	Sentiment, 'mine', familiarity
'Necessities'	Possession	Convenience

Surrender of attachment is facilitated by appreciating that 'value' is a superimposition that depends on abstract significance and what a thing or attribute symbolizes. Thus, it will be found that a specific loss or gain can be compensated for by substituting an equivalent in the same or a higher class.

Some forms of grief have to do with real or imaginary loss of personal attributes, such as youth, physical strength, health, or even lost opportunities and regrets over unfruitful pursuits, past failures, or unfortunate choices. Grief over past errors or misjudgments resolve via recontextualization as part of the learning process called 'being human'. Regret is also a consequence of giving reality to the hypothetical, e.g., "I should have," "I could have," or "If only I had chosen differently," etc. These also include the illusion that the hypothetically 'better' decision would have brought benefit or greater happiness. These suppositions also ignore that evolution is on a learning curve and that there are negative as well as positive unknown karmic influences on choices. There is an inherent fallacy in the proposition that "I could have" or "should have" because, in reality, if one really "could have," they obviously "would have" if all conditions were favorable to a better choice.

Compassion for self as well as the nature of human life is conducive to the healing process. Grief is consequent to clinging to prior perceptions. There is major benefit from making the decision to rededicate oneself to the present and focus on it without making value judgments or dire presumptions about the future. If unimpeded, the human psyche is creative and inventive. Each level of consciousness has its own innate problems but also its concordant solutions. The desire to undo the past is understandable but futile and blinds one to the opportunities of the present. A limitation in one area of life is simultaneously the opening of opportunities and options in other areas. Loss often turns a person from looking without for happiness to turning within for reevaluation of assets and previously bypassed choices. Thus, loss can be turned to profit as a spur to spiritual growth and evolution. That a loss can be a 'blessing in disguise' takes time to ripen into a discovery. The refusal of the opportunity leads to bitterness and a devolution of the intrinsic value of life. Acceptance of the vicissitudes of human life leads to greater understanding and compassion.

Love is the opportunity to surrender the personal will to God and to reassess what is the overall purpose of the gift of human life.

The Dualities of Grief

While some degrees of grief are inevitable in the course of life, chronic Grief requires relinquishment of dualistic positionalities upon which it is based as a long-term attitude or prevailing state of consciousness.

The Dualities of Grief

Attraction	Aversion
Cling to	Let go of
Live in past	Live in the now
Undo	Accept
Bargain with God	Accept limitation - karma
Hope to change, entreaty	Surrender
See as loss	See as opportunity to move on
Refuse, deny	Work through
Anger, resentment	Acceptance
Self-blame	Accept limitation
Feel empty	Replace with new values
Lessened	Compensate
Equate 'other' or 'that' as source of happiness	See happiness as internal
Dependent on externals	Depend on self
Resist	Transcend
Despondency	Hope
Go back in time	Move forward to options
Emotionalize	Minimize
Seek sympathy	Sufficiency of self
Avoid, control	Accept, work through
See loss as permanent	See loss as temporary
See source of happiness as 'out there'	See source of happiness as 'in here'
Irreplaceable	Future has promise
Life full of problems	Life full of solutions
Bitter	Faith and hope

CHAPTER 5

Fear

(Calibration Level 100)

Introduction

At the level of 100, more life energy is available. Fear of danger runs much of the world, spurring on endless activity. Fear of enemies, old age or death, and rejection, along with a multitude of social fears, is a basic motivator in the lives of most people.

From the viewpoint of this level, the world appears hazardous, filled with traps and threats. Fear is the favored official tool for control by oppressive totalitarian agencies. The proliferation of fears is as limitless as the human imagination. Once one focuses on fear, the endless fearful events of the world feed it. Fear becomes obsessive and may take any form, e.g., fear of the loss of a relationship leads to jealousy and a chronically high stress level. Fearful thinking can balloon into paranoia or generate neurotic defensive structures, and because it is contagious, it can become a dominant social trend.

Fear limits growth of the personality and leads to inhibition. Because it takes energy to rise above Fear, the oppressed are unable to reach a higher level without assistance. Thus, the fearful seek strong leaders who appear to have conquered their fear to lead them out of its slavery.

Fear is an emotion, but as a pervasive lifestyle, it is limiting. Realistic fear (i.e., caution) subserves survival in contrast to irrational fears, which indicate psychological intrapsychic problems. Socially serviceable fear is an accepted and normal concomitant to all human life. Its pervasiveness is expressed in almost every area of life, from locked doors and fire alarms to health and eating habits and the whole financial structure of society. In addition, it is a recurrent focus of the media where it plays a major role in human affairs, especially survival.

From an evolutionary viewpoint, fear arose as a requisite of animal survival, which, in the human, progressed through capacity for cognition into expressions that have meaning, including expression as abstractions.

The capacity to analyze and abstract the perception of time and its concept of the future provides an endless variety of real or imaginary conditions along which fear can be projected. Thus, the multiplicity of fears promulgates endlessly via the mechanism of imagination and fantasy. Whereas guilt, shame, and regret represent the past, fear is an anticipation that is focused on the future.

Because the basic mechanism of fear is of animal origin and a prerequisite to survival, it is built into the very structure and physiology of the human brain (see Brain Function chart, Chapter 9). Fear also eventuates into the fear of the emotional and physiological symptoms of fear itself. These can result in adaptive skills, but when out of control, they can escalate to dread, terror, and paralyzing panic.

Although fear adds safeguards that are woven into all aspects of ordinary life, its operational fluctuations are accepted as normal. Fear as a prevailing mode of behavior is uncomfortable and a hindrance that limits reality testing, resulting in a decrease in the level of consciousness.

As a predominant level of consciousness at calibration level 100, fear becomes a limitation and a habitual, prevailing, subjective state of expectancy, which can then be projected onto almost any aspect of life. This results in hyperarousal of the brain's survival mechanisms, which results in a higher alert level of the diffuse 'reticular activating system' that triggers release of stress hormones expressed as the adrenaline/cortisone balance, along with other neurotransmitters. Fears that are related to protective countermeasures support survival. Unrealistic fears, however, can become incapacitating.

From an evolutionary viewpoint, it can be seen that human life starts with the infant's already experiencing fear (being dropped or the loss of a maternal figure). Fear continues on throughout life and ends with the fear of death itself, along with fear of the unknown. In normal life, fear is assuaged by myriad defense maneuvers and compensations that make life tolerable or even pleasant, yet, lurking in the shadows are fears that are inexplicable, including those of accidental or catastrophic events.

Research literature indicates that religious/spiritual alignment with faith is capable of reducing overall levels of fear. The spiritual energy shifts brain dominance to a more benign system processing by which stress hormones are replaced by endorphins and levels of serotonin and other neurotransmitters.

Pathological/Clinical Fear

The clinical degrees of fearfulness are expressed as anxiety disorders, including phobias, PTSD, inhibitions, or excesses of compensatory mechanisms, such as withdrawal, dependency, or substance addiction. Widespread use of tranquilizers and alcohol attests to the problem of uncomfortable and excessive anxiety, which also includes genetic and other factors of both individual and group inheritance. In response to the need, a variety of treatment modalities has arisen, including deconditioning, individual and group counseling, and the various psychotherapies, including psychoanalysis. Morbid fear also underlies other psychological difficulties, such as obsessive-compulsive disorders, hypochondriasis, and hysteria.

Transcending Fear

The processing out of negative feelings is similar to that of recovery from other negative attitudes and states. In this process, fears are allowed to arise without resistance, and their emotional energy is surrendered as it arises. A simple technique is called "And then what?" In this process, one starts with a fearfulness and then surrenders to a consequence if such a fear should actually happen. For example:

"I'm afraid I'll lose my job."
"And then what?"
"Then I won't have any money."
"And then what?"
"And then we'll be thrown out of the house."
"And then what?"
"And then we'll become homeless."

"And then what?"

"And then we won't have any money for food and we could starve to death."

"And then what?"

"And then we'll get sick and die," and so on.

As each fear consequence is surrendered (it *can* be, for multitudes do that very thing), the train of fears always terminates and ends up with the fear of physical death itself. Interestingly, the 'near death' experience subsequently eliminates all fear of death (also experientially true in the author's own life). Almost all social, psychological, and physical fears are unconsciously just elaborations of the fear of death, from which they all arise. It may take only a short time, or it could take hours, days, or even longer to go through the whole list of horrors. Finally, when death is accepted and surrendered to God, the core of the fears drops away. This final curative surrender obviously brings up one's contextualization of Divinity, and surrendering physical life to God then brings up the last stack of fears, which relate to Destiny—fears of a punitive God and anthropomorphic depictions and legends of Divinity. It is helpful to remember that if God were not All Merciful, we probably would not even be alive today.

Even primitive belief systems of punitive, jealous, vengeful, and angry gods also provide resolutions by which redemption and salvation can be granted. Within rational and confrontable realms, these include absolution by confession, penance, acceptance of a Savior, institution of a major change of behavior, prayer, entreaty, and basically surrendering one's will to God.

It is useful to realize that all life, from moment to moment, is based on faith by whatever name it may be called. Even the atheist clings to the belief system out of faith that the beliefs are authentic and valid. Research on the calibrated levels of consciousness verified the validity of the world's major religions and spiritual belief systems (*Truth vs. Falsehood*, 2005).

Peace can be the consequence of surrender to the inevitabilities of life. The religious/spiritual skeptic can look within and observe that the inner fundamental irreducible quality of life is the capacity of awareness, consciousness, and the substrate of subjectivity. Without consciousness, the individual would not 'know' or even 'know' if they 'know', so that consciousness is a priori awareness of existence, irrespective of the content of that existence. Thus, consciousness itself can be accepted as an obvious reality, without the elaboration of being Divine (as recommended by the Buddha). To 'be' is one thing; to *know* that one 'is' obviously requires a more transcendent quality.

All fear is a product of the ego as an evolutionary stage, concomitant to physicality. Nonsentient life continues on by means of design and actualizing mechanisms that operate out of the predominant attractor field, e.g., colonies of coral. But with the evolutionary awareness of one's existence arises a 'me' as separate from an animal class. Thus, fear arises concomitant with choice and the awareness of consequences. Fear propagates in the individual by resistance and recedes with acceptance that can be facilitated by restructuring the fear so it is seen as an asset.

Upon examination, aside from the content of fear, fear itself is feared because it is an unpleasant physiological, emotional, experiential reaction. This is the basis for President Roosevelt's famous quote, "We have nothing to fear but fear itself." Therefore, in processing out fear, the physical concomitance has to be accepted through nonresistance. By this means, the sensations themselves expire (queasy feeling in the stomach, shaking muscles, perspiring, rapid pulse, etc.). Thus, fear can be reduced to physicality itself.

Clinically, fears can be transcended fairly easily in the hypnotic state. One therapeutic modality is to teach the sufferer self-hypnosis, which is a relatively simple technique that can be readily learned in one session. Self-hypnosis is also a tool for past-life regression and recall. Skepticism remains until the actual past-life experience begins to rerun itself, enabling the core issues to become apparent, thus bringing great relief. Fears can be converted to rational predictions and calculations that result in the preservation of life without resort to the emotionality of fear itself. Finally, there can be an addiction to the excitement of fear and the concomitant imaginary melodrama.

Consciousness research reveals that the precise timing of physical death is set at the very moment of birth—not the 'how', but the 'when'. (Calibrates as 'true'.) It is helpful to realize that the individual is linear and thus limited, whereas the Self is nonlinear and unlimited. It is also helpful to realize that actual, real death is not a possibility as life can only shift from one dimension to another but cannot be extinguished. That which is linear (form) is the receptacle of life but not its source, for life and the Source of life are nonlinear and therefore not subject to time or dimension. The elimination of fear requires subjugation of the imagination that originated in childhood when differentiation between reality and fantasy was not yet developed. Emotionalized, fearful images are thus in the imagination and not subject to restraint. They can become elaborated into superstitions and fearful images that are reinforced by fairy tales and the programming influence of the media. Children's cartoons customarily contain endless frightening images and graphic elaborations and are therefore a frequent source of children's fears. Importantly, brain research indicates that a child's brain cannot distinguish real from televised violence (Lohmann, 2004). Adults enjoy horror films because they get to process fears from the safe distance of the spectator. This imaginative capacity of the human mind, however, can be used therapeutically in desensitization programs via 'virtual' techniques.

Fearfulness tends to be self-reinforcing and is a limitation to the development of adaptive skills. Fear of failure results in inhibitions and stultifies development of social confidence. Fear of social disapproval leads to withdrawal and guardedness or emotional neediness. Denial of fear can result in its seeming opposite by overcompensation as bravado and unnecessary risk-taking behaviors.

Fear and Spiritual Evolution
    Jesus Christ said that fear is the last hindrance to be overcome. From the viewpoint of consciousness

research and its evolution, all fear is a product of the persistence of the ego and its failure to relinquish its sovereignty to the will of God. Active surrender to God's will is by choice and is a decision of the will, which is therefore quite different from passivity, apathy, or resignation. To consciously choose alignment with Divinity and Truth is reempowering and shifts identity from the self to the Self, resulting in an increase in confidence, courage, and personal dignity rather than self-abasement or self-denigration. Total surrender brings peace; partial or conditional surrender brings lingering doubt.

When the ego/self is progressively surrendered, it is dissolved into and replaced by the Self, which is timeless and self-effulgent, obliterating all doubt forever. The same realization occurs in people who have had a near-death experience or those with advanced consciousness who have gone through transformative realizations. Consciousness research confirms that death is not a possibility. Life itself is supported by its eternal Source from which it cannot be separated. That which is linear, circumscribed, and limited in time comes into existence because of that which is eternal and nonlinear (calibrates at 1,000).

Fear and Religion

Fears arise with the awareness of consequences in the future for transgressions, errors, and moral lapses that may have been temporary or perhaps even long term. There is fear of Divine Judgment as well as fears of anthropomorphic depictions of an angry or even a vengeful God. The more primitive the view of Divinity, the more fearful are the images. The fears are associated and combined with guilt and expectation of punishment or even Hell itself. These are increased by mythological belief systems that become enculturated.

The higher the level of consciousness, the lower the fear of God. Traditionally, man is depicted ambiguously as innocent because of ignorance ("they know not what they do"), as well as guilty by virtue of the ego's animalistic instincts. The ignorance is intrinsic to the structure and limitations of the dualistic ego/mind, which is unable by limited evolutionary development to discern appearance from essence. Thus, without a Savior, Avatar, or Great Teacher, the human in the world is at a serious disadvantage. Even the religions themselves tend to be in conflict, with the exception of the principle of monotheism. Thus, the human is in conflict, operationally at risk, and beset by temptations from both within and without.

The Judaic-Christian and Islamic religions provide resolutions of salvation and redemption, while Buddhism and Hinduism stress spiritual evolution from the limitations of the linear ego to higher nonlinear levels of spiritual identification. However contextualized, the consequences of sin/error/limitation/ ignorance are counterbalanced by Divine Mercy, Love, and Compassion.

From consciousness research, it becomes confirmably clear that the fate of one's soul is the consequence of one's own choices and decisions rather than by retribution of an angry deity. Thus, like a cork in the sea that rises to its own innate degree of buoyancy, or an iron filing that moves automatically within a universal electromagnetic field, each spirit determines its own evolutionary position within the nonlinear context of the overall infinite field of consciousness.

Divine Justice is innate and autonomous as a consequence of Creation itself. In addition, the overall omnipresence of Allness includes ever-present options for salvation. The Justice of God is thus perfect in that it also affords perfect freedom as well as the opportunity for the evolution of consciousness and spiritual awareness. (The above calibrates at 945; in contrast, anthropomorphic depictions of God calibrate at 75.)

The Dualities of Fear

Fear is a basic survival mechanism and intrinsic to the evolution of the ego from the earliest primitive animal life forms. There is short-term realistic fear that is in contrast to fear as a prevailing, dominant level of consciousness. Fears have an early onset in the young child and proliferate throughout life unless countered by an overall feeling of security. To feel adequate in response to life requires surmounting the irrational fears that emerge as a result of the ego's numerous positionalities.

The Dualities of Fear

Attraction	Aversion
Excitement of danger	Stay 'cool'
Panic, overreact	Self-control
Dramatize	Handle calmly
Emphasize	Deflate
Gain attention, help	Self-sufficient
Survive	Trust God
Protect	Lose, loss
Control	Surrender
Emotionalism	Think clearly
Exaggerate	Minimize
Imagine	Stay logical
Project to future	Live in the now
Proliferate	Suppress imagination
See enemies	See safety
Resist, defend, avoid	Accept
Elaborate, escalate	Reduce perceptions
Harbor	Work through
Justify	View realistically
Project cause	Own responsibly
Death	See life as eternal
Focus on body	Focus on spirit
See life as physical	See spiritual as reality
Loss of youth, money, possessions	See source of happiness as intrinsic
Loss of love of others	See Self as Source
Depend on self	Trust in God, Self

CHAPTER 6

Desire
(Calibration Level 125)

Introduction

There is yet more energy available at the level of Desire. Desire motivates vast areas of human activity, including the economy. Advertisers play on desires to program us with needs linked to instinctual drives. Desire moves us to expend great effort to achieve goals or obtain rewards. The desire for money, prestige, or power runs the lives of many of those who have risen above Fear as their predominant life motive.

Desire is also the level of addictions, wherein desire becomes a craving more important than life itself. The victims of Desire may actually be unaware of the basis of their motives. Some people become addicted to the desire for attention and drive others away by their constant demands. The desire for sexual approval has produced the huge cosmetics and fashion industries that extol glamour and allure.

Desire has to do with acquisition and accumulation, which is often insatiable because it is an ongoing energy field. Satisfaction of one desire is merely replaced by the unsatisfied desire for something more, e.g., multimillionaires often remain obsessed with acquiring more and more money.

Desire is obviously a much higher state than apathy or grief. In order to 'get', one first has to have the energy to 'want'. Television has had a major influence on many oppressed people, inculcating wants and increasing their desires to the degree that they move out of Apathy and begin to seek a better life. 'Want' can start us on the road to achievement. Desire can therefore become a springboard to yet higher levels of awareness.

Clinical

Constructive desire results in the pleasing fulfillment of chosen options based on their completion in view of the resources of reason, followed by an act of the will, and these in turn affect the overall level of consciousness. Thus, wantingness and desire can be replaced by choice and decision.

The downside of desire is expressed by its compulsory quality, which can lead to constant craving and drivenness. When expanded by emotionality, it can become experienced as 'needs'. The consequence of a life of endless pursuit and anxiety about the acquisition of the externalized, artificial sources of satisfaction is increased exposure to fear of loss.

The evolutionary origin of the pattern and drive of wantingness extends back to the earliest animal life form, which lacked an internal source of energy that therefore had to be sought externally by trial and error. Thus, needs and wants became linked with survival and fear. In the human, desires and wants become elaborated with social and abstract expression and result in compulsory pursuit or even the resort to high-risk behaviors.

Cravings can be continuous due to a failure of the internal satisfaction mechanism by which there never seems to be enough, and acquisition becomes a lifestyle of endless pursuit. Wantingness is an offshoot of the original drive of hunger/thirst, which can be a self-propelling behavior pattern of chronic frustration. In classic esoteric terminology, the wantingness and desire are energetically located in the chakra of the solar plexus, which results in the parlance that a person 'is driven by their solar plexus'. Pathological forms of chronic wantingness are well known in society as an endless drive for relationships, sex, materialism, hoarding, addictions, and more. Constant desire for approval leads to 'people pleasing' behaviors, subservience, and obsequiousness. Social craving is often compensatory to self-doubt, low self-esteem, and the need to constantly provide external sources of pleasure.

Social expressions of needing and wanting may attach to external concepts, political positions, and the need to control others for the sought-for feelings of importance and public attention. Thus, wanting and neediness are inordinately narcissistic, albeit seemingly altruistic social expressions and positionalities. Social neediness also expresses personality traits of manipulation, competition, and status seeking.

Desire and the Ego

Due to its evolutionary origin, the ego develops the acquisitive function of 'getting', which is biologically necessary for survival. The source of satisfaction is therefore located as being 'out there', whereas the actual source of pleasure itself is an internal brain mechanism that is merely triggered by the acquisition of a 'want'. In its more benign expressions, its wantingness and neediness are for social and emotional nurturance, such as that provided by the family, tribe, or pack.

Socialization results in motivations to achieve dominance, control, and capacity for attraction. In the human, elaborations become socially expressed in pursuit of rank, status, possessions, and a competitive lifestyle that leads to jealousy and envy. The basic problem with this level of consciousness is the inner feeling of lack that results in chronic dissatisfaction, feelings of incompletion, and constant seeking behaviors. The vulnerability of the ego's wantingness is its presumption that fulfillment depends on acquisition from external sources. The exaggerated need results in an overestimation of externals and their unrealistic inflation as to importance. Thus, wantingness leads to insatiability, frustration, and anxiety, as well as greed, avarice, and chronic acquisitiveness.

The problem of Desire is linked to the ego's proclivity to project specialness onto perceived objects, persons, or qualities. Thus, the desired person, attribute, or possession is inflated, romanticized, and glamorized with exaggerated magical attributes (as described in the classic book, *Glamour: A World Problem* [Bailey, 1950]). Thus, the ego becomes infatuated with its own projections, facilitated by the specific energy of glamour itself. This gives the desired object, person, or quality a magical allure and seductive attraction that most people ruefully discover is an illusion (e.g., adolescent romantic crushes).

The amplified hypertrophic desire then becomes a craving and a drivenness that defies rationality. When the illusory magical promise dissolves into reality, there is a feeling of bitterness or loss and mourning. The media specialize in glamorization of products as well as personalities in which 'presentation' is far more important than the underlying reality. Thus, media hype is a major and influential industry. ("Any publicity is better than none at all.") The result is an endless craving and desire to stay in the limelight, as 'getting attention' is one of the ego's allures. The ego is the main hero/heroine in the inner movie of one's life.

The ego's inner anxiety about fulfillment of its projected needs leads to an insatiable greed for power and control over others that emerges in its most expanded form as dictatorships, narcissistic megalomania, and grandiosity, all seeking to dominate the entire world. Frustration of egoistic desires has led to rage, revenge, and the killing of millions of innocent people throughout history. This is a consequence of the insatiability of egocentricity that results in barbarism and totalitarian militant extremism. The condition is called 'malignant messianic narcissism' because the core of the nonevolved ego secretly envies and hates God and sees Divinity as a rival. The clever ego expresses its inner grandiosity by seeking to replace Divinity by declaring itself to be God (Nero, Caesar, etc.), or claiming special Divine authority by declaration as being Divinely ordained and therefore authorized.

The usurping of Divinity is seen in the despotic public figure displays of the 'great leader', etc., who frankly expect to be worshipped. Potentates required bowing and kneeling in their presence and assumed the title of 'lord'. Kings ruled by 'Divine right' and from a throne that was always higher than the seats of everyone else. The throne itself symbolized the claim to sovereignty, unlimited power, and the 'Divine Right of Kings'.

The paradox of the messianic claims of world leaders over time is that few of them maintain a calibrated level high enough to indicate actual intrinsic power. Instead, they rely on force (munitions, secret police, army, and terrorism).

The Downside of Desire: Frustration, Envy, and Jealousy

The feeling of inner lack and the drive to compensate for it by externals in its social expression leads to compulsion and the desire for symbols of importance, prestige, rank, 'being noticed', popularity, and others. These drives lead to rivalry, status seeking, social climbing, and endless desires for possessions by which money becomes an end in itself. The desire to 'be somebody' is contextualized as specialness and implied superiority that lends attraction to anything so symbolized. Other avenues may be sought through extreme behaviors to gain headlines and media attention. An obvious source of desire for status originates from sibling rivalry and the school years in which competition and achievement are rewarded. The motivation to 'be somebody' at any cost is the basic, admitted motivation of celebrity murders (e.g., John Lennon's killer).

The disorder of unfulfilled wantingness can reach extreme and pathological proportions, such as seen in the chronic criminal or militant political extremists who cannot wait to 'claim credit' for acts of violent extremism and horrific, grotesque acts of conduct for which they want public acknowledgement and seek attention via the media. Another expression is the serial killer who leaves a signature and taunts the authorities by achieving fame and simultaneously frustrating apprehension. The obsessive need for approval extends to both public and self-images and may express itself as perfectionism or excessive ambition.

Desire as Bondage

Happiness and satisfaction ensue from fulfillment of choices, whereas wantingness brings anxiety and tension. The attachment is to the pursuit of inner sensation of the reward system by the brain itself, which early in evolution was linked to the senses. Addiction and compulsory wantingness are the human elaborations of the means (activities, thoughts, etc.) of triggering the hoped-for brain response. Thus, the Buddha said that the basic primary bondage is to the senses.

Gluttony was included in the list of the Seven Deadly Sins because of its bondage to the body and its pleasures by which food or sex became the most common addictions. Later on in civilization, these included alcohol and drugs to artificially trigger the brain's reward system.

Desire as Addiction

Repetitive satisfaction of the desire-satiation cycle leads to habituation, which may escalate in vulnerable individuals to craving and addiction. The escalation is to the same level as instinctual drives and may even become prioritized above normal survival instincts. When satisfaction of cravings becomes dominant, inhibition by reason becomes futile and inoperative, as is seen in the pursuit of dangerous high-risk ventures that have a history of high fatality rates (e.g., climbing Mt. Everest; riding in a barrel over Niagara Falls; going for a deep-sea diving record, etc.). Even the likelihood of death from volcanic lava or suffocation in an avalanche is insufficient to control the drivenness of insatiable craving and the thrill of flirting with death as is also seen in the desperate extremes of criminality (Bonnie and Clyde).

Addictions supersede rationality and self-preservation despite even severe consequences. Compulsions quickly return when the opportunity for satisfaction returns as is seen in compulsive gambling, pedophilia, drug and alcohol addiction, criminality, kleptomania, sexuality, arson, psychopathic behaviors, eating disorders, compulsive shopping, and bullying, as well as in irrational extravagance, hoarding, and more.

Research in brain neurochemistry has revealed genetic neurotransmitter mechanisms in addictions that respond to pharmaceutical interventions. In general, the addictions are all operationally similar in that they trigger the brain's release of the neurotransmitters associated with pleasure. Essentially, all addictions are the consequence of addiction to the pleasure response itself by whatever means. (A recent clinical discovery was that even anti-Parkinson's disease drugs might trigger compulsive behaviors, such as gambling, sex, or shopping. [Tanner, 2005].)

These behaviors may range from predatory multi-billionaire financial schemes to serial child rape and murder, but the underlying mechanism is the same. The particular type of behavior selected is in accord with karmically influenced genetic and cultural factors that result in the individual's level of consciousness. Addictions are not extinguished by negative consequences, no matter how dire. Therefore, they are not comprehensible to the average normal person who expects that a prison term will deter criminality. Most recidivist criminals relapse into crime within only a few days after release from prison due to the drivenness of the compulsion, as is characteristically seen in child predators.

The Ego as an Addiction

By understanding addiction, the way is open to comprehend the tenacity of the ego. The self seeks pleasure and becomes addicted to the pleasure it receives from positionalities. This response cycle then becomes habitually reinforced, resulting in a dominant brain pattern that persists despite negative consequences to self or others. Even the satisfactions of negativity are primarily due to the *addiction*. This explains the chronic nature of social/spiritual/emotional pathology that dominated whole civilizations for centuries. Even today, that pathology dominates seventy-eight percent of the world's population, for to let go of negative behaviors and emotions would represent a *loss* of pleasure and satisfaction.

The pay-off of pride is obvious; the pay-offs of greed, acquisition, and pomposity are equally clear. People cling to hate and endlessly seek justification for it for centuries. Injustice collectors abound, as do martyrs, hate mongers, sadists, masochists, and losers, as well as demagogues and tyrants of all sorts. The hate of violence is intoxicating, and killers of the innocent are *jubilant*. Political, religious, and philosophical conflicts are so addictive that entire cultures and populations go to their deaths for the major pleasure of 'being right' and getting even.

While the above are examples of extremes, the same underlying mechanism of secret pay-off pleasure is derived from stubbornness, resentment, guilty self-recrimination, and, as bizarre as it may seem at first glance, suffering itself. Other forms are chronic guilt, endless fears, obsessions, compulsions, and the endless fears of ordinary life called 'worries'. Even defeat and loss can be paradoxically gratifying as punishment or as evidence of the cruelty of fate. Ego positions have the characteristics of disowning responsibility and placing blame 'out there'. In the end, the ego pay-off is the energy by which the ego persists because it lacks the pleasure of the input of spiritual energy. The ego's pay-off is its substitute for Divinity, and it thus maintains its sovereignty and is convincing in its secret silent belief that *it* is the source of one's life itself, i.e., that *it* is God.

Recovery from Addiction to the Ego

In and of itself, the ego is incapable of transcending its own coils. It is the circuitous trap of the house of mirrors of illusion. Of its own, the ego would never seek salvation. It is only by the awakening of spiritual energy that the levels of consciousness can be transcended. The mechanism for salvation is via the will, which invites the intervention of Divinity.

The ego became dominant as the result of its

ancient atavistic origin as being essential to primitive survival. To the ego, a 'want' is interpreted as a 'need' and a 'have to have'. Thus, its seeking can become frantic, and all caution can be thrown to the winds. Desires are thereby escalated to being desperate and demanding any sacrifice, including even the deaths of *millions* of other people. It *must* have what it wants at any cost and will find many excuses to justify itself. It gets rid of reason with clever rhetoric bolstered by blame and demonizes others, for the ego has to *win* at all costs because throughout millions of years of evolution, it *did* die if it did not get its wants and needs fulfilled. The ego has a long, long memory and millions of years of reinforcement.

Transcending Desire

Because the problem is internal rather than external, attempts to control compulsive cravings with 'will power' (the ego) rarely succeed, nor does gratification of the endless desires, which only gives temporary relief. As is well known, the more destructive forms of compulsive drives respond best to faith-based treatment programs and groups whose basic foundation follows the successful example established by the twelve-step groups. All such organizations stress the same basic concepts of humility, inner honesty, responsibility, and surrender to a power greater than oneself. Failure to respond to such programs is due to the unwillingness to drop the resistance that emanates from the core of the ego itself, to which surrender is anathema unless the pain of the disorder reaches unbearable proportions.

Less severe but troublesome degrees of being driven can be transcended by substituting preferences for demands and surrendering each impulse to God as it arises. Another practice is the "And then what?" spiritual process in which each dreaded and anticipated consequence is surrendered to God. At first, this process seems impossible, but upon investigation, 'impossible' turns out to be merely unwillingness itself. Thus, surrendering depends on 'wanting to' rather than 'can't'.

Another example of the "And then what?" process is as follows: "If I give up such-and-such, then I'll be bored, unhappy, isolated, become nobody, destitute," and so on goes the list of presumed intolerable conditions, which, upon examination, reveals that none of them are intolerable, and the intolerability is merely due to the resistance itself and not the condition (e.g., if it were reality based, nobody would be happy unless they were rich and famous).

Unwillingness and resistance frequently take the form of the "I can't" excuse in order to avoid responsibility and the surrender of an ego motive. This can be uncovered by asking, "If someone held a loaded gun to your head to shoot you if you didn't surrender, then would you do so?" The answer, of course, is that you *could*, so the problem is 'would', not 'could'. Note that even a 'bare bones' ascetic lifestyle is acceptable if elected and chosen. There are many spiritual communities of worldly renunciates or followers of 'less is more' principles. Simplicity as a choice is acceptable but resented if imposed.

The more evolved the person's level of consciousness, the less the pressure of needs. With major evolution, wants and needs disappear because the satisfaction arises not from what one has but from the realization of the Source of one's own existence, which is therefore not dependent on any externals or artificially altered brain physiology. The evolved person experiences the joy of the feeling of inner freedom.

In following a sequence of "And then what," eventually the bottom fear that triggers the entire series turns out to be fear of death itself. It is this fear of death that is repressed and unconscious behind the myriad fears to which man is prone. With surrender of life itself and its embodiment to the will of God, the inner radiance of the Self shines forth, and one's survival is surrendered to God with the emergence of joy. A prerequisite to the successful elimination of the fear of death is a surrendering to God at great depth and simultaneously praying for Divine Grace.

The emergence from restrictive limitation goes through the classic steps from 'having' to 'doing' to 'being'. Becoming the fulfillment of one's spiritual potential eliminates all needs or wants, for the source of happiness resides within where it always has been. The ego's sources of happiness are provisional, temporary, transitory, and illusory, which is a Reality that can only be verified experientially. The Self wants nothing for it is innately totally complete as it is the primordial Source of everything that exists.

Thus, aside from basic physical needs for survival, 'lack' is a perception. The spiritual challenge is to discover the Source of happiness. Many very rich and successful people frankly acknowledge that, other than physical conveniences, they are basically no happier than they were as penniless students; thus the perennial attraction and popularity of the opera, *La Bohème* (Puccini, 1896). Personal happiness is believed by the ego/self to be conditional, which brings up fear. To 'want nothing' is free of fear and therefore an immune, fearless state. Eventually even the desire to 'have' a body disappears and it is seen to be an encumbrance although useful for exploring the linear domain.

Operationally, the body could be viewed as a temporary 'space probe' of the linear dimension that subserves spiritual evolution in the process. Attachment to it is based on the illusion of identification with it as 'self' and as the source and locus of life. From the viewpoint of higher states of consciousness, the body may seem like a nuisance and limitation, as well as a distraction. That also then has to be surrendered. Eventually identification with the body disappears and it then goes about spontaneously as an 'it' rather than a 'me'.

Replacement of Desire

The mind thinks that desire and wanting are necessary motivations for achievement of goals. This belief stems from the old, evolutionary animal crave-reward system. Above consciousness level 200, goals are reached not by wantingness but instead by decision, commitment, and choosing as an act of the will. The goal then becomes inspirational, which results in alignment of priorities that eventuate, as in spiritual work, with dedication and letting go of resistances. Decision adds value to the process of effort necessary to realize a goal. It is not necessary to 'crave' it but merely to decide to follow the necessary processes to actualization.

This is facilitated by surrendering resistances that may arise if the ego/mind pictures them as 'sacrifices'.

The Positionalities of Desire

Each level of consciousness is associated with presumptions that reinforce the perceptions of that level and result in resistances. These characteristically take the form of dualistic pairs of attractions and aversions.

The Dualities of Desire

Attraction	Aversion
Special	Common
Win, gain	Lose
Wealth	Poverty
Control	Passive
Get	Lose
Crave	Frustrated
Force	Weakness
Approval	Criticism
Success	Failure
Fame	Anonymity
Stubborn	Give in
Aggression	Submission
Resist	Change
Defend	Surrender
Acquisition	Poverty
Conquest	Lose
Popularity	Unnoticed
'Have to have'	Prefer
Important	Ordinary
Feel 'high'	Just normal
Exceptional	Average
Noticed	Ignored
Excitement	Boredom
Glamorous	Common
Change world	Change self
Possession	Simplicity
Display	Bland
Superior	Common

These are the recognizable drives that are classically associated with the solar plexus chakra. They find widespread social acceptance and reinforcement. Collectively, they emerge as attitudes and motivations that have to be surrendered as attachments. The necessary processes are willingness plus contemplation, reflection, and meditation, but the subsequent reward is great and opens the door to many unexpected benefits that recontextualize the subjective qualities of life.

CHAPTER 7

Anger

(Calibration Level 150)

Introduction

Anger can lead to either constructive or destructive action. As people move out of Apathy and Grief to overcome Fear as a way of life, they begin to want. Desire leads to frustration that in turn leads to Anger. Thus, Anger can be a fulcrum by which the oppressed are eventually catapulted to freedom. Anger over social injustice, victimization, and inequality has energized great movements that have led to major changes in the structure of society. Note that it was the movements and not the anger itself that brought about constructive benefits.

Anger, however, expresses itself most often as resentment or as a lifestyle that is exemplified by irritable, explosive people who are oversensitive to slights and become 'injustice collectors', as well as quarrelsome, contentious, belligerent, or litigious.

Anger that stems from frustrated want is based on the energy field below it (Desire). Frustration results from exaggerating the importance of desires. The angry person may, like the frustrated infant, go into rage. Anger easily leads to hatred, which has an erosive effect on all areas of a person's life.

Anger as an emotion is prevalent throughout society as a transient reaction, but anger as a level of consciousness is indicative of dominance by a pervasive, negative energy field that is reflective of the ego's distorted perceptions. A primary aspect of the distortion is a narcissistically-oriented worldview and expectations that the world should cater and conform to one's wishes and perceptions. Inasmuch as the world is not centered or concerned with a specific individual per se, the result is chronic frustration and resentment.

The narcissistic ego is competitive and prone to feel slighted and insulted with even minimal provocation, as the core of the ego sees itself as sovereignty that expects priority and agreement or compliance with its expectations, as well as satisfaction of its wants or proclivities. This results in chronic resentment and seething anger that lurk just below the surface and express as surliness, sulking, or attitudes of 'sour grapes', a 'chip on the shoulder', or a 'hair trigger'. Anger may also take more disguised, sophisticated social positions that lead to the acting out of the role of the chronic protester and self-appointed critic who angrily attacks perceived enemies. Periodically the repressed anger emerges as overt behavioral aggression or even physical assault, as well as expressions such as bullying and public riots. As resentments pile up, periodic temper tantrums or rages may emerge. They are commonly expressed in relationships as spousal or child abuse. Chronic anger often results in an overly aggressive personality that attempts to coerce others by intimidation and dominance. The ensuing lifestyle is characteristically described as 'stormy'.

The Ego Mechanisms of Anger
The ego structure is dualistic and splits the unity of Reality into contrasting pairs and seeming opposites

that are therefore the product and content of perception, which consists of projections. This is a basic defect of the mind, as noted by Descartes, who clarified that the mind confuses its own mentations (*res interna, res cogitans*) with the external reality of nature as it is (*res extensa/externa*). (This basic defect is covered extensively in Section I of *Truth vs. Falsehood.*) The personal self is therefore operationally a victim of its own projected dualistic perceptions. Below calibration level 200, this is a prevailing limitation in which the mind is unable to differentiate between its emotionalized perceptions (opinions) and the external world as it actually is. This impairment affects seventy-eight percent of the world's population and forty-nine percent of America's population.

The angry person then sees that which does not serve the ego as the enemy. The angry person is therefore always on the defensive and prone to emotionalized excitement that is propagated by the energizing of the primarily animal left-brain mechanisms (see Brain Function chart, Chapter 9). The cycle of misperception, followed by anger and resentment, then fuels the body's overall sympathetic nervous system and triggers fight-or-flight responses (Cannon, 1929), with increases in adrenaline and cortisone. Thus, the angry person's overall nervous system is set for the classic alarm reaction and stress response (Selye, 1978) of increased heart rate, sodium retention, and increased blood pressure. The ego is fed by the pay-off of negative emotions and thus clings to negativity for survival. While the spiritualized brain is supported by spiritual energy, the animalistic, ego-oriented left brain relies on the sources of animal energy throughout evolutionary time. The positionalized ego fears admitting a mistake and avoids responsibility to forestall the anger's turning inward. A major defense of the ego is to project a punitive conscience (its 'superego') onto the outer world and then live in fear of it in the form of fears of vengeance. Thus, the angry ego fears truth, honesty, and balance, which would reduce its dominance, and therefore considers forgiveness or seeing the innocence of others as anathema. The angry person's ego sees relationships as a battleground for dominance, control, and primitive attitudes and actions. The resistance to giving up pejorative attitudes is that, subjectively, the ego extracts pleasure from negativity, which propagates and motivates the personalities that calibrate below 200.

In contrast, people above 200 dislike anger in themselves or others and are made uncomfortable by it. Socially, anger is a detriment to family, workplace and other relationships as well as personal health. To people who feel inwardly weak and vulnerable, anger seems like strength, whereas to strong people, anger is seen as a primitive, vulgar weakness that is disliked and viewed as immature, 'low class', and an embarrassing childish social faux pas.

In and of itself, anger is merely a subjective emotion that does not actually of itself accomplish anything in the world as would the use of reason and restraint. Anger is used by the ego as a substitute for courage, which actually only requires being resolute, determined, or committed.

The ego, like a primitive animal, puffs up with anger

and unconsciously seeks to make itself appear strong and formidable. The ego's position propagates itself because its secretly sought pay-off is the emotion itself. This self-propagating mechanism is further strengthened by clinging to the past to justify and nurture grudges and vitiate the guilt that would otherwise result from self-honesty about one's true motives. The fallacy of milking the past is indicated by its low calibration level, which is due to the fact that in actuality, the past no longer exists. One can actually only 'know' the present, and at best, that is only a fleeting perception because truth is a consequence of not only linear content but also of context.

Clinical Expressions

Chronic anger often results in destructive social consequences, such as marital discord or divorce. Outbursts that occur in the workplace result in a spotty employment record, and counseling is frequently advised. Therapy is often court ordered as a requirement of probation for infractions of the law, especially in the expression of anger as criminality. Research shows that the pattern is usually evident in early childhood and leads to problems with siblings and classmates. Chronic belligerence leads to social rejection that increases chronic resentments and anger and justifies what may even erupt as homicide.

A variety of the lifestyle is seen in the clinical expression as the 'explosive personality disorder', as well as 'borderline personality disorder', where rages can be triggered by seeming trivialities. Another expression of clinical anger is seen in the 'passive-aggressive personality disorder' in which passivity is a disguised form of aggression as resistance, with periodic eruption into overt anger. Aggressive resistance derives from the childhood age of two where it emerges as the classic two-year-old's "No." Overt hostile aggression is a characteristic of psychopathic personalities in which the absence of conscience allows for overt acting out of primitive aggression and results in a low capacity for self-control and intolerance of delay. There is also the incapacity to assess consequences for one's own actions or to take responsibility for them.

Severe character disorders often become worse when expectations or demands are not fulfilled quickly. Paradoxically, fulfillment of expectations tends to inflate the ego so that the angry, impatient person and the psychopathic personality do not suffer from low self-esteem, as commonly believed but, on the contrary, have inflated egos. The progressive fulfillment of this inner grandiosity has dramatically disastrous consequences to society, of which the narcissistic messianic tyrant is the most glaring example. Satisfaction of narcissistic, egoistic expectations does not satisfy or quell the demands but only escalates the aggression. Thus, placations do not stop aggression but instead feed into it. The greed of the ego is insatiable, and its frustration can result in the merciless, arbitrary death of literally millions of ordinary, innocent citizens as well as whole armies and entire populations.

Beneath the hostile, angry, raging ego is the blood-lust of the merciless 'berserker' of ancient times, as well as the savage 'militant' of the current decade. The deep roots of this anger/hatred bloodlust are atavistic

(Freud's 'Id' and instinct of *Thanatos*). The inflated ego is devoid of reality testing as well as amelioration by reason, logic, or rationality.

The charismatic messianic leader is adept at feeding the bloodlust with propaganda. The psychological explanation for the release is the sanction of authority or society in which Freud's classic superego (conscience) is drowned by crowd agreement. This is historically demonstrated in the Roman arena; via the guillotine; during the massacre of civilians in Manchuria; in the bullring; or in the massive malevolence demonstrated by Pol Pot, Chairman Mao, Adolf Hitler, and others. The position of being a dictator pulls up the nascent megalomania of the primitive, unconscious aspects of the ego from the unconscious. The core of the ego is its delusional belief that it is God (Nero, Caesar, the Great Leader). The paradox is that whereas the reality of Divinity is infinitely merciful, its fraudulent usurpation results in massive cruelty, death, and the opposite of mercy. Chronic anger requires justification, and thus, the common expression of the angry personality is seen in the classic injustice collector who nurses grievances and, by paranoid extension, collects grievances to justify hostility.

It is notable that in faith-based recovery groups, such as the twelve-step programs, a basic dictum is that there is no such thing as a 'justified resentment'. The ego also likes to cite spurious misinterpretations of history to justify its extremism

It is a basic dictum that perception finds what it seeks (e.g., the Internet search engines). Thus, the deliberate promulgation and propagation of historical justification continues on self-servingly over the centuries at the cost of the lives and freedoms of the populace. This is characteristic of religious hatreds that go on for millennia. As noted by Mahatma Gandhi, an eye for an eye makes the whole world blind. Thus, the political power of extremist leaders is based on the continuation and propagation of hatred, anger, resentment, and injustice collecting. To such politicized movements, peace obviously would be the greatest threat possible (witness the career of Yasser Arafat who started out calibrating at 440 and ended up calibrating at 65). The deliberate propagation of dissent and hatred is the downside exploitation and subversion of the liberty of free speech (e.g., play the card of race, sex, class, age, etc.).

Transcending Anger
To the normal person, anger is seen as a detriment. It is a transitory annoyance and viewed as disruptive. The obvious antidotes are those of compassion, acceptance, love, and the willingness to forgive. Transcendence requires the willingness to surrender primary positionalities:
1. Harboring chronic resentments and milking 'injustices'.
2. Unrealistic expectations of the world and relationships, including expectations of convenience, agreement, approval, compliance, and others.
3. Surrendering self-centeredness as a lifestyle and focusing on changing oneself instead of the world.
4. Willingness to surrender the residual infantile expectations (of age two) of self, others, and the

perceived imperfect world, e.g. "God grant me
the serenity to accept the things I cannot
change; courage to change the things I can; and
wisdom to know the difference" (as per the 12-
step program).

5. Taking responsibility for bringing inner infantile
   attitudes to the surface and subordinating them
   to mature and essentially more gratifying
   processes, such as reason, balance, and concern
   for others.

6. Realize that resentment or anger is not about
   what others 'are', but about what they 'are not'
   (i.e., 'not' generous, rather than stingy; 'not'
   unselfish, but selfish; 'not' careful, but thought-
   less, etc.)

7. Accepting human fallibility and limitation that, in
   a portion of the population, is due to an inborn
   incapacity to be self-honest.

The processing out of anger requires inner honesty
and the willingness to surrender what is not integrous
and essentially unworkable and replace it with self-confidence. Another process is to utilize the "And then
what?" process where one surrenders the seemingly
impossible scenarios to God. Compensatory attitudes
that are far more powerful than anger are dedication,
reason, humility, gratitude, perseverance, and tolerance.
It is also helpful to see that the inner ego has become
addicted to the artificial 'high' of anger, with its puffed-
up animal characteristics. It is also educational to select
a successful role model and pattern oneself in accord
with those traits, such as determination, commitment,

skill, and integrity. One does not become a success by envying and vilifying it but by imitating it. Thus, the angry person has to go back and make up for what was missing in their own education and development.

Blockages

As with other levels, positionalities result in conflicting dualities that require the surrender of the transitory pleasure of indulgence of the attractions and the resistance to the aversions. Willingness enables the surrender of short-term self-indulgence for long-term spiritual growth.

The Dualities of Anger

Attraction	Aversion
Act out feeling	Self-control
Intimidate	Forgive
Hold on	Let go
Punish, get even	'Go Scot free'
Self-vindication	Exoneration
Dump on others	Restraint
Excitement, 'stirred up	Stay 'cool'
Emotionalize	Think
Dramatize	Ignore
Express	Stifle
Prove self	Dismiss
Be right	Be wrong
Enlist support	Keep to oneself
Puff up	Appear weak
'Macho'	'Wimp'
Growl, show teeth	Be calm
Excitement	Peace
Snarl	Reason
Threaten	Compromise
Judgmentalism	Acceptance

CHAPTER 8

Pride

(Calibration Level 175)

Introduction

People feel more positive as they reach this level, and the rise in self-esteem is a balm to all the pain experienced at lower levels of consciousness. Pride is far enough removed from Shame, Guilt, or Fear that to rise out of despair is an enormous jump. Pride as such generally has a good reputation and is socially encouraged, yet, as we see from the Map of the Scale of Consciousness, it is sufficiently negative to remain below the critical level of 200. Pride feels good only in contrast to the lower levels.

Because "Pride goeth before a fall," it is defensive and vulnerable as it is dependent upon external conditions, without which it can suddenly revert to a lower level. The inflated ego is vulnerable to attack. Pride remains weak because it can be knocked off its pedestal into Shame, which is the threat that fires the fear of loss of pride.

Pride is divisive and gives rise to factionalism, resulting in costly consequences. Man has habitually died for Pride for which armies still regularly slaughter each other. Religious wars, political terrorism and zealotry, and the ghastly history of the Middle East and Central Europe are all the price of Pride and hatred for which all of society pays.

The downside of Pride is arrogance and denial. These characteristics block growth. In Pride, recovery from addictions is impossible because emotional problems or character defects are denied. The whole problem of denial is that of Pride; thus, Pride is a very sizable block to the acquisition of real power, which displaces Pride with true stature and prestige.

Discussion

As the level of consciousness rises, so does the presence of experienced happiness. Approximately twelve percent of the people at the level of Anger feel happy about their lives, but at the level of Pride, the percentage rises to twenty-two percent. Yet, Pride, like Anger and Fear, is still a defensive posture because of its intrinsic vulnerability that requires its positions be guarded and defended. Pride is gratifying yet a block to moving on to the solid ground of Courage, which is beyond fear because of its invulnerability. The ego inflation of Pride is the core of its vulnerability in that the ego overestimates its importance and thus miscalculates its value as a guide to function, survival, and interaction with others. The self-esteem of Pride rests on an inflated and exaggerated opinion rather than on reality. Thus, the ego searches for confirmation, which rests on the insecure premises of opinion.

Pride is operationally serviceable as a transitory self-reward for successful accomplishment and therefore a normal response that is learned in childhood via parental approval and rewards for good behavior. Thus, as a reward system, it facilitates maturation and acculturation. The error occurs when the ego assumes that it is the 'me' that is being rewarded rather than the behavior itself. This leads to the seeking of the reward of admiration by which actions become subservient to the goal of winning approval. The motivating pattern persists in most adults to varying degrees, but with progressive maturity, the pattern becomes internalized and self-reward occurs by virtue of the authority of internalized parental figures and standards. With further maturity, the opinions or approval of others diminish in importance and are supplanted by self-approval, and life is then lived according to internalized standards. At a more mature level, although the approval of others is nice, it is not deterministic of behaviors, as expressed in the common dictum, "I have to live with myself."

Socialized Pride

Pride is often dependent on social image and its expressions via possessions, publicity, titles, wealth, etc. Social status and its symbols motivate subcultures, which have their own intrinsic earmarks of success. These may include everything from style of language and dress to 'whom you know', as well as address, size of house, automobile, and the appurtenances of wealth.

Although America and other democracies are hypothetically classless societies, in practice, social class is a strong reality. Other than age and sex, it is one of the first things that people notice about each other. Each subculture has its own ranking system of 'ins' and 'outs' and stratifications. These appear in nuances of roles and privileges, as well as responsibilities and expectations, with consequent rewards and obligations as a result of complex system motivators. Values can automatically accrue to certain activities and qualities, such as education, personality traits, and styles of behavior and speech. These become codified within subcultures, each of which also has its own accepted internal codes.

The social pressure of subcultures is quite strong and often determines the content of internalized behavioral patterns that define success or failure and affect pride, self-esteem, and perceived social value. The same behavioral style that leads to approval or success in one subculture may spell failure and rejection in another. Thus, appropriate is the wisdom of the dictum, "When in Rome, do as the Romans do." Paradoxically, there are subcultures that emphasize conformity to their characteristics of nonconformity.

Each subculture has its own intrinsic, unwritten philosophy interwoven with attitudes and belief systems that are expressed as an orientation towards presumptive values, goals, and range of options. These contextualize and express as a calibratable, evolutionary level of consciousness in which the overall field is dominated by an attractor field of invisible but strong energy to which the individual consciousness becomes entrained and dominated. The presence of the field is intuited and recognized by subtle signals. These express as emotional and psychological behavioral attitudes that become a visible and articulated lexicon resulting in presumptions and expectations. Thus, attitudes are visible shorthand expressions of specific levels of consciousness.

While pridefulness, in contrast to self-esteem and confidence, is considered an asset in some subcultures, in general, it is a social deterrent in society at large. Pride expressed as arrogance and personal superiority tends to be an antagonistic social positionality for it is seen as vanity with its implied air of superiority, (i.e., 'politically correct', or 'elite').

Pride is self-admiration, which implies that others, by comparison, are inferior or have less worth, rank, or value. The transparency of this veneer is quickly apprehended by more mature people who consider it to be an embarrassment and a socially detrimental attribute. Egoistic pride as 'specialness' triggers resentment in others and in society in general. In contrast, the truly successful people are accepted because mature success is accompanied by humility and gratitude rather than an air of superiority.

Pride is guarded because of its vulnerability as well as high visibility. Its downside is envy, competitiveness, jealousy, and their consequences of hate, malice, and vindictiveness. The fragility of pride stems from its narcissistic core, which sees true importance as a threat and an implied loss of stature. Thus, vanity results in sensitivity to slights or comparisons that lead to fear of attack and social paranoia with its nascent hostility that can rapidly become overt. This tendency is expressed socially in the 'hate the leader' syndrome or in the hatred of success, such as in the 'hate America' syndrome.

This downside of narcissism is expressed in children who envy and are hostile towards the winners in their class and results in the derision of high performance by fellow students. The hostility of narcissism finds profitable cultural expressions where it is exploited for political or financial gain and attention-getting. The paradox is that the anti-celebrity hostility arises out of the critics' own inner celebrity-seeking motivations.

A consequence of self-importance based on pride is its need to be constantly fed and propped up to offset the inner doubt and deficiency of wholeness and completeness that ensue from fulfilling the requirements of integrity. Pride is 'sensitive', competitive, feels threatened, and becomes enflamed by hostile jealousy that accrues to social status or attention to others. Pridefulness is therefore the motivation of the self-appointed critic's use of sarcasm, ridicule, supposed satire, and the whole industry of attacking public figures and the reputations of acknowledged leaders.

The Internet has become very visibly the domain of contentious vilifiers of integrity. These represent inflation of narcissism expressed as 'opinion'. Because the narcissistic ego is not aligned with integrous truth, its forms of expression become strident and fallacious and therefore calibrate extremely low.

The primitive, prideful ego is greedy, and its transparent Achilles' heel eventually attracts the consequences of hubris, which is the theme of many great classics of history. That "Pride goeth before a fall" is society's rueful epithet to vainglorious causes, as history attests.

Because of the pervasiveness of Pride as an expression of the human ego, some forms of pride are accorded social acceptance or even approval and accepted as normal. The most prominent is the status of personal opinion in its multiple expressions as 'free speech'. This cloak of implied approval excuses everything from gross prevarication to various forms of mendacity. When examined as a function of the ego, opinion reveals itself to be nothing more than an idea

to which self-importance has been added because it is
'my' opinion. An opinion is an idea that has acquired
the glamour of self-importance and is therefore more
attractive than just reason, logic, or facts.
Opinion is often rationalized by rhetoric in order to
justify a positionality such as is represented by skepticism (cal. 160), which denounces the nonlinear
domain because it is unable to comprehend it. The
innate prideful narcissism of the ego precludes the
capacity to understand the abstract, so reasoning at this
level is limited to materialistic linear reductionism that
negates the reality of consciousness levels 500 and
over. This is a consequence of limited brain physiology
(as per chart, Section 2 Overview).

Skepticism fails in its attempt to discredit its
targets because, in order to do so, it would have
to comprehend the subject being criticized. Thus,
quantum mechanics or the Theory of Relativity cannot
be disproved by Newtonian physics. Skepticism
and cynicism lack the erudition that would give argu-
mentation validity.

Humility is the antidote to most errors of self-
deception. Pride precludes recognition of the enormous significance of context and especially of paradigm. Therefore, every major advance in human
knowledge has been derided, as historically demonstrated (e.g., the Wright brothers at Kitty Hawk,
germs as the cause of infection instead of miasmas,
etc.).

Due to the innate structure of the ego, it is intrinsically incapable of discerning truth from falsehood
and confuses perception with reality. Thus, the ego is

the victim of its own limitations. What 'seemed like a good idea at the time' is often the source of regret later on, as everyone knows. Thus, the value of consciousness calibration is that the relative, actual truth of a statement can be derived by a system that evaluates truth in accord with an absolute scale of validity. A free society that gives free rein to the whole gamut of human expression, from the blatantly fallacious to that of advanced wisdom, actually hopes that over time, wisdom and common sense will prevail over excess and rhetoric. When inflated, however, falsity becomes elaborated, and the consequences of falsity may take decades or even centuries of suffering before the falsity is revealed.

Ego-Dynamics
The intrinsic source of Pride is the narcissistic energy of the ego by which it self-propagates via images and symbols through a circuitous self-reinforcing pattern. Importance is an emotional value with a complexity of components signifying worth or importance that is always relative and therefore subject to error as well as contradiction. The ego fears deflation by negation and therefore constantly seeks reinforcement by approval and agreement as well as accolade. This is overtly expressed by the endless exploitation of the media by which image eclipses and replaces reality by creation of a virtual seductive, glamorized, and distorted replacement. The wise person avoids ostentatious display as it more often attracts envy and jealousy rather than admiration.

Pride is fragile and, therefore, its defenses are often rigid and extreme to the point of paranoia. That which is inflated is subject to deflation, which quickly triggers shame. Thus, humility is misinterpreted by the ego as being the equivalent of humiliation, whereas, in reality, humility is the strongest safeguard against humiliation or vulnerability. This is a basic tactical wisdom in the martial arts where taking a positionality is a flaw that leads to defeat because a fixed posture is one that gives the opponent a pattern for attack.

In ego-dynamics, a rigid set of expectations results in brittle self-esteem. The structure of Pride is linear and therefore vulnerable, whereas the Self is nonlinear and thus not subject to linear attack.

While the ego is conditioned, the Self is not subject to conditions, for it is self-fulfilling, without limitation, definition, or qualities, and is beyond adjectives. The ego's self-evaluation is based on claims and opinions, whereas true self-esteem arises by virtue of the energy of integrity and truth. The Self is complete by virtue of its completion and identification as 'is-ness', which is unconditional.

Transcending Pride

Pride is a needless burden and a fragile prop that is not only vulnerable to deflation but also, paradoxically, it even provokes and attracts attack. It is based on a false presumption that one's intrinsic worth is a definable variable. Self-acceptance results from surrendering self-doubt. All that exists is intrinsically equal by virtue of its creation and the source of that creation itself.

Worth or value is based on linear value judgments, all of which are merely arbitrary adjectives. All 'add-ons' are suppositions, as are social symbols or public accolades, which are ephemeral and transitory. To try to prove or claim self-worth is to lose it.

The pattern of vulnerability arises in childhood out of the helplessness of infancy where self-esteem is consequent to the opinion of others and their satisfaction of wants. Thus arises the illusion that power and worth are provisional. In normal development, dependency on outside sources of gratification is withdrawn and instead internalized as self-approval. This is afforded by a benign conscience and realistic expectations of the performance of realistic goals and standards.

Realistic self-esteem arises from fulfilling integrous principles so that intention becomes an important factor, which in itself is less vulnerable than idealized results. The fortunate infant receives unconditional love, even though the pride of approval may be conditional. Insufficient approval in childhood brings later insecurity.

It takes courage to jettison the props of Pride and, with humility, accept one's inner reality, which is of an invulnerable source. To accept the inner core of one's existence as a self-existent reality requires letting go of any definitions of self as a 'who' and, instead, seeing oneself as a 'what'.

The antidote to Pride is to choose humility and integrity instead of a positionality, such as being important, 'right', getting even, indulging in blame, or seeking admiration. All credit for accomplishments is given to God as the Presence of the Divinity within instead of to the ego, and therefore accomplishment results in gratitude and joy rather than vulnerable pridefulness.

The underlying error of spiritual Pride is the ego's presumption and claim of sovereignty as the author and agency of performance and results of action. Its claim for recognition is analogous to a light bulb's claiming credit for light, whereas the source of its power is from the impersonal energy of electricity itself.

Processing Pride

All exists by virtue of Divine Ordinance; thus, by virtue of the Source of Creation, everyone is a child of God. Pride is the replacement of Reality by illusion. The equality of All that Exists is a consequence of the gift of Existence itself. It is therefore only necessary to 'be', which is already a given. Gratitude easily replaces Pride, which is self-rewarding and eclipses all judgmentalism from within and without.

Inner peace is the consequence of humility and acceptance of one's karmic inheritance, with its intrinsic gifts as well as limitations. It is very helpful to know that even one's human existence is the consequence of assent by the will. The Buddha taught, "Rare is it to be born a human; rarer still is it to have heard of Enlightenment; and most rare is it to pursue Enlightenment."

Like any limiting ego position, it is not the position itself that requires relinquishment but the emotional pay-off or energy that holding onto that position provides to the ego. To realize that Pride is a limitation is already a great step in itself.

Notable is that Pride is intrinsically a statement of lack, and it is therefore constantly needy and seeking to be fed and propped up to compensate for its insufficiency. Also notable is that the more it is fed, the more voracious its appetite, which eventually becomes insatiable. Frustration of pride easily leads to rage; thus arose the wise adage to be cautious with the prideful for they can become spiteful or vengeful.

The spiritually wise reject the temptation of ego inflation of flattery, titles, worldly success, pomp, wealth, worldly power, and other temptations of illusion. Lastly, there is the paradoxical, concealed temptation of pride in one's humility, i.e., the so-called spiritual ego, where even piety or humility can be a display.

Assumed poverty can also be a form of ostentation and can be worn as a badge out of spiritual pride. True asceticism is a matter of economy of effort or projected value. It is not the possessions themselves but the importance attached to them. Thus, one can be wealthy but unattached to the wealth itself, which is a matter of indifference, e.g., "to wear the world like a loose garment," as suggested by St. Francis of Assisi. The capacity for happiness is not dependent on possessions once one's basic physical needs are met. Rates of happiness are correlated clearly with calibrated levels of consciousness (as per chart). The less the 'wants' prevail, the greater the experience of freedom. As one's level of consciousness advances, possessions can become an encumbrance. Wealthy people frequently live very simple lives in just two or three rooms of huge estates and have not even been in the other parts of their mansions for many years.

As with the other levels of consciousness, there are concordant presumptions and positionalities that reinforce their prevalence as a consequence of dualistic pairs of attractions and aversions. Each has its anticipated rewards and fear of losses.

A major overall posture, such as humility, facilitates all inner spiritual work. It is generally overlooked because the mind focuses on the content of prevailing issues rather than on the overall context within which spiritual endeavor is pursued. Humility is not just an attitude but also a reality based on facts. With inner honesty, a devotee needs to realize the limitations inherent in just being a human. A 'person' does not really know 'who' or 'what' they are, where they came from, or their destiny, and they are unaware of a multitude of karmic factors, both individual and collective.

The mind is unaware of multiple aspects of the psyche and the influence of multiple unseen energies of the interacting attractor fields of consciousness. Thus, the mind, unaided, is unable to really know if that which is desired will turn out to be a blessing or a hindrance.

"I, of myself, really know nothing" is factual, for at best, the mind has impressions and presumptions. Life 'makes sense' only in retrospect. Spiritual practices accompanied by devotion provide additional strength and enlist unseen support. Thus, faith and trust plus willingness and intention are time-honored guides. In today's world are the added reassurances of the validation of spiritual truth and realities via consciousness calibration. Truth is also reinforced by the testimony of those who have trodden the path, which can also be validated experientially and by consciousness calibration.

Dualities of Pride

Attraction	Aversion
Vain, proud	Humility, humble
Be more	Be less
Important	Nobody
Admired	Looked down on
Status	Common, ordinary
Noticed	Ignored
Special	Ordinary
Better than	The same
Superior	Inferior
Attractive, fashionable	Dull
Be right	Wrong
Opinionated	Silent
Thrill	Dull, pedestrian
'Insider'	Excluded
Exclusive	Common
Succeed	Fail

The surrender of the above list results in a great expansion of inner freedom and release from numerous fears and inhibitions. Paradoxically, the imaginary 'loss' of the attractions eventuates as great overall gains that are not vulnerable to loss and exist independently of the world or passing events. These are understood to be the consequence of cause and effect as a byproduct of 'doingness'. With surrender of perceived 'gain' or 'loss', karmic possibilities actualize by assent and as a consequence of what a person has become. As one evolves, what the world admires can be seen as an encumbrance, and what the world sees as a loss is a spiritual freedom. Inner peace results from surrender of both attractions and aversions.

Section Two

Calibration Levels 200-500
Linear Mind

Section Two – Overview

The Physiology of Truth:
Transition from Lower to Higher Mind

Introduction

At the lower consciousness levels, the ego dominates life based primarily on the techniques and emotions of animal survival, which are aligned with pleasure, predation, and gain. As consciousness evolved over time, some animal species, as well as portions of humankind, rose to consciousness level 200, which is the major demarcation that heralds reliance on power rather than force.

In human consciousness, this transition reflects the increasing influence of spiritual energy, which is transformative. Its influence is accompanied by progressive awareness and responsiveness to the energy of love, and as a result, behaviors, emotionality, and mentalizations become increasingly benign. The energy of love is also aligned with progressive awareness of truth and the underlying Reality from which Existence and Creation emerge as the evolution of both physicality and spirituality.

While physicality and force represent evolution in its linear expressions, spiritual energy, as well as the basic energy of life itself, is nonlinear and shows the contrast between form and essence. The ability to distinguish between these contrasting qualities emerges as spiritual awareness and the capacity to recognize spiritual reality as truth.

The capacity for survival was facilitated by intelligence, which is the quality of life consciousness that is capable of first comprehending the linear domain, and as it progresses, being able to comprehend abstract principles. In hominids, the evolutionary progress of this capacity was enabled by the emergence of the forebrain, which became dominant with the evolution of the bipeds. This emerging mental intelligence of cognition was primarily utilized below consciousness level 200 in the service of the animal instincts of survival, aggression, and dominance. It was therefore subservient to the limited linearity of form. As consciousness evolved over level 200, the energy of life and awareness became progressively aligned with the nonlinear realities of love, benevolence, and the search for spiritual truth. It is only at level 200 that the intrinsic worth of 'others' becomes a reality.

Brain Physiology and the Function of Truth

The capacity to recognize and comprehend truth is concordant with the levels of consciousness as reflected not only in the evolution of brain anatomy but, more importantly, also by changes in the physiology of the human brain and its prevalent patterns of processing information. These, in turn, depend on underlying, unseen spiritual energy fields. In humans, critical and profound changes occur in the brain's physiology and patterns of processing information at consciousness level 200. These can be summarized as follows:

Below Consciousness Level 200:

The left brain (in right-handed people) is dominant in information processing (the right brain in left-handed people). Input is directly processed via the relay centers (thalamus) to the emotional/instinctual centers (the amygdala) via a fast track, and only belatedly from the prefrontal cortex via a slower track. Thus, emotional response occurs before intelligence and cognition have a chance to modify the response.

Memory of an event is stored in the hippocampus region of the brain as learning and for recall. This left-brain process is akin in function to the animal brain in that it is directed towards personal survival, and thus, in the human, it subserves the ego. From this orientation, 'others', including family or tribal (pack) members, are seen primarily as objects or means to personal survival. Also of great importance is that the information supplied by the delayed input of intelligence from the prefrontal cortex is not only slower to reach the response center, but when it does, it has already become subordinated to the previously elicited emotional response. Thus, the intellect becomes primarily a tool of animal drives and self-serving goals. Subsequent responses are therefore primitive, survival oriented, and routed through the fight-or-flight patterns with their neurohormonal consequences, such as the release of cortisone or adrenaline that, in turn, stress the physiology of the acupuncture and immune systems.

This left-brain, self-centered response system is accompanied by the transitory weakening of the body's musculature and a negative or weak muscle response. The body's energy system, however, quickly recovers and restores the acupuncture balance so that the overall energy system is again poised for the next stimulus response cycle. The stress-reaction patterns

were described by Hans Selye (1956, 1974) as follows:
1. Alarm reaction.
2 Stage of resistance.
3. Stage of exhaustion and physiological
   impairment (catabolic).

Left-brain dominance is also reflected by limited or even nonexistent spiritual awareness since it is programmed for animal survival. The memories of this sequence of events are stored in the brain's region of the hippocampus; thus, later recall will reawaken memory of the sequence as it was contextualized by the ego's primitive survival goals and techniques. Memories are therefore negatively emotionalized and stored, along with fear, anxiety, anger, resentment, or pleasure of gain.

Above Consciousness Level 200:
The right brain in right-handed people (the left brain in left-handed people) becomes dominant above consciousness level 200. Input is fast-tracked via the relay center to the prefrontal cortex and hence to the emotional center. (As we shall see later, this occurs even more rapidly through the prefrontal region of the etheric brain.) Perception is therefore modified by intelligence, and the overall meaning of the event is contextualized according to the prevailing level of consciousness. Generally, recall is that of a more benign event than would have been recorded by a strictly left-brain response. With right-brain spiritualized brain processing and physiology, the neurohormonal response is anabolic, which releases endorphins and balances the acupuncture system. There is also the

release of oxytocin and vasopressin to the amygdala (emotional center) that relates to maternal instincts, paternal behavior, pair bonding, and social capacity via the 'social brain' (Moran, 2004) of mammals. At the same time, the muscle response is strong and positive. The propensity to process information via the healthier pathways is influenced by early life training and exposure to classical music, aesthetics, and religious affiliation, all of which affect neuronal patterning and connections.

Brain research shows that the nondominant brain hemisphere is stimulated by art, nature, music, spirituality, and aesthetics, resulting in increased altruism, inner calm, and higher levels of consciousness (Matthews, 2001). Further research on Tibetan Buddhist monks demonstrated the brain's 'neuroplasticity' and changes of physiology as a result of meditation (Begley, 2004).

These major and significant differences can be summarized in chart form (reprinted for convenience from *Truth vs. Falsehood*) as follows:

BRAIN FUNCTION AND PHYSIOLOGY

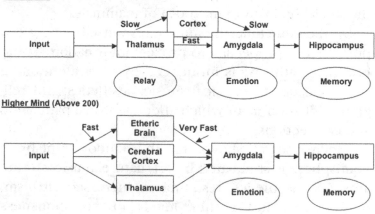

BRAIN FUNCTION AND PHYSIOLOGY

Lower Mind (Below 200)

Higher Mind (Above 200)

Below 200	Above 200
Left-brain dominance	Right-brain dominance
Linear	Non-linear
Stress—Adrenaline	Peace—Endorphins
Fight or flight	Positive emotion
Alarm—Resistance—Exhaustion	Support thymus
(Selye—Cannon: Fight/Flight)	
▼ Killer cells and immunity	▲ Killer cells
Thymus stress	▲ Immunity
Disrupt acupuncture meridian	Healing
Disease	Balanced acupuncture system
Negative muscle response	Positive muscle response
▼ Neurotransmitters—Serotonin	
Track to emotions twice as fast as through prefrontal cortex to emotions	Track to emotions slower than from prefrontal and etheric cortexes
Pupil dilates	Pupil constricts

Importance:
Spiritual endeavor and intention change the brain function and the body's physiology and establish a specific area for spiritual information in the right-brain prefrontal cortex and its concordant etheric (energy) brain.

Mental Changes at Consciousness Level 200

Consciousness levels are aligned with calibratable energy fields that, in nonlinear dynamics, are termed 'attractor fields'. These dominate a particular level of the concordant energy field associated with a specific level of consciousness and influence degrees of intelligence. The attractor field that is aligned primarily with survival is termed 'Lower Mind' and calibrates at level 155. It is concerned with physical survival, emotional pleasure, and personal gain. It is denoted as being essentially aligned with self-interest.

As consciousness continues to evolve, it becomes increasingly aware of the importance of others, and with a greater capacity of discernment, eventually arrives at level 275, denoted as 'Higher Mind', which is capable of dealing with nonlinear abstractions and essence. It is therefore more perceptive of principles and the subtle qualities of essence.

Attitudes

These reflect the degree to which perception, emotion, mentation, and rationality are influenced at different levels of consciousness. The world is experienced and viewed quite differently from Higher Mind at consciousness level 275 in contrast to Lower Mind at level 155. These levels profoundly influence all aspects of life. The degree of difference is almost equivalent to describing two different, contrasting civilizations with different levels of the quality of interpersonal relationships, pleasure, happiness in life, worldly success, philosophies, politics, and most importantly, the level of spiritual awareness and alignment.

As is apparent, Lower Mind focuses on the linear specifics of a situation and sees them in terms of self-interest. In contrast, Higher Mind includes the overall context and is thereby aware of the abstract nonlinear meaning, including spiritual significance.

For convenience, the following have been selected from previously published research and lecture materials.

Table 1: Function of Mind—Attitudes

Lower Mind (Cal. 155)	Higher Mind (Cal. 275)
Accumulation	Growth
Acquire	Savor
Remember	Reflect
Maintain	Evolve
Think	Process
Denotation	Inference
Time = restriction	Time = opportunity
Focus on present/past	Focus on present/future
Ruled by emotion/wants	Ruled by reason/inspiration
Blames	Takes responsibility
Careless	Disciplined
Content (specifics)	Content plus field (conditions)

Lower Mind (Cal. 155)	Higher Mind (Cal. 275)
Concrete, literal	Abstract, imaginative
Limited, time, space	Unlimited
Personal	Impersonal
Form	Significance
Focus on specifics	Generalities
Exclusive examples	Categorize class—inclusive
Reactive	Detached
Passive/aggressive	Protective
Recall events	Contextualize significance
Plan	Create
Definition	Essence, meaning
Particularize	Generalize
Pedestrian	Transcendent
Motivation	Inspirational, intention
Morals	Ethics
Examples	Principles
Physical & emotional survival	Intellectual development
Pleasure and satisfaction	Fulfillment of potential

All gradations exist between the contrasting pairs that reflect intensity, e.g., there is a difference between craving, wanting, desiring, 'must have', and demanding in contrast to the options of preference, hoping for, wishing, choosing, favoring, or accepting. The difference in just this one single quality alone can spell the distinction between homicide, rage, depression, and misery versus contentment, relaxation, and being easy-going in one's expectations.

Psychology, psychiatry, and brain chemistry research now pay much attention to the study of attitudes, which demonstrates how important they are to human happiness, satisfaction, and success (Szegedy-Maszak, 2004; Arehart-Treichel, 2005; Moran, 2004, et al.). 'Attitude' can be defined as a habitual mindset that relates the perceived self to the perceived world and others. In our society, attitudes are studied within the so-called field of 'self-improvement' for which there are workshops and voluminous literature. The common collective experience is that expectations of self and others become modified with growth and progressive maturity, along with spiritual evolution. Thus, the cultural field of growth attracts the progressive segment of society recently labeled 'cultural creatives' (Ray and Anderson, 2000). As a simple exercise, merely surveying the contrasting lists, including the one that follows, has a freeing effect as it brings various options to awareness that have been overlooked.

Table 2: Function of Mind—Attitudes

Lower Mind (Cal. 155)	Higher Mind (Cal. 275)
Impatient	Tolerant
Demand	Prefer
Desire	Value
Upset, tension	Calm, deliberate
Control	Let go, surrender
Utilitarian use	Sees potential
Literal	Intuitive
Ego-self directed	Ego, plus other-oriented
Personal & family survival	Survival of others
Constrictive	Expansive
Exploit, use up	Preserve, enhance

Lower Mind (Cal. 155)	Higher Mind (Cal. 275)
Design	Art
Competition	Cooperation
Pretty, attractive	Aesthetics
Naïve, impressionable	Sophisticated, informed
Guilt	Regret
Gullible	Thoughtful
Pessimist	Optimist
Excess	Balance
Force	Power
Smart, clever	Intelligent
Exploits life	Serves life
Callous	Merciful
Insensitive	Sensitive
Particularize	Contextualize
Statement	Hypothesis
Closure	Open-ended
Terminal	Germinal
Sympathize	Empathize
Rate	Evaluate
Want	Choose
Avoid	Face and accept
Childish	Mature
Attacks	Avoids
Critical	Accepting
Condemning	Forgiving
Skepticism	Comprehend

Table 2 reveals further options and possibilities that benefit self-awareness. Limiting attitudes have been called 'character defects', and groups that support spiritual growth have noticed that these defects begin to diminish as soon as they are recognized and owned.

The benefit of accepting one's defects instead of

denying them is an increase in an inner sense of self-honesty, security, and higher self-esteem, accompanied by greatly diminished defensiveness and neurotic 'sensitivity' to perceived 'slights'. A self-honest person is not prone to having their feelings hurt or 'having a bone to pick' with others. Honest insight has an immediate benefit in the reduction of actual as well as potential emotional pain. A person is vulnerable to emotional pain in exact relationship to the degree of self-awareness and self-acceptance. When people admit their downside, others cannot attack them there. As a consequence, one feels emotionally less vulnerable and more safe and secure.

Most domestic arguments stem from the refusal to own or take responsibility for even simple character defects, such as forgetting an errand or some triviality, which, oddly enough, constitutes the majority of interpersonal conflict. Most bickering represents the endless mutual accusations over trivialities that emotional maturity and honesty would have prevented in the first place. Battered spouses and marital homicide start out over mundane issues and then escalate as they trigger the release of the narcissistic ego to which 'being right' is astonishingly more important than even life itself.

The key to painless growth is humility, which amounts to merely dropping pridefulness and pretense and accepting fallibility as a normal human characteristic of self and others. Lower mind sees relationships as competitive; higher mind sees them as cooperative. Lower mind gets involved with others; higher mind becomes aligned with others. The simple words "I'm sorry" put out most fires painlessly. To win in life means to give up the obsession of 'who's at fault'.

Graciousness is far more powerful than belligerence. It is better to succeed than to 'win'.

Table 3: Function of Mind—Attitudes

Lower Mind (Cal. 155)	Higher Mind (Cal. 275)
Guarded	Friendly, charitable
Cynical	Optimistic, hopeful
Suspicious	Trusting
Selfish	Considerate
Stingy	Generous
Calculating	Planning
Devious	Forthright
Quixotic	Stable
Fussy, choosey	Easy to please
Short of money	Adequate for needs
Insists	Requests
Excess	Balance
Rude	Polite, gracious
Extremes	Compromising
Rush, hurry	'Keep moving'
Avarice	Money isn't everything
Lust	Desire
Ungrateful	Appreciative
Downgrades	Compliments
Condemn	Disapprove
Sexist	Humanist
Stultified	Progressive
Focused on self	Concern for others & the world
Opportunistic	Fits life plan
Complacent	Self-improvement
Vulgar, gross	Restrained, subtle
Prevaricate	Honest, truthful
Envy	Appreciation, respect
Grim, heavy	Sense of humor, lighthearted

The strength to adopt positive instead of negative attitudes is already available in the province of the will. The entreaty of Divinity for assistance results in a transformative process that becomes more powerful with practice because the personality is now aligning with a strong, positive attractor field rather than with the weak linear ego. In practice at the beginning, what may seem false or artificial becomes surprisingly natural and easy because it is aligned with and supported by Reality. The linear ego/self struggles to survive but the power of the spiritual Self is supported by the infinite field by which life evolves and survives. Love summons support; anger repels it. With the throwing off of the lead weights of resistance, a cork automatically rises to the surface of the ocean as a consequence of its own buoyancy.

Personality Traits: Character Formation
The learning and adaptation of constructive and more mature attitudes result in a more pleasant personality that is aligned with greater overall satisfaction with self and others. The rate of subjective happiness at level 155 is only fifteen percent, but by consciousness level 275 (Higher Mind), the rate quadruples, to sixty percent.

It will be discovered that the ego consists of interlocking building blocks and that to move even one unsettles the whole pile, which then begins to fall of its own gravity. Even a seemingly small effort can have very major effects, and one discovers that just a simple smile can totally change one's life. The many thousands of people who follow self-improvement and spiritual pathways confirm the reality of this discovery.

Following is a list of 'winner' attitudes, all of which

are quite simple to choose and have extremely long-term benefits (adapted from *Truth vs. Falsehood*). Life lived in the energy field of a calibration level over 200 is quite different from life lived below that level.

Positive Personality Traits – Part I

Available	265	Equitable	365
Balanced	305	Ethical	305
Benign	225	Fair	305
Calm	250	Faithful	365
Considerate	295	Firm	245
Content	255	Flexible	245
Cordial	255	Friendly	280
Decent	295	Genuine	255
Dependable	250	Glad	335
Diligent	210	Happy	395
Diplomatic	240	Hard Work	200
Easygoing	210	Healthy	360

The table above reveals qualities that are valued and supported by all successful societies throughout time that calibrate over 200. The road to spiritual awareness is supported by the fact that higher motivations are reinforced by energies that reflect power, whereas egoistic positions are weak, limiting, and exhausting. Just as negative qualities are intertwined with each other, positive qualities are as well, so that progress in one area brings surprising improvements in other areas that were not even consciously addressed.

From consciousness research, it is learned that adopting a positive attitude immediately invites in the attractor field of an entire field of consciousness that then unwittingly begins to alter the personality and bring benefits to one's own life as well as those of others.

Positive Personality Traits – Part II

Helpful	220	Protective	265
Honest	200	Rational	405
Honorable	255	Reliable	290
Humane	260	Respectable	250
Humility	270	Respectful	305
Idealistic	295	Responsible	290
Kind	220	'Salt of the Earth'	240
Nice	255	Sane	300
Normal	300	Sense of humor	345
Open	240	Sensible	240
Orderly	300	Stable	255
Patient	255	Supportive	245
Persistent	210	Thoughtful	225
Pleasant	220	Tolerant	245
Pleasing	275	Warm	205
Polite	245	Wisdom	385
Positive	225		

The transition from Lower Mind to Higher Mind results in a drop of unemployment from almost fifty percent to only eight percent. Also, the rate of poverty drops from 22 percent to 1.5 percent, and dramatically, the rate of criminality drops from 50 percent to only 9 percent. Similar major benefits are reflected in all the other important areas of life, including educational level, income, marital success, reputation, personal appearance, social approval, initial impression, language style, and political and social views. All of these reflect the assumption of personal responsibility and thus result in a major change in the rate of traffic violations, credit rating, percent of home ownership, physical health, longevity, and very importantly, personal satisfaction.

While these advantages are very evident and obvious on the personal level, they become even more so when expressed collectively. The society that calibrates at level 155 is characterized by the predominance of underprivileged characteristics, such as poor economic development, a low rate of literacy, high birth and infant mortality rates, and unemployment rates. It is also represented by the exploitation and repression of civil rights, rampant corruption, and gross extremes in the distribution of wealth. These societies demonstrate pervasive poverty, lack of civil freedoms, the prevalence of violence and oppression, and collectively, they are depicted as undeveloped or even quite primitive.

Experiential 'Reality'

The ego/mind presumes and is convinced that its perceptions and interpretations of life experiences are the 'real' thing and therefore 'true'. It also believes by projection that other people see, think, and feel the same way, and if they do not, they are mistaken and therefore wrong. Thus, perception reinforces its hold by reification and presumptions.

As has been described, each level of consciousness is in accord with and a reflection of a dominant attractor field of consciousness by which meaning and value are contextualized. Each person therefore lives in a world of their own making, reinforced by seeking agreement and a variety of rationalizations. The disparity is compensated for positively by empathy, compassion, acceptance, and the wisdom of maturity. A negative attitude, in contrast, sees differences as sources for anger, resentment, and other negative feelings.

The question arises as to whether the experiential differences are limited just to *res interna* (perception) or are due to external differences in the experiences themselves. By clinical observation, people not only perceive wide variation in accordance with their levels of consciousness but actually experience quite different events. To those who are unfriendly, other people actually *are* often cold and unfriendly; and to a warm, loving person, the exact, same environment is cordial and supportive. Thus, by virtue of what we *are*, we subtly influence events around us. Because of a benign attitude, loving people attract positive events, and the opposite is equally true (with karmically-influenced variations). Even animals can intuit intention, and humans are guided by subliminal signals that reflect intention, attitude, and levels of consciousness. Within limits, we tend to experience the reflection of what we have become.

The skeptic is dubious about the validity of spiritual realities because they do not have experiences such as the miraculous and therefore negate the reality of higher dimensions within which they are common occurrences. The literal mechanistic mind sees all such phenomena (the *siddhis*, etc.) as 'woo-woo' at best, or even delusional, and it cannot understand the capacity to comprehend essence. Each level of consciousness thus tends to be self-ratifying, which elucidates why the evolution of consciousness appears to be slow.

Summary
From all the foregoing, it is starkly obvious that transcending consciousness level 200 is of very major and

critical importance in every area of life, both individually and collectively. From a spiritual viewpoint, it is
even more critical as level 200 denotes the transition
from being dominated by falsehood to becoming
aligned with truth. As previously noted, of great significance is that as yet, seventy-eight percent of the
world's population calibrates below 200 (forty-nine
percent in the United States). Because of the enormous
increase in power of the levels over 200 (a logarithmic
progression), a population committed to integrity
counterbalances the negativity of the majority of the
population worldwide. Thus, civilization survives in
order to continue to evolve.

CHAPTER 9

Courage

(Calibration Level 200)

Introduction

At the level of Courage, spiritual energy profoundly alters the experience of self and others; therefore, it is the level of the onset of empowerment. This is the zone of exploration, accomplishment, fortitude, and determination. At the lower levels, the world is seen as hopeless, sad, frightening, tempting, or frustrating, but at the level of Courage, life is seen as exciting, challenging, and stimulating.

Courage implies the willingness to try new things and to deal with the vicissitudes of life. At this level of empowerment, one is able to cope with and effectively handle the opportunities of life. At level 200, for example, there is the energy to learn new job skills, and growth and education are now attainable goals. There is the capacity to face fears or character defects and to grow despite them, and anxiety does not cripple endeavor as it does at the lower stages of evolution. Obstacles that defeat people whose consciousness level is below 200 act as stimulants to those who have evolved into the first level of true power.

People at this level put back into the world as much energy as they take from it. At lower levels, populations as well as individuals drain energy from other individuals and society without reciprocating. Because accomplishment results in positive feedback, self-reward and self-esteem become progressively self-reinforcing. This is where productivity begins.

Crossing over level 200 is the most critical step in the evolution of human consciousness and its concordant quality of both inner and outer life. The development of the capacity to align with a recognized truth rather than personal gain clearly separates truth from falsehood. The decisive choice to make this step is that of accepting responsibility and being accountable for one's decisions or actions. This also indicates a shift from being dominated by primitive emotions, which become attenuated by intelligence and verifiable validity rather than the self-serving emotionality that results in fallacious and distorted reasoning. Thus, courage represents conquering the fear of loss of gain as well as its replacement by more long-term rewards of truth.

At level 200, there is intuitive acceptance of the truth of accountability as a spiritual and social reality. This is accompanied by the emergence of awareness of responsibility for the destiny of one's soul and not for just the body and the satisfactions of the ego. Truth is now seen as an ally instead of an enemy. Alignment with truth rather than gain brings strength, self-respect, and true empowerment rather than ego inflation. The dictum, "What gains a man to win the world but lose his soul?" now becomes an axiom that guides decisions and choices of options.

Courage brings inner confidence and a greater sense of personal power because it is not dependent on external factors or results. To choose integrity and self-honesty is self-rewarding and reinforcing. There is a greater sense of inner freedom due to the relief from guilt and fear that subtly accompanies all violations of truth, for on the unconscious level, the spirit knows when the ego is lying and violating premises that operate out of conscious awareness. This emanates from an archetype in the collective unconscious, as described by the Swiss psychoanalyst Carl Jung (cal. 520). The accumulation of unconscious spiritual debt (karma) progressively pulls down the calibrated level of consciousness of those who violate truth. They then have to compensate by defensive pride, anger, guilt, shame, and the fear of ultimate Divine Judgment.

Steadfastness and integrous performance result in inner gratifications that accrue from the satisfactory fulfillment of inner standards. At this level, it is the effort and intention, not just the result, that are important. "To thine own self be true" progressively dominates choices, decisions, and the emergence of an inner sense of honor. The long-term goal of life becomes the development of inner potentials, such as strength, rather than the acquisition of externals.

Although courage is both recognized and rewarded by society, the social approval becomes only secondary, for integrous people know that it is possible to fool the world but not oneself. Because of the greater awareness that occurs at level 200, temptations to violate integrity for gain are recognized and rejected, whereas below level 200, they are rationalized for the quick payoff of gain with no regard for consequences.

From consciousness calibration research, it is verified that everyone knows unconsciously when they are being lied to, which is quickly revealed by the muscle test that instantly discerns truth from falsehood. This weakening of the body's musculature response and the alterations of the energy flow through the acupuncture system indicate that the awareness of the difference between truth and falsehood is intrinsic to life energy and is reflected in the body's response, even if the mind denies it.

The energy of consciousness at level 200 is aligned with integrity of reason, and therefore, distorted deceptions of rhetoric are rejected as being weak and faulty. With this forward step in evolution, there is a major diminution of emotionality and wishful fantasy. Life thereby becomes less dramatized, and the transitory pay-offs of negative ego positions lose their appeal because they are now devoid of reward. In return, there is a greater equanimity and overall feeling of security that can only be acquired by adherence to inner honesty. By trial and error, it is discovered that the cost of compromise is not worth the risk to the confidence to which integrity becomes accustomed.

Social Expressions

Concern for others and the capacity for social responsibility arise above level 200. That seventy-eight percent of the world's population is below consciousness level 200 (in America, forty-nine percent), explains why the world is as it is, with its endless conflict, wars, poverty, crime, etc. Research indicates that the source of these problems is endogenous rather than exogenous.

Self-honesty brings relief from the negative emotions of lower energy fields. Anxiety, fear, insecurity, and guilt diminish as do frustration, resentment, and anger. Negative emotions are now unwelcome and unpleasant in both oneself and others. Argument, conflict, and discord are no longer attractive because they have lost their ego inflation. Transitory difficulties of social realities are accepted aspects of human life rather than being seen as personal insults. There is a progressive distaste for violence and the theatrics of political and

ideological extremism, as the comfort of inner-calm
homeostasis is preferred to the excitement of adrenaline.
With maturity, there is the development of a sense
of humor that replaces hostile attacks and outbursts.
The peace and quiet that seem boring to lower levels
of consciousness are now preferred as are periods of
calm during which to think and contemplate.
Reflection now becomes more important than emotionalized reactivity. Desires are less demanding, and the
quality of patience replaces drivenness and intolerance
for delay of gratification. At level 200, life becomes
more deliberate and impulsiveness diminishes.
Personal happiness becomes an achievable goal, and
gratitude replaces resentment, self-pity, and blaming
others. The subjective experience of the world changes
for the better, and people seem more friendly and
hospitable. The glamour of specialness fades as an attraction, and excesses are replaced by balance. Courage leads
to exploration and self-development, and it facilitates
personal growth and the evolution of consciousness.

The critical key to moving into the strength of
courage is the acceptance of personal responsibility
and accountability. This major move requires relinquishment of a victim/perpetrator dualistic fallacy that
socially undermines integrity via blame and excuses
based on dualistic, moral, and social relativistic fallacies
and theories by which an external 'cause' or social
condition replaces integrous personal autonomy and
self-honesty. Thus, courage also includes rising above
identification with the rationalizations that characterize
social belief systems that calibrate below 200 and are
based on presumptions of blame and excuses. Even if
there is or has been an external 'cause', it still behooves

the individual to rise above it. Society is rife with well-publicized examples of such invocation of courage, even in the face of severe calamities (e.g., Mccain, 2005). Experientially, the most common challenge to courage is fear, plus concordant self-doubt and the fear of failure. Courage does not mean absence of fear but the willingness to surmount it, which, when accomplished, reveals hidden strength and the capacity for fortitude. Fear of failure is diminished by realizing that one is responsible for the intention and effort but not the result, which is dependent on many other conditions and factors that are nonpersonal.

Strong intention plus dedication assisted by inspiration surprisingly can bring success despite prior failures. This reveals the inner capacity for bravery and fortitude that greatly increases self-esteem and confidence. Many of life's travails can only be traversed by 'white-knuckling it', which builds self-confidence.

Ego Dynamics

Level 200 tends to be self-reinforcing due to inner balance, alignment with integrity and truth, and successful functioning. Its inner dictum is to 'stay on course' and, like a ship, right oneself from the temporary effects of the waves of life. The lower emotions still erupt periodically and require correction, but they are now unwelcome rather than sought or valued.

The calibrated level of consciousness is a consequence of alignment with spiritual principles. It directs one's destiny and is analogous to the setting of a ship's compass. By alignment with integrity, there is the acceptance of character defects, which are seen as challenges for self-improvement rather than as excuses for blame, self-pity, or resentment. At level 200, goals are value driven, and their achievement is both realistic and feasible.

The function of the psychological ego, as seen by psychoanalysis, is to align the personality with the social reality of the external world and to simultaneously balance the personality component of the conscience (Freud's superego) with the 'ego-ideal' (internalized standards) against the primitive instinctual animal drives (the 'Id').

Lack of success in this requisite function leads to pathological conditions and traits, such as the projection of inner disapproval, fear, or primitive instincts onto others in the external world (e.g., blame or paranoia). Failure to control instincts results in upsurges of repressed rages, as well as fear and depression. An excessive or sadistic superego can also be projected onto others and result in rigid character traits, self-hatred, and self-punitive guilt. These mechanisms are important to know and best described by Anna Freud in *The Ego and Mechanisms of Defense* (1971).

Successful self-inquiry requires a realistic appraisal of the limitations of human development and tolerance for both ambiguity and the normalcy of being less than perfect. By the inner increase of spiritual power, the pay-off of lower ego positions is rejected for the pleasure that is innate to their replacement by honesty and integrity. Equanimity itself is found to be both gratifying and pleasurable, as well as to increase self-confidence.

From level 200 on up, responsible social relationship is now possible. While the lower emotional levels lead to involvement with others, at 200, the intention now shifts to alignment with others and the rewarding principle of mutuality rather than egocentricity.

Without the interference of narcissistic distortions,

the capacity for reality testing replaces perceptual illusions and pretenses. Without the constant interference of discord, there is the emergence of harmony as an operating principle that enables getting along with others and coordinating activities. The consequence is an increase in social approval and acceptance. Each in turn reinforces integrous goals and motivations. Anxieties and uncertainties are accepted as normal and concomitant to growth (new job, new relationship, etc.).

Because of the alignment with truth at 200, there is improved capacity to discern truth from falsehood, and the intellect advances markedly, developing the capacity to detect the substitute of emotionalized rhetoric for valid, confirmable validity. There is therefore the ability to detect pretense and the illusions by which imagination and fantasy replace logic and balance. Because below level 200, truth has been sold out for gain, there is the incapacity to discern truth from falsehood, and fallacies are accepted uncritically as being convincing. Thus, below 200 there is actually a significant loss of reality testing as well as intellectual capability. (People below calibration level 200 are unable to use the muscle test for truth and get false results.)

While below level 200 there is the capacity to process 'facts' (linear), there is not yet the capacity to discern truth, which is nonlinear and depends on the capacity for abstract thought. Lower Mind uses facts to support positionality, whereas Higher Mind respects balance, meaning, and concordance of levels of abstraction. Thus, progressively, meaning is aligned with levels of truth as a consequence of disciplined rules of logic and reason rather than wishful thinking.

Below level 200, facts are assembled without

respect for categories of equal value, and contrary evidence is ignored or rationalized away. Thus, higher mind is subject to discipline, the laws of dialectics, and the requirements of intellectual integrity. The discernment of truth thus depends on recognition of context, which profoundly influences and categorizes meaning and significance. While facts, when logically assembled, can be cited as 'proof', truth is of a different level of abstraction and can only be substantiated by other means of confirmation. Even at best, the human mind, in and of itself, is intrinsically unable to discern 'fact' from truth and truth from falsehood. The discernment of truth is supported by humility and the spirit of balanced, integrous inquiry. A classic example is that of the Wright brothers who were ridiculed by the 'fact' that aircraft are heavier than air and therefore unable to fly. That selected facts can lead to very erroneous conclusions is well exemplified by the argument of skepticism.

Transcending Level 200

The view of God at 200 is that of confidence, justice, balance with authority, and the provision for mechanisms to compensate for a lack of perfection through salvation, to accept responsibility for defects, and to strive for morality. This more benign view of Divinity replaces the lower levels' anthropologic, projected images of God as prone to extreme human weaknesses, such as pride, harshness, judgmentalism, vengeance, anger, partiality, and jealousy of seeming ethnic and geographical favoritism.

At level 200, religion is respected and seen to be an option rather than a threat. Primary principles are to avoid sin, accept spiritual responsibility, and reject temptation (e.g., as in the Lord's Prayer). Prayer is seen as both worshipful and confirmatory of God's will, and to ask for guidance is natural as a consequence of humility and acceptance of character defects. Thus, morality tends to be a major focus that often reflects itself in socially responsible attitudes and respect for traditional values. Although there is still fear of Divine Judgment, it is ameliorated by faith in God's fairness, mercy, and forgiveness in response to contrition and the promise of salvation.

The dedication to sinlessness and integrity brings character defects into awareness, resulting in spiritual humility and the awareness that without God's help, the ego and its limitations are difficult or sometimes seemingly impossible to overcome. The fear of sin, although not overwhelming, is still a serious consideration. This leads to religious affiliation and observances that are seen as rational as well as comforting. Respect for authority results in acceptance of and compliance with religious/spiritual concepts, along with an understanding of the necessity for faith.

Courage is the result of an act of the will by which the decision is made to accept inner honesty and integrity as axiomatic principles of life to be followed despite all resistances, temptations, and obstacles. Duty to self and others results in alignment with spiritual principles and the courage to overcome those obstacles and resistances. By intention and successful practice, the vicissitudes of life, both internal and external, become opportunities for increasing strength. This is the foundation for trust in oneself, in God, in spiritual truth, and in life itself, established as a rock-like foundation.

CHAPTER 10

Neutrality

(Calibration Level 250)

Introduction

Energy becomes very positive at the level termed Neutral because of release from the positionalities of the lower levels. At the levels below 200, consciousness tends to see dichotomies and take on rigid positions that are impediments in a world that is complex and multifactoral rather than black and white. Taking dualistic positions creates polarization, which then creates opposition and division. As in the martial arts, a rigid position becomes a point of vulnerability—that which does not bend is liable to break.

Rising above barriers or oppositions that dissipate one's energies, the Neutral condition allows for flexibility and a nonjudgmental, realistic appraisal of problems. To be neutral means to be relatively unattached to outcomes. Not getting one's way is no longer experienced as defeating, frightening, or frustrating.

At the Neutral level a person can say, "Well, if I don't get this job, then I'll get another." This is the beginning of inner confidence. When sensing one's power, one is not easily intimidated or driven to prove anything. The expectation that life, with its ups and downs, will be basically okay if one can roll with the punches is an attitude of level 250.

People at Neutrality have a sense of well-being; the mark of this level is a confident capability to live in the world. This is the level of safety. People at the Neutral level are easy to get along with and safe to associate with because they are not interested in conflict, competition, or guilt. They are comfortable and basically emotionally undisturbed. This attitude is nonjudgmental and does not lead to any need to control other people's behaviors. Correspondingly, the level of Neutral results in greater freedom for self and others.

Discussion

Courage has the motivation, power, and strength to overcome resistances, face challenges, and work through them with fortitude and determination, which in turn reinforces the capability to actualize decisions. Courage is required because the level of Courage still sees problems or difficulties that require effort and determination to work through them. Thus, seeming obstacles may really be projected anticipations; however, they do not arise from reality but from residual positionalities. Courage can anticipate difficulties to be handled, such as discomfort, reluctance, uncertainty, or anxiety.

In contrast, the level of Neutrality does not project dualistic perceptions because it has dropped positionalities, such as the obstacles to courage created by doubt, anticipatory anxiety, or unfamiliarity. Freedom ensues from not having an emotional investment in outcomes or insistence on narcissistic goals, such as having it 'my way'. Neutrality is not interested in egoistically winning, controlling others, or acquiring gain. It is content to attract rather than promote. Neutrality is benign and not inclined to proselytize or prize the glamour of importance; neither does it minimize nor diminish itself out of false humility. It is not interested in persuasion, coercion, intimidation, or threat. In Neutrality, one is free from trying to 'prove' anything about oneself. In addition, it is not attracted to causes to promote or defend; therefore, Neutrality is peaceful and values tranquility and calm. It is also a level that is devoid of demands, pressure, or narcissistic needs.

A general attitude of this level is that of being interested but not emotionally involved, thus allowing for an easygoing and pleasant attitude because there is nothing really 'at stake'. Devoid of the need of 'winning' or 'gaining', Neutrality is relatively self-sufficient and content to be what it is. 'Take it or leave it' is an attitude of confidence and intrinsic worth that needs nothing from others.

The level of Neutrality is comfortable and relatively free of anxiety for it does not place survival value on preconceived outcomes. Thus, the source of happiness is not projected externally onto others or the outside world, which brings about relatively conflict-free inner security and freedom. Neutrality is also reasonably free from the social anxiety of feeling threatened and is therefore devoid of paranoia. The laissez-faire attitude allows for easygoing cordiality because there is nothing at stake requiring agreement by others. The freedom of Neutrality is the consequence of the letting go of positionalities, conditions, and expectations. Narcissistic demands and egocentric needs are no longer dominant. Therefore, the level of Neutrality does not suffer from lack nor is it driven by desire, wantingness, or the compulsion to 'do' something or take sides in social issues; thus, it includes flexibility.

In Neutrality, there is trust in God as being nonjudgmental and benign, resulting in reliance on Divine wisdom that makes allowance for man's limitations. Thus, God is really the source of freedom because Divinity no longer seems to be a threat to be feared or hated and therefore denied.

The social expressions of this level of consciousness are those of easygoing coexistence. Neutrality is not interested in conflict or participation in revolutionary movements, protests, or conflict. This may be misperceived as passivity, whereas, in actuality, it is stability that neither promotes nor resists change. The equanimity of Neutrality thus offers a counterbalance to the excesses of social change and a refuge from emotionality that allows for reflection and calm evaluation.

Ego Dynamics of Neutrality

Positionality results in dualistic perceptions that are the result of egoistic distortions and the inherent limitations of the ego's capacity for accurate mentation. Projected perceptions are confused with reality and given emphasis by imaginary gain or loss. In contrast, Neutrality is the consequence of nonattachment and is therefore relatively devoid of distortions of projected superimposed values, opinions, etc.

It is important to differentiate nonattachment from detachment. Detachment indicates withdrawal as well as negation, leading to indifference, which in itself is a defense against the fear of attachment. Progressive detachment leads to ennui, flatness, and a decrease in aliveness and the joy of existence. If followed consistently, detachment as the pathway of negation leads eventually to the Void, which is often misunderstood to represent Enlightenment or the described Buddha state of *anatta*, from the Sanskrit. While the Void is a very impressive state, in contrast, Allness is the ultimate state. The Void is nonlinear, which is impressive, but void of Divine Love, which is also nonlinear. The true conditions of Allness versus nothingness are experientially very, very different. (Discussed in Chapter 18.)

The pathway to the state of Enlightenment is via nonattachment rather than negation. In understanding this, it is important to realize that the nonlinear energy of consciousness itself is intrinsic within the linear, and that nonattachment means nondependence on form. Nonattachment means neither attraction nor aversion. In contrast, detachment often leads to aversion and avoidance, as well as devaluation. Nonattachment allows for the freedom from the attraction of projected values and anticipations such as gain. Without fear of either attraction or aversion, Neutrality allows for participation and the enjoyment of life because, experientially, life becomes more like play than a high-stakes involvement. This is consistent with the teachings of the Tao, in that the flow of life is neither sought nor resisted. Thus, life becomes effortless and existence itself is pleasurable, without conditions, and easygoing like a cork in the sea. It is 'wearing the world like a loose garment', as St. Francis of Assisi recommended.

Experientially, daily life is an amusement in which nothing of any great significance or importance rests on outcomes. With no stakes involved, there is no fear of loss or ego-inflation of seeming gain.

Whereas Courage sees challenges, Neutrality sees principles and guidelines rather than demands or rigid rules. In Neutrality, it is okay to accept or decline an option, as there is nothing to prove, nothing to gain, and nothing to lose. Consequently, Neutrality allows for flexibility and freedom from judgmentalism or anticipatory consequences.

From a psychoanalytical viewpoint, at the level of Neutrality, the positive aspects of healthy, normal ego functions are successful in balancing both inner and outer functions. Primitive impulses are recognized and rejected as unfavorable options. The intellect is free of distorted emotionalities, allowing healthy reality testing and social accommodation to ensue. The conscience (superego) has been attenuated so that it is not necessary to project inner attitudes onto others. Human nature, including its animalistic drives, is accepted as normal and therefore does not have to be rejected, repressed, denied, or projected onto others. Thus, Neutrality is nonjudgmental about the downside of physical, emotional, and social life.

The level of Neutrality is accompanied by feelings of security and safety as a consequence of nondefensiveness and nonpositionality, with the resulting freedom from fear, guilt, or judgmentalism. There is also relief from the incessant demands of narcissistic needs or imperatives. Neutrality is neither cynical nor pessimistic, nor, on the other hand, does it proselytize for optimistic goals. It accepts progress, change, and evolution of consciousness with neither resistance nor anticipation but instead floats along the river of life by decision and acceptance rather than by what could be misperceived as passivity or indifference.

Transcending Neutrality

The peace and calm of Neutrality are a welcome relief to those who have transcended the lower levels and survived their inner anguish. This might be viewed as a recuperative level for the spirit/soul that has struggled out of the swamps of despair, depression, anguish, guilt, fear, and frantic searching for gain, approval, and earthly riches, only to have them turn into ashes. Instead of regret, Neutrality looks at the past as informative and ruefully educational. Many people elect to spend this lifetime at this level of recuperation and inner healing.

While Neutrality is subjectively a very favorable state as compared to those below it, it is not yet an expression of the joy and radiance of Divinity or that of love or compassion as an upliftment to life. Neutral is neither destructive to life nor resistant, but neither is it an active contributor. It serves life by nonresistive participation and declines to be a deterrent. This level is essentially silent, neither adding to nor detracting from the panorama of life.

In Neutrality, one is grateful to have escaped the inner house of mirrors by the process of letting go and surrendering. There is freedom from the drivenness of 'have to's' or 'must's'. It is no longer necessary to be a 'winner', or 'successful', or to acquire approval or acceptance. It is not necessary to be 'right', nor does one feel compelled to 'do something' about the world's problems. Eventually, however, because of alignment with spiritual principles, consciousness again evolves by virtue of inspiration, which seeks agreement by the will. The inner balance then moves from neutral to the more positive side of the scale as a consequence of intention that is supported by faith and the upliftment of positive purpose.

Because of nonresistance, the spiritual energy of lovingness again stirs the soul, which now seeks ever higher levels of awareness and expression. The potentiality for the development of unconditional love and compassion attracts an increasing appreciation of beauty and spiritual progress as a consequence of worship and prayer. Thus, by nonresistance, the door is opened for the Grace of Divine energy that propels the evolution of consciousness by which the personal will becomes affirmative and is drawn to Divinity by attraction and the progressive inner warmth of the Radiance of Divine Love itself. The activation of spiritual potentiality is a consequence of nonresistance, which is like the flower that opens and responds to the warmth of the sun by virtue of its intrinsic qualities imbued by Creation itself.

CHAPTER 11

Willingness
(Calibration Level 310)

Introduction

This very positive level of energy may be seen as the gateway to the higher levels of awareness. Whereas jobs, for instance, are performed adequately at the Neutral level, at the level of Willingness, work is done well and success is common in all endeavors. Growth is rapid here; these are the people chosen for advancement. Willingness implies that one has overcome inner resistance to life and is committed to participation. Below level 200, people tend to be close-minded, but by level 310, a great opening occurs. At this level people become genuinely friendly, and social and economic successes seem to follow automatically. The willing are not troubled by unemployment; they will take any job when they have to, or create a career, or become self-employed. They do not feel demeaned by service jobs or by starting 'at the bottom'. They are helpful to others and tend to volunteer, contributing to the good of society. They are also willing to face inner issues and do not have major learning blocks.

At this level, self-esteem is high and reinforced by positive feedback from society in the forms of recognition, appreciation, and reward. Willingness is sympathetic and responsive to the needs of others. Willing people are builders of and contributors to society. With their capacity to bounce back from adversity and learn from experience, they tend to become self-correcting.

Having let go of Pride, they are willing to look at their defects and learn from others. At the level of Willingness, people become excellent students and represent a considerable source of power for society.

Discussion

Spiritual dedication and effort bring unanticipated rewards that confirm the validity of the commitment. The seeming sacrifices turn out to be well worth the effort. Spiritual gratification is an unsuspected source of pleasure that brings a greater sense of well-being, which is the consequence of an increase in the flow of spiritual energy. There is a greater sense of aliveness and appreciation for life as its quality progressively improves. The experience is subjective, nonlinear, and subtle but all pervasive. Confidence and optimism replace doubt, mistrust, resistance, and cynicism. Struggle is replaced with ease, and life itself becomes innately attractive and pleasing.

With relinquishment of resistance, less effort is required to function in the world. The intrinsic rewards of spiritual growth become self-activating motivation that evolves into enthusiasm as a consequence of the more positive view of self and life. There is an attraction to positive participation in activities that are constructive. Life is enjoyed instead of resisted and is accompanied by positive anticipation. Motivation is the consequence of inspiration instead of the desire for gain. It is found that surrendering the negative pay-offs of egocentric positionalities and goals results in much greater inner rewards.

Willingness is cheerful, helpful, and voluntary. It has

the extra energy that would otherwise be wasted on resistance, delay, and complaints. Willingness energizes fulfilling the needs of others, and thus its social expression is benevolent and humanitarian. It is also the attitude of the 'good Samaritan' as well as social trust, which, in its social expression, varies from decade to decade.

The energy of Willingness is also the level of the Golden Rule: "Do unto others as you would have others do unto you." In successful relationships, this results in a mutuality of partners as helpmates and companions. This mutuality is the result of alignment with each other's welfare rather than just the more animal-driven emotional involvement that often has a fractious downside. With mutuality, partners proceed side by side, whereas with involvement, the relationship is better described as 'entanglement', with pulling in different directions for control.

Willingness is supportive rather than competitive for gain or dominance, and relationships involve service to each other's growth and goals rather than to just one's own. Willingness is therefore harmonious and is expressed as the 'win-win' attitude instead of the lesser levels that view life as a 'win-lose' dichotomy.

To contribute to the welfare and happiness of others is gratifying, and leads to the discovery that generosity is its own reward. Some people are so limited that they experience this phenomenon only with their favored pets, but at least that is a start. True generosity expects no reward for there are no strings attached. The capacity for Willingness is latent in the overall populations and invisibly surfaces as a response to major catastrophes. True benevolence does not seek credit nor is it motivated by ego inflation. Many truly charitable people see it as an honor to be allowed to serve others and are unaware that it simultaneously subserves the accumulation of karmic merit.

Willingness attracts abundance and supportive feedback, not as a result of seeking but in response to that which it is because 'like goes to like'. Thankfulness is a consequence of a giving attitude, which adds to the attraction.

The true-life story of an acquaintance named Greta exemplifies all the above. She came to the United States from Ireland with only a limited grade-school education and no skills and thus sought work as a maid. She found a job as an upstairs maid on the large estate of a very wealthy and socially prominent family. Her cheerful willingness and dedication to the family's welfare resulted in her progressive promotion to housekeeper. She tended to all the needs of the family, traveling around the world with them in luxurious style. The father of the family had many investments and he occasionally gave Greta a 'tip' at dinnertime about the stock market. Peculiarly enough, Greta's stocks always skyrocketed. As time went on, his occasional recommendations resulted in the expansion of Greta's portfolio, with its relatively frequent stock splits.

Eventually, she traded a block of stocks for some Manhattan (New York) real estate and subsequently became a millionaire in her own right. Despite her now considerable wealth, Greta continued with her dedication to the family as they grew up, had their 'coming out' parties, got married, etc.

One day she received a call from a distant uncle who was visiting from Ireland. He called a number of family members to meet with him in New York City, which was a bit of a trip, but Greta was the only one who agreed to do so. She met him for lunch, and then he went back to Ireland. A few years later, he died and left an enormous estate (worth many millions of dollars) to Greta out of gratitude for her friendliness. Greta continued on as the family housekeeper and was a multimillionaire many times over by the time she finally died. Her funeral was attended by many hundreds of people whom she had befriended over the years. In her will, she left a great deal to charity, along with enough to make all of her children and relatives extremely wealthy also. Apropos of Greta's story, a recent remark by another acquaintance said, "You know, a million dollars just doesn't go very far anymore."

Willingness (cal. 310) stands in contrast to 'do-gooderism' (cal. 190), which seeks control and imposition of presumptive values on others.

Ego Dynamics of Willingness

By spiritual alignment and dedication, the level of spiritual energy rises and strongly activates the right-brain chemistry and physiology (as per the chart on Brain Function). This alters perception and releases anabolic neurotransmitters and endorphins in the brain. The world is therefore seen as more benign, friendly, and supportive. Fulfillment of goals is facilitated by virtue of their internalization rather than projection to external conditions. Thus, gain is internalized and valued as successful internal growth and the gratification of reaching developmental goals.

Benign intention motivates actions and decisions that lead to choosing positive options. Integrity of intention is concordant with a benign conscience and results in self-approval and healthy self-esteem that is independent of the opinions of others or external gains. This results in autonomy and the gratification that occurs through the fulfillment of inner potentials.

A concomitance to spiritual alignment is the inner urge to grow and seek perfection, which becomes an inner way of life. Spiritual perfection becomes an 'ego-ideal' that influences by attraction rather than promotion.

As a consequence to the relinquishment of the narcissistic ego, there is a reduction of distortions of perception that are the result of self-seeking positionalities. It is easier to accept the imperfections of humanness, which, at the level of Pride, would have been handled with anger, denial, guilt, or projected externally. With a benign conscience, mistakes and errors can be acknowledged and corrected without defensiveness or loss of self-esteem. There is a concomitant increase in the capacity for humor and the ability to laugh at oneself and human foibles (i.e., "To err is human, to forgive divine").

The level of Willingness is effective in the world because it is not impeded by resistance, and when coupled with dedication, it is capable of breaking through the inner barriers of the belief system of "I can't" to "I can." Other mottoes are "Just put your head down, keep going, and go for it," or "When the going gets tough, the tough get going," or "Walk straight ahead, no matter what," or "Create your own opportunities." Central to all

these mottoes and many philosophies is the willingness
to accept personal responsibility, accountability, and the
refusal to place blame or responsibility externally.

Transcending the Level of Willingness

Success at level 310 results in inner conviction of
capability and dependability that affirms personal
worth. The resultant optimism encourages further
growth and validation of the practical as well as the
subjective value of alignment with the pursuit of spiritual truth and its principles. The increase of inner
strength confirms the operational reality of spiritual
tenets, for by their fruits are their truths revealed.
Effective attitudes and actions are self-rewarding and
reinforcing. Successfully transcending prior limitations
encourages further spiritual exploration and reinforcement of basic principles.

The limitation of this level is the focus on the personality and the identification with it as the self,
whereas in reality, the growth is due to the radiance of
the Self. It is by virtue of the progressive illumination of
the Self that the willingness to surrender limitation is
energized. The illusion is that the personal 'I' is due
credit. Thus, the belief that the basic reality is the personal self is yet to be transcended. The positive momentum of Willingness, however, leads fairly easily to its
transcendence. Willingness sees its principle tenets and
convictions as a propelling force as though the source
lies within. Thus, the belief is that the personal self is
the cause of success.

The primary limitation is the identification of the
source of one's life as a separate personality that

becomes identified as volition itself. The understanding yet to be realized is that everything happens as a consequence of potentiality's manifesting as actuality when conditions are appropriate, and that the will and intention are the trigger but not the primary cause of this evolutionary stage.

The spiritual practice of selfless service is classically termed 'karma yoga', which, when combined with prayer and devotion, is transformative. It was the pathway of Mahatma Gandhi.

Willingness supports intention and facilitates the purification process of spiritual evolution, which often requires the willingness to face inner discomfort for the sake of reaching a higher goal. Willingness summons forth the extra energy required for the effort of overcoming obstacles and resistances. It also requires commitment to periods of endurance to reach the higher goal. It includes a positive attitude toward the process of learning itself and the acquisition of necessary spiritual information and commitment. Willingness is a positive attitude as contrasted with the attitude of willfulness, which is a form of resistance. Surrender of positionalities is a consequence of willingness and is therefore an important quality of serious inner spiritual endeavor.

CHAPTER 12

Acceptance
(Calibration Level 350)

Introduction

At this level of awareness, a major transformation takes place with the understanding that oneself is the source and creator of the experience of one's life. Taking such responsibility is distinctive at this degree of evolution, characterized by the capacity to live harmoniously with the forces of life.

Below consciousness level 200, there is the tendency to see oneself as a victim at the mercy of life. This stems from a belief that the source of one's happiness or the cause of one's problems is 'out there'. The enormous jump of taking back one's own power is completed at this level with the realization that the source of happiness is within oneself. At this more evolved stage, nothing 'out there' has the capacity to make one happy, and love is not something that is given or taken away by another but is created from within.

Acceptance is not to be confused with passivity, which is a symptom of apathy. This form of acceptance allows engagement in life on life's own terms, without trying to make it conform to an agenda. With Acceptance, there is emotional calm, and perception is widened as denial is transcended. One now sees things with less distortion or misinterpretation, and the context of experience is expanded so that one is capable of 'seeing the whole picture'. Acceptance essentially has to do with balance, proportion, and appropriateness.

The individual at the level of Acceptance is less interested in judgmentalism and instead is dedicated to resolving issues and finding out what to do about problems. Tough jobs do not cause discomfort or dismay. Long-term goals take precedence over short-term ones; self-discipline and mastery are prominent.

The level of Acceptance is not polarized by conflict or opposition; it sees that other people have equal rights and therefore honors equality. While lower levels are characterized by rigidity, at this level social plurality begins to emerge as a form of resolution of problems. Therefore, this level is free of extremes of discrimination or intolerance. There is an awareness that equality does not preclude diversity. Acceptance includes rather than rejects.

Discussion

Consciousness levels below 350 reflect the domination of perception by emotionalized positions and presumed values. At levels below 200, the emotions are harsh, destructive, and adversarial, and thus prone to conflict and strife. At level 200, the emotionality moves away from negativity to a more positive view of the world and self and becomes supportive of life. By level 310, the emotionality and volition are predominantly positive but still represent emotional drives. At level 350, by acceptance, tranquility replaces disturbing emotions so that the interference of emotionality fades into the background rather than determines feelings.

At level 350, the narcissistic ego's demand to control others is silenced by virtue of the cessation of value-driven judgmentalism and its innate desire to promulgate its views. Dualistic mentations diminish, as do judgments predicated on perceptions based on the dichotomy of good and evil. Choice presents itself as freedom of options rather than as opposing moralistic categories.

At the world's level of consciousness, to choose vanilla means to see chocolate as a rival, an enemy, or a quality to be hated. At level 350, there is the freedom to see that they are merely alternate options and one can choose one flavor without demonizing the other. Thus, there is release from the coercion that ensues from labeling options as severe degrees of desirability or aversion.

Critical to this level is the utilization of the previously achieved capacity for Willingness (which was acquired at level 310). The success of level 350 is based on the willingness to apply the principle of forgiveness in order to counterbalance morality and judgmentalism. Thus, vindictiveness is replaced by mercy, which allows for greater inner, as well as interpersonal and social, harmony and well-being. Error is seen to be in need of correction, forgiveness, and compassion rather than the justification for punitive attitudes or actions.

The surrender of judgmentalism is resisted by the ego's inflationary self-importance gained by viewing itself as righteous and a sovereign arbiter of moral worth. Acceptance does not require denial but instead replaces it by realistic perception and recognition of its innate limitation. It does not feel compelled to 'take a stand' about what is perceived or to take action and feel compelled to 'fix it'. Therefore, Acceptance can see and accept the limitations of human life and the world of distortions without losing its balance and equanimity.

Acceptance is a result of wisdom as well as surrendering positionalities in that it accepts that the varied expressions of life are in accord with Divine will and that Creation is thereby multitudinous in its expressions as evolution. Acceptance does not get caught in the 'either-or' of 'black and white' duality and is able to bypass the temptation of judgmentalism. Acceptance sees that perceived qualities are innate to the human condition and are reflective of individual as well as group karma and innate to the species Homo sapiens. Society includes an admixture of different levels of evolutionary development, including a panorama of options and alternate ways to go in the existential 'house of mirrors'.

Acceptance at level 350 is harmless because it does not seek to judge, control, change, or dominate others. It is not out to 'save the world', or to condemn it in its multitudinous expressions. By surrendering the wish to change or control others, there is a reciprocal freedom of not being controllable by others' opinions and values, nor is there a desire or need for their approval. With freedom from the need of approval by others, there is release from the compulsion to seek and crave social agreement. This is, however, in contrast to and different from passivity or indifference, which innately devalue others as a protective maneuver.

Ego Dynamics of Acceptance

Acceptance applies to the inner as well as the outer world. With spiritual education, it becomes apparent that the ego, by virtue of its innate structure, is prone to perceptual error, and that by the willingness to surrender a positionality, these distortions of perception are transcended. The maturity of Acceptance includes the ability to tranquilly accept both personal and human limitations without loss of self-esteem because value judgments have lost their validity and are now seen to be primarily arbitrary, personalized choices. Thereby, personal opinions become dethroned and lose their tendency to dominate by sheer emotional pressure.

The conscience (superego) then becomes benign as it has been 'defanged', and therefore it is no longer necessary to deny it, fear it, or project it onto the world. By acceptance instead of moralized denial as repression, animal drives are accepted as just being part of nature to be counterbalanced by positive human characteristics. By transcending judgmentalism, the most primitive instinctual drives do not have to be compartmentalized or otherwise distorted and attributed to others. At the same time, primitive drives still exist and are acknowledged but not acted upon. Acceptance precludes pretense and allows for realistic objectivity.

At this level, unemotional discernment replaces judgmentalism, which itself is usually highly emotionalized by anger, indignation, or vituperative denunciation and attack. While it is obvious that there are many elements and forces in the world that are deleterious to human life and happiness, it is not necessary to hate or demonize them but instead to merely make appropriate allowances and avoid them. Thus, what was formerly demonized now appears to be more like bad weather, a tidal wave, or a force of nature to be reckoned with but not hated. Life survives not by hating lightning but by avoiding where it is likely to strike.

Surrendering judgmentalism results in freedom from pejorative and hateful emotions that in themselves bring up either conscious or unconscious guilt or unconscious fears of retaliation and paranoia. Humility avoids the ego inflation by which the narcissistic core of the ego sees others as 'wrong' and the self as 'right' and therefore superior.

Humility results in surrendering the ego's self-importance and narcissistic gain that arise from judgmentalism. To decline the role of moral arbiter allows the surrendering of that function to God ("'Judgment is mine,' sayeth the Lord") and results in detachment from the world's endless debates over moral, ethical, legal, political, religious, ethnic, judicial, and social positionalities. While the ego would like to view that putting in one's 'two cents' worth' is a glorious celebration of the rights of free speech, etc., humility acknowledges that humanity has managed to survive this long without one's personal opinions and advice.

Self-honesty requires examining the ego's ulterior motives that are concerned with a vainglorious image, expressed as rhetoric and argument. Humility observes that the world is as it is, despite the millions of self-appointed experts in it. There is usually resistance to this humble realization because the ego loves to get on a soapbox.

Does acceptance then mean that one's personal life is of little worth, value, or significance? On the contrary, with humility, it loses false value and accepts its true power and function that increase spiritual energy and power, thereby influencing the world, especially through the collective consciousness of mankind. The spiritual power and integrity of every individual help raise the sea and all the ships on it. Moralistic exhortation brings about its opposite as counterforce, whereas the integrity of humility radiates power to which there is no opposite.

In surrendering the egotism of the ego, it is also necessary to realize that failure to condemn is not the same thing as condoning, nor is condemning a moral obligation. Everybody knows that crime is 'wrong', which has hardly resulted in its cessation.

Transcending Level 350

By relinquishing emotionalized judgmentalism, the way is clear to enter into harmony and peacefulness as a consequence of the decrease of the pressure of emotionality. Forgiveness and mercy allow for contemplative reflection and the emergence of the balance of discernment and understanding. The resistance to emotion-free clarity is the consequence of the ego's reluctance to give up its narcissistic role of self-importance as judge and arbiter of worth and morality. The ego pretends to be pious and secretly feeds on its 'holier than thou' attitude, which is the energy it absorbs and prizes. It fears it will diminish in worth, value, and importance if it surrenders positionality and thus become only a servant of God instead of being God in its own secret estimation. Thus, the core of resistance is the ego's carefully concealed illusion and claim to omnipotence and divinity.

The ego fears loss of its illusory sovereignty, which is actually only grandiosity. Of greater importance than pomposity are sagacious wisdom and astute observation and analysis, which are the faculties of the intellect and intelligence, unimpaired by emotionality and bias. Emotions obscure comprehension, significance, and meaning, which can only fully evolve and develop at the higher level of consciousness that is free of emotionality and positionalities. Thus, the level of Acceptance clears the way for the next evolutionary step to Reason and Logic.

The narcissistic ego is humorless and reveals its true nature by its 'sensitivity' and other neurotic traits. It lacks the capacity to laugh at oneself and the foibles and paradoxes of human life. Thus, developing a sense of humor assists the evolution of consciousness through deflating the ego's puffed-up self-image by which it imbues its emotionalized opinionating and vanity. Humility precludes making a fool or spectacle of oneself to gain attention or control others by bombastic shouting and gesticulation. Acceptance declines drama and allows calm plurality without getting marginalized by the inflation of pumped-up positionalities that, by their very inflation, attract argument and attack. Acceptance brings peace by inclusion rather than by rejection or denunciation, thus offering the security necessary for the development of rationality and the intellect.

CHAPTER 13

Reason
(Calibration Level 400)

Introduction

Intelligence and rationality rise to the forefront when the emotionalism of the lower levels is transcended. Reason is capable of handling large, complex amounts of data and making rapid, correct decisions; of understanding the intricacies of relationships, gradations, and fine distinctions; and of expert manipulation of symbols as abstract concepts become increasingly important. This is the level of science, medicine, and generally increased capacity for rationality, conceptualization, and comprehension. Thus, knowledge and education are highly valued. Understanding of information and logic are the main tools of accomplishment that are the hallmarks of level 400. This is the level of Nobel Prize winners, great statesmen, Supreme Court Justices, Einstein, Freud, and many other important figures in the history of thought as represented in *The Great Books of the Western World* (for convenience, reprinted from *Truth vs. Falsehood*).

The shortcomings of this level are the failure to clearly distinguish the difference between symbols (i.e., *res cogitans*) and what they represent (*res externa*), and the confusion between the objective and subjective worlds that limits the understanding of causality. At this level, it is easy to lose sight of the forest for the trees, to become infatuated with concepts and theories, and to end up missing the essential point.

Calibrations of The Great Books
of the Western World

Aeschylus 425	Faraday 415	Marx 130
Apollonius 420	Fielding 440	Melville 460
Aquinas, Thomas	Fourier 405	Mill, J. S. 465
460	Freud 499	Milton 470
Archimedes 455	Galen 450	Montaigne 440
Aristophanes 445	Galileo 485	Montesquieu 435
Aristotle 498	Gibbon 445	Newton 499
Augustine 503	Gilbert 450	Nicomachus 435
Aurelius, Marcus	Goethe 465	Pascal 465
445	Harvey 470	Plato 485
Bacon, Francis	Hegel 470	Plotinus 503
485	Herodotus 440	Plutarch 460
Berkeley 470	Hippocrates 485	Ptolemy 435
Boswell 460	Hobbes 435	Rabelais 435
Cervantes 430	Homer 455	Rousseau 465
Chaucer 480	Hume 445	Shakespeare 465
Copernicus 455	Huygens 465	Smith, Adam 455
Dante 505	James, William	Sophocles 465
Darwin 450	490	Spinoza 480
Descartes 490	Kant 460	Sterne 430
Dostoevsky 465	Kepler 470	Swift 445
Engels 200	Lavoisier 425	Tacitus 420
Epictetus 430	Locke 470	Thucydides 420
Euclid 440	Lucretius 420	Tolstoy 420
Euripides 470	Machiavelli 440	Virgil 445

Intellectualizing can become an end in itself (e.g., 'relativism' and its negative impact on academia). Reason is limited in that it does not afford the capacity for the discernment of essence or the 'critical point' of a complex issue.

Reason is disciplined by the dialectic of logic as a necessity to discern the linear truth of confirmable facts. It produces massive amounts of information and documentation, but it lacks the capability to resolve discrepancies in data and conclusions. All philosophical arguments sound convincing on their own. Although Reason is highly effective in a technical world where the methodologies of logic dominate, Reason itself, paradoxically, is the major block to reaching higher levels of consciousness because it attracts identification of the self as mind. Transcending this level is relatively uncommon in our society (only four percent do so), as it requires a shift of paradigm from the descriptive to the subjective and experiential. That a shift of paradigm is requisite to understanding higher levels of consciousness and spiritual reality is not as yet recognized by even such fields of study as 'science and consciousness' or 'science and theology' that seek for confirmation of spiritual realities (nonlinear, which calibrate from 500 and up) in the limited linear domain of the 400s.

Discussion

The consciousness levels of the 400s represent the emergence of the capacity to synthesize and utilize linear abstractions and symbols of great complexity and to extract significance and meaning as well as predictive verification. Intelligence comprehends hierarchical fields of organizational rank and discerns value as to reliability, implied worth, or significance. It stratifies prioritization via sequence to classification systems that are analogous to paradigm, domain, category, class, species, subspecies, genus, and then finally, a specific example. This complex function is analogous to a rapid sorting system that is simultaneously capable of integration and selection. Although the content is linear, its overall direction and source of functioning are nonlinear, and its overall domination is in accord with the power of the consciousness level of the field itself.

In addition to the above colossal capability, the complex processing functions simultaneously and automatically give a variable weight to each piece of data with ascribed degrees of credibility, importance, plausibility, worth, and value. Thus, they draw on an enormous data bank, both individual and collective, created by humanity over the ages.

The capacity to think and reason spawned the academic fields of science, psychology, philosophy, metaphysics, and psychoanalysis, as well as spiritual and esoteric psychology. The word 'dynamic' was added to aspects of all of these to increase the emphasis on the importance of function. Superimposed on the above were learning theory, behaviorism, operant conditioning, feedback and reward systems, facilitation, and inhibition. Through research, science elaborated further to describe and correlate patterns of functioning with neuroanatomy, neurochemistry, the tuning of the autonomic (sympathetic/parasympathetic) nervous system, brain hormones, neurotransmitters, and their modification by experience in genetics.

While all the foregoing represents an impressive mass of information, the basic question remains the same as it has throughout all of history: What does it all 'mean' (i.e., hermeneutics)? Pondering the implied subtleties of meaning has occupied the greatest minds of history and produced the great wealth of philosophy and its central issues, such as epistemology, theology, and metaphysics, which addressed the problem directly as does ontology (the science of 'being').

With the evolution of consciousness, reason, logic, and the intellect are energized by alignment with commitment to truth, which is actually an aspect of Divinity and the invisible source of the power of the field of mind itself. The gift of the alignment with truth results in comprehension and the accumulation of wisdom and sagacity in the exercise and application of the function of reason. Thus, it is still up to the individual will to choose the degree to which reason is prioritized in relation to emotionality. The individual is free to ignore reason or to follow its dictates and interpretations of reality vis-à-vis imagination, wishful thinking, fantasy, or emotional options and their degree of expression.

Thus, thinking and reasoning occur in an overall field of an evaluative emotional tone that may be facilitating or limiting. The overall emotional tone also reflects collective social input and varies from culture to culture. Within each culture, it is distributed in various subgroups that emphasize or detract from the value of reason and the intellect. In general, higher education has had a social-status value superimposed on its innate and intrinsic worth. It reached its highest esteem in the Golden Age of ancient Greece in approximately 500-300 B.C. and then received valuable input over the centuries in Europe. It declined during the last century in academia in both Europe and America via politicalization and the inroads of philosophical/moral relativism (as described in *Truth vs. Falsehood*).

A mature culture endorses education and learning as positive life-supporting patterns evidenced by the spreading popularity of the self-improvement movement. The 'cultural creatives' movement is an example (Anderson and Ray, 2000) that has an overall positive impact on society in general. The consciousness calibration level of the United States is currently at 421, which is evidence of the major influence and importance of the consciousness level of the intellect. Of significance is that at the level of Reason, the calibrated level of 'happiness' is at approximately eighty percent, which is in marked contrast to its low percentages below level 200 (one to twenty-two percent).

Humanitarian efforts to assist the disadvantaged emphasize education as the most effective way out of poverty. The higher the educational level, the lower the birthrate, infant mortality, disease, and other concomitants of deprivation. This is dramatically demonstrated by the recent emergence of the economic 'Celtic Tiger'. After centuries of abject poverty, the Irish economy surged to become the current leader in Europe as a consequence of establishing free higher education and concomitant progressive economic and political/legal reforms.

Ego Dynamics of Reason

The combination of reason, logic, and education is a strong counterbalance to offset the pressures of the primitive narcissistic core of the ego that feels threatened by the higher values of personal and social integrity. An enemy of rationality is the self-servingness of narcissism itself, which warps and distorts reason to facilitate its own ends. At lower levels of consciousness, the mind is merely used as another weapon to enforce positionalities, control others, and allow for the acting out of rationalized animal instincts. The reason of the intellect can be distorted as rhetoric to serve emotional, egoistic goals rather than those that are integrous (e.g., the philosophies of relativism [cal. 180], or Marxism [cal. 130]). The distortion of truth to subserve positionalized agendas is characteristic of Lower (ego) Mind rather than Higher Mind (see Overview, Section II).

Lower mind substitutes narcissistic intellectualization for the disciplined dialectic of logical truth. The best example is the decline in the level of academia consequent to the corrosive inroads of 'moral relativism', which is succinctly described in the following quotation from the *Philadelphia Trumpet* (June 2005):

Moral Relativism

Moral relativism is the belief that defining right and wrong is an individual and personal choice. Denying the presence of absolute law, this ideology teaches that every decision is a matter of personal feeling.

Moral relativism means that adultery, for example, is not objectively wrong. While I may believe that adultery is wrong and that it destroys marriages, you are entitled to believe it is right and strengthens a marriage. The same reasoning applies for murder, stealing, pedophilia, and every other facet of human life. With this ideology, there is no absolute definition of right and wrong—only what you perceive to be right and wrong.

This distorted principle has made great inroads into our universities. Created by secularists, moral relativism is a by-product of the evolutionist theory, which itself permeates university culture, especially the sciences. By denying the existence of God, the theory of evolution sowed the seeds of moral relativism. If there is no God, secularists reason, then there is no absolute law.

Using moral relativism as their weapon, liberal secularists can destroy any absolute law they desire. Even the laws that govern society can be destroyed. Most people recognize that American law, ideology, and morals are essentially governed by Judeo-Christian belief in the Ten Commandments. Since there is no God, according to secularists, then all we have are ten Suggestions; there is no law. With no absolute laws, defining right and wrong is a strictly personal matter.

This is why Ward Churchill, Harris Mirkin, and other secularist faculty members can espouse such ideologies as anti-Americanism and pedophilia. If a person doesn't believe in absolute law, then he or she is not required to believe that pedophilia is wrong. Moral relativism destroys the law that defines right and wrong, moral and immoral.

These are a few examples of the immorality and moral relativism that pervade our universities. The idea that it is the individual's responsibility to decide right and wrong is firmly entrenched in the minds of today's university students.

It is also notable that the current Pope, upon taking office, declared that the foremost problem threatening the world is that of moral relativism, which replaces Divinity by declaring the sovereignty of the narcissistic ego. The impact on society has been noted by many current social commentators (e.g., Bruce, 2003).

Consciousness levels in the 400s denote that although emotions are still present and taken into account, they no longer dominate or replace logic and reason. 'Thinkingness' is merely random mentation, whereas reason is constrained by the dialectics, discipline, and limitations of the rules of logic, which are well represented by mathematics.

Lower Mind is less evolved and characteristic of children, immaturity, and lack of education. In its more primitive condition, mentalization subserves emotionalities and personalized needs and wants. Thus, Lower Mind subserves communication of subjective states or opinions, which are not in the same category as the mental constructions of Higher Mind that are intended to represent more objective, verifiable statements that thereby require higher standards of validity or proof. Thus, Lower Mind is ruled by 'wants', and Higher Mind is disciplined by accountability that requires adherence to standards of truth, with concomitant requirements of ethics and responsibility. To present falsity as purported truth is excused in children but can have major consequences in adult life. 'Postmodern' philosophies (Marcuse, Chomsky, et al., as listed in *Truth vs. Falsehood*, page 209) calibrate between 135 and 185 because they are attempts to distort reason in trying to justify and legitimize falsehood as truth and pretend that they are of equal validity. Thus, the downside of the intellect is that it is subject to the distortions consequent to naïveté and wishful thinking that subvert meaning to narcissism (e.g., "A word means just what I choose it to mean," says Humpty Dumpty in Carroll's *Through the Looking-Glass*).

Falsification of reason is indicative of nonintegrity and is also a primary characteristic of psychopathic personality traits. Mendacity by public figures constitutes a major focus of the current media, which thrives on scandal. The superego, or conscience, also constrains the intellect, and therefore integrous reason and logic are a consequence of morality and ethics that reflect context and not just content. Lower Mind characteristically ignores context because it would impose a constraint on emotionalized distortions of truth (a ruse frequently employed in political rhetoric).

As becomes obvious, violation of truth can also be a consequence of purposeful distortion of the meaning of words by virtue of politicalization and social theories that calibrate below 200 (e.g., 'new think', language police, political elitism, etc.). Disciplined reason and logic adhere to the dictionary definitions of words.

The adherence to reason and logical truth as a social standard has declined in the judiciary and in public discourse as a consequence of the exploitation of the concept of 'free speech' to mean that anyone can say anything they wish to with no consequences, and that actions and behaviors are 'symbolic speech'. By legitimizing any and all behaviors as a 'right', the road to anarchy and degenerative social disruption is aided and abetted. Historically, the great empires thus crumble from within by moral decay. Actually, the First Amendment prohibits only the government from censoring speech. In the social arena, adherence to truth is no longer a requirement, thereby giving greater voice to the expressions of illogical premises that have exploitive media value rather than intrinsic worth. As fiction replaces truth, the calibrated levels of consciousness reflected by communications have declined although some have resisted the trend for which, paradoxically, they are now criticized rather than being respected (see *Truth vs. Falsehood*, Chapter 9).

Mentalization is the processing of symbols at random. Linear thought is prone to error as it deals with content. The content is known by virtue of the quality of awareness, which is the attractor field of consciousness by which contextualization occurs. Content *thinks*; the field *knows*. In contrast, Self *is*.

The distortion of integrous reason to subserve egoistic goals is the prime source of social conflict, moral discord, and human suffering. The negation of reason, with its intrinsic strengths, allows for the release of atavistic propensities of the animal instincts relegated to the primitive aspects of the ego, which sees logic, proof, and rationality as thwarting its intentions. The massive consequences to the distortion of logic and reason are evident not only throughout history but also in the world today. Whereas truth is aligned with survival, falsehood accounts for the death of tens of millions of lives in just the last century alone.

With maturity, the intellect is integrated with positive emotions that add value and motivations, such as the pleasure of accomplishment. Spiritual alignment results in prioritizing spiritual principles by which to resolve conflict. In so doing, it brings Reason to its highest development. To commit to the endeavor to serve the highest good means to subordinate it to God's will.

The perceptions of 'good' or 'bad', as Socrates noted, are often primarily the result of desire or illusion rather than any objective reality. If desired, a circumstance or an option appears to be 'good'; if not desired, it is rejected as 'bad'. Thus reason counterbalances emotionalized distortion, as its intention is to discern truth rather than rationalize fallacy. Spiritual principles are often accorded preference over more limited intellectualizations by which faith in reason is supplanted by faith in God.

Reason and logic (i.e., science) are of great value within their appropriate paradigm. By level 500, via spiritual alignment, subjectivity also progressively becomes a major focus of experience that emphasizes the values of forgiveness, mercy, love, and devotion. It adds a different understanding to meaning and value that thereby influences the selection of options and choices as perceived by the intellect.

Transcending the Limitations of the Intellect

The intellect accumulates, sorts, processes, and assimilates spiritual and religious information. It seems to be a paradox that at the same time, it can become a limitation to the evolution to a higher consciousness level, which requires transcending the mind. The limitation of the mind is evidenced by its structure in that the functional ego is linear, dualistic, and dominated by the Newtonian paradigm of causality that reinforces the illusion of a separate, personal 'I' as a self-actualizing causal agent.

The transition from the consciousness level of the 400s to the level of the 500s is a paradigm jump from the mental realm of linear symbols to nonlinear subjectivity. The mind is satisfied with the acquisition of knowledge but then discovers that alone it is insufficient to bring about transformation, which requires a further step to convert data into an inner experiential reality.

The intellect is used to being satisfied by hearing 'about' a subject and may naïvely conclude that the information itself should be sufficient. While this is often partially true, at other times, the transfer from the acquisition of information to subjective experience comes about through spiritual practice, meditation, contemplation, and devotion, assisted by prayer.

By rejecting egocentricity and by spiritual declaration, practice, and commitment, the spiritual energy flows into the energy system as lovingness rather than as personal love limited to personal relationships. The transformative energy fields from 500 up are calibratable, nonlinear, self-effulgent, radiant, and beyond objectively verifiable scientific definition.

Hindrances are the result of clinging to limitations for their personal gain, such as pride in intellectual acquisition of information itself. Although the shift from the mental to the truly spiritual is volitional and proceeds by consent, it is not controllable as was the acquisition of the mental material and information. The transition is best described as the classic passage from 'have' to 'do' to 'be' and is facilitated by surrendering the attempt to control the process. It is more important to place faith and trust in spiritual intention and surrender to Divinity by which potentiality transforms into actuality when conditions permit.

Thus, surrender is a necessary and almost constant attitude that is subserved by humility at great depth. A resistance that is often unrecognized is attachment to the familiar by what can be called 'paradigm allegiance'. For instance, this limitation is demonstrated, as previously noted, by conferences and publications dedicated to the fields of 'science and religion' or 'science and consciousness' that are academic and therefore calibrate in the mid-400s. They characteristically preclude recognition of the primary importance of subjectivity, the realm of the Self, only by which can spiritual realities that calibrate at 500 or over be recognized or understood.

The limitation of academic science is most markedly obvious in its ambivalence and distrust of first-person experiential testimony and information (Ginsburg, 2005). Scientific intellectualization about the 'reality' of personal experience reflects a dithering about the academic respectability and credibility (from the Newtonian paradigm) of human experience. Thus, true spiritual reality is excluded from study albeit the presumed goal of such projects. This is like looking for the lost car keys at night under the lamppost 'because the light is better there', or looking for ghosts with a Geiger counter.

Of obvious major importance is that, by virtue of paradigm blindness, the world's primary source of spiritual information—the historical record of the world's great mystics and enlightened major spiritual teachers (including its greatest Avatars)—is excluded. Science is linear; Spiritual Reality is nonlinear, which one would think should be clearly obvious.

By spiritual intention, the intellect can be sanctified so that it becomes a springboard and roadway to understanding spiritual reality instead of a dead end or a roadblock. Spiritual study utilizes the intellect to reveal that the intellect itself has to be transcended from 'knowing about' to 'becoming', which it accomplishes by spiritual practice, discipline, and devotion.

Mentalization: Thinkingness

A major deterrent to spiritual evolution and transcending identification of the self with mind is the processing of data, symbols, and words via random mentalization, which is presumed to be 'thinking'. During meditation, this mental chatter is frustrating and becomes a source of anxiety. To try to silence the mind via will power is ineffective, and the results are limited and brief. By understanding the source of the flow of mentalization, it can be transcended, revealing the silence out of which thinkingness arises.

Mentalization is of egocentric origin, and its primary function is commentary. Unless requested, thought is a vanity, an endless procession of opinion, rationalization, reprocessing, evaluating, and subtle judgment by which the thoughts are given value or importance via presumed significance because they are 'mine'. The ego is enamored of its life story and its central character.

It is confrontive to the intrinsic vanity of the ego to

accept that unless requested to solve problems, its mentalizations are superfluous and of no intrinsic worth or value. Thus, 'importance' is a self-appointed vanity, and the ego presumes by inflation that it has the 'right' and is entitled to intrude upon peace and silence with endless childish babble and chatter. The mind has an imaginary audience and carries on a monologue for self-adulation and presumptive importance. The undisciplined mind has an observation commentary or opinion on everything. Who cares? Who asked for it? Its thoughts are frequently repetitive, plebian, monotonous, and mundane.

It is a relief to let the mind become silent and just 'be' with surroundings. Peace results, and appreciation and calm prevail. In order to realize that a running commentary is not necessary or even authorized, the will gives the mind permission to be silent. When devalued and humbled, the vanity basis of thinkingness collapses, and in its place one discovers the joy of inner silence, which actually constitutes ninety-nine percent of the mind. Only one percent is actually chattering.

The well-disciplined mind should only speak when requested to perform a task. Untrained, the mind becomes an unruly 'on stage' performer and a nuisance. The self needs to learn respect for the Self and the Silence of the Presence. By observing the mind, it becomes apparent that it represents the disruptive, unruly child who constantly seeks attention.

It is usually fruitless to try to block thought or force the mind to be still without removing its motivation and pay-off. Its motivational roots can be identified and surrendered. It is then surprisingly possible to make a

decision: *just do not think about anything.* This is
made possible by aligning with the Infinite Silence out
of which thinkingness arises. It is located not between
but just before the emergence of thoughts.

A useful technique to bypass mentalization is that
of creative visualization in which the desired goal is
envisioned and held in mind periodically. Potentiality
tends to manifest when conditions are favorable, and
intention (plus karmic propensities) is a contextual
influence. In ordinary mentation, logic and sequence
are seen as causal and also needful of effort.
Envisioning is influential on outcome by entirely
different (and easier) mechanisms.

Section Three

Calibration Levels 500-599
Spiritual Reality

Section Three – Overview

Transcending Linear Duality

Introduction

While the transition of consciousness level 200 is the major obstacle to most of humanity (approximately 80 percent worldwide and 50 percent in the United States), the transcendence of the domination of the linear mind at consciousness level 500 is relatively infrequent (only 4 percent of the world's population), and the evolution of consciousness to Unconditional Love at level 540 is rarer still (0.4 percent).

Below consciousness level 200, awareness is dominated by negative emotions, but between 200 and 400, the emotions become progressively positive. Then, in the 400s, logic and reason prevail over emotion. There is another major paradigm jump at consciousness level 500, from emotionalized, conceptual linear content to the predominance of nonlinear context. The more powerful fields of consciousness levels 500 and up reprioritize meaning, significance, and value. The move is from what the world considers 'objective' to experiential subjectivity as the dominant quality of awareness experience.

The transition is one of changing the focus of importance from the descriptive qualities of the observed to the subtle qualities of the observer. This subjectivity recontextualizes the observed in terms of pleasure, satisfaction, significance, and prioritized worth. The shift profoundly influences decision and choice, as well as long-term goals that influence relationships, career choices, and innumerable decisions in life.

Shift of Paradigm

Importantly, level 500 indicates that the subjective condition called Love has now become not only significant but also dominant, not just as a feeling and emotion, but as the guiding principle. While the energy of Love may be focused as a consequence of interest or motive, it represents a breaking away from restriction and limitation of self-interest. Love serves, whereas ego seeks to be served in its pursuit of gain. To Love, the long-term satisfaction and pleasure of givingness replace the evanescent, short-term ego satisfaction of gain.

The energy of Love has a unique, timeless quality that gratifies potentialities that are subtle and difficult to logically describe. As Love becomes progressively spiritualized, it emerges as an alignment with Divinity, which is the ultimate source and province of Love. It thereby becomes viewed as holy, sacred, and the substance of devotion, religious faith, and mystical awareness.

From consciousness level 500 and up, the attraction of beauty, peace, and inner quietude becomes increasingly important. The spiritual principles of the great teachers become incorporated into one's lifestyle and eventually become dominant. Conflicts arise, not about whether to be forgiving, loving, or compassionate, but about how they can best be instituted and fulfilled. Thus, the linear specificity and content of actions become dominated by the power of the overall field of context. Eventually, the Divinity of life itself becomes self-revealing, and all of life becomes valued.

The advance of paradigm is characterized by a shift from reliance on perception and mentalization to the discernment of essence. This transition is a consequence of and in concordance with what has been classically termed the 'opening of the third eye of the Buddhic body', which represents the emergence of spiritual vision.

While perception focuses on linearity, spiritual vision represents the capacity to discern the inner reality that reflects the overall field. Its closest experiential relative in ordinary life is frequently alluded to as intuition, which implies that it is not the consequence of linear, logical processing.

The etheric, spiritual energy bodies emerge progressively and concomitantly with the advance of consciousness levels from 'lower mental' to 'higher mental', then to 'causal' and progressively to the Buddhic, Christ, and Atmic bodies. Within each body, the energy concentration is analogous to the chakra system. At the highest levels, they correlate with Christ consciousness, and finally, at the crown chakra of the Atmic body, with unrestricted dominance of the Divine consciousness of Enlightenment via the identification with Divinity innate as the Self. It is by this level of consciousness that God Transcendent and God Immanent are recognized as the overall Unity out of which All Existence/Awareness/Creation arise, and the awareness out of which subjectivity and consciousness occur.

Calibrated Level of Consciousness

The energy of each predominant level of consciousness is set by the spiritual will whereby alignment arises. As mentioned previously, it is comparable to the setting of the compass of a ship, in which destiny (i.e., 'the future') becomes dominant and influences the decisions of the present by virtue of underlying intention.

The periodic fluctuations of emotions, like choppy waves at sea, call only for correction and do not mean that the destination has been affected or changed, which is only accomplished by the will. Periods of unanticipated difficulty are to be expected that may seem like 'setbacks' but merely mean that some trend (often primarily unconscious) has surfaced for recognition in order to be processed. Similar periods in any inner uncovering process, such as psychoanalysis or inner-depth analysis, can occur consequent to any investigation of the self, such as the Fourth Step in the Twelve-Step Program ('take an inner moral inventory'). The self-honesty arising from the self-examination requisite to 'know thyself' requires not only courage but also the willingness to relinquish self-judgment and to surrender to God.

The general human experience throughout time has been that true, inner self-honesty at great depth is possible only with God's help, for understandably, the ego alone is quite unlikely to cooperate with its own demise and extinction as the moving, dominant force in one's life.

Initially, spiritual work has to do with transcending emotionalities and perceptual positionalities, which are considered to be primarily personal, but at higher levels, the limitations are those of context and paradigms.

When described, these may sound abstract, but operationally, they are the obstructions to ever-higher awareness. Thus, they pertain to the overall fields of constraints that are generally out of awareness and that could, academically, sound as though they belong to the realms of theology, metaphysics, epistemology, or ontology and discernment of the nature of existence/beingness itself.

The framing of paradigms of subjective awareness is often by unconscious presumptions that are ordinarily beyond conceptualization or even attempts at description. These become more problematic at the level of the ephemeral and ineffable, which are primarily fundamental to the basic experiential qualities of existence as a reflection of consciousness.

Questions arise as to the source of the capacity to even realize Existence or Beingness, and whether such qualities are innate or are superimpositions by silent paradigm presumptions. One asks, By what quality does the abstract even become discernible, and is not that knowingness itself merely a higher level of abstraction? Again, although these may seem academic to the intellect, experientially, they are a priority and profoundly transformative as the light of the levels of consciousness.At the highest levels, they represent the last clouds that hide the radiance of the sun of Divinity.

While consciousness level 600 formally denotes the onset of the states classically referred to as Illumination/Enlightenment, Realization of the Self is characteristic of the consciousness level of the 700s. In the mid-800s, there is the obstacle of the illusion of the Void to be bypassed, and then, with the actual death of the limitations of context, the splendor of full Enlightenment bursts forth; it *is* Gloria in Excelsis Deo and fulfills the promise of the world's great Avatars.

CHAPTER 14

Love

(Calibration Level 500)

Introduction

The 500 level is characterized by the development of an energy field that is progressively unconditional, unchanging, and permanent. It does not fluctuate because its source within the person who loves is not dependent on external factors. Lovingness is a way of being in and relating to the world and is forgiving, nurturing, and supportive. Love is not intellectual and does not proceed from the mind; love emanates from the heart. It has the capacity to lift others and accomplish great feats because of its purity of motive.

At this level of development, the capacity to discern essence becomes predominant; the core of an issue becomes the center of focus. As reason is bypassed, there arises the capacity for instantaneous recognition of the totality of a problem and a major expansion of context. Reason deals with particulars, whereas love deals with wholes. This ability, often ascribed to intuition, is the capacity for instantaneous understanding without resorting to sequential symbol processing. This seemingly abstract phenomenon is, in fact, quite concrete and is accompanied by a measurable release of endorphins in the brain.

Love takes no position and thus is global, rising above the separation of positionality. It is then possible to be 'one with another' as there are no longer any barriers. Love is therefore inclusive and progressively expands the sense of self. Love focuses on the goodness of life in all its expressions and augments that which is positive. It dissolves negativity by recontextualizing it rather than by attacking it. As such, it is benign, supportive, and nurtures life; consequently, it is the level of true happiness.

Discussion

In terms of the evolution of consciousness, this level reflects transcendence of identification with the limiting linear domain and its positionalities to the awareness of subjectivity as the primary state that underlies all experience. Thus, the sense of reality moves from what is perceived to the condition or faculty by which it is experienced.

Whereas the ego focuses on content, the spirit values context. The ego values quantity, and in contrast, the spirit values quality. By consciousness level 500, approximately ninety percent of the people experience happiness as a basic quality of life. The barriers to Love that arise from animal instincts no longer pressure for dominance, nor does the narcissistic core of the ego predominate, which is a consequence of humility and the relinquishment of egocentricity. Thus, personal self-interest is no longer dominant as selfishness or neediness. The view of the self is that of benign adequacy and alignment with Love as a primary goal and lifestyle.

The energy field of Love is innately gratifying in and of its own quality. It is discovered that Love is available everywhere and that lovingness results in the return of love. Although love may start out as conditional, with spiritual intention it becomes a way of life and a way of relating to life in all its expressions. As Love progresses, it seeks no return or gain for it is self-rewarding by virtue of its completeness since it has no needs. The capacity for Love grows so that the more one loves, the more one can love, and there is no end point or limitation. In addition, it is discovered that to be loving is also to be lovable.

At lower levels of consciousness, what is perceived as love is conditional and identified with possession, passion, romance, and desire, which are projected onto people or objects to give them an exciting specialness and glamour that tend to fade after the prized object or relationship is obtained. As the excitement of acquisition fades, so does the allure of the exaggerated desirability. Infatuations tend to be frantic with a fear of loss that leads to despair. Interference with the possession can result in very severe emotional reactions such as rage, jealousy, or even murder and suicide. Thus, there is a drivenness, possessiveness, or jealousy that can be imbalanced and excessive, leading to obsession due to the projected, exaggerated, and inflated emotional image. Society tends to look upon such excesses as a temporary madness ('madly in love'), with its transitory but intense loss of reality testing, along with immunity to rational intervention or caution.

The emotionality of infatuation releases adrenaline and sex hormones, and the much-celebrated phenomenon calibrates amazingly enough at only 145, which reveals that its origin is primarily the mating instinct from the animal nature. In contrast, the consciousness level of Love is accompanied by the release of endorphins. The frantic nature of the mating instinct is a reflection of nature's way of propagating the species, and very often, after a temporary mating, a couple parts, although some species, such as swans, mate for life. Love also appears in the animal kingdom as an accompaniment to the wagging tail of the dog and the purr of the cat, and it also expresses as maternal love in its self-sacrificial nature.

Because the conditions of Love and passionate desire are frequently confused, the following chart can be helpful in the differential diagnosis, which is often puzzling to the participants and observers. As becomes evident, the contrast is between ego involvement (the self) versus consensual alignment of Self that indicates mutuality of the higher intention of serving the relationship rather than just the personal ego's want-ingness or cravings.

Diagnostic Differential: Infatuation vs. Love

Quality	Passion/Attraction (Level 145)	Love (Level 500+)
Locus	Self/ego	Self/spirit
Origin	Animal instinct	Spiritual state
Mental function	Impaired reality testing	Uplifted
Intention	Mate, get	Bond, enjoy
Duration	Transitory	Permanent
Hormone/endocrine	Adrenaline/sex hormones	Endorphins
Emotions	Excess/imbalance	Calm/balance
Brain physiology	Left brain-physical	Right brain-etheric
Stability	Impaired/desperate	Enhanced
Emotional	Frantic, fearful, torment	Self-fulfilling
Body functions	Impaired; loss of appetite and sleep	Improved
Description	Addiction, craving	Fulfillment, content
Pathology	Suicide, stalking, despair, depression	Well-being
Judgment	Impaired	Improved
Perception	Exaggeration, glamorized	Illuminated
Intention	Possess, capture, control, own	Be with
Emotional	Frustration, anxiety	Gratitude, satisfied
Productivity	Disrupted	Enhanced
Self-image	Inflated	Positive
Loss	Depression, rage, hate, blame	Grief, regret, longing
Balance	Erratic, overstimulated	Steady
Social image	Inflated	Enhanced
Intellectual function	Romanticizing, Lower Mind	Realistic, Higher Mind
Consciousness level	Lowers	Raises
Style	Involvement	Alignment
Pattern	Individualism	Concordance
Relatedness	Demanding, limiting	Harmonious, expansive
Good	Satisfy, own	Fulfill, complete

Ego Dynamics of Love

The capacity for Love increases as the limitations of the narcissistic ego's perceptual positionalities are surrendered. This is accompanied and supported by an increase in spiritual energy that emanates from the Self, in contrast to desire, which emanates from the self. Love emerges as a consequence of spiritual alignment and accord with spiritual principles and practices and is accompanied by the increased spiritual energy. Perception is replaced with vision that allows for the awareness of the intrinsic value of all that exists.

Love is a quality of Divinity and as such illuminates the Essence and therefore the lovability of others. From calibration levels 500 to 539, the love is still subject to conditions and partialities based on considerations and qualitative values, as well as the influence of belief systems.

The limitations may be frustrating to spiritual aspirants who try to 'see past the behaviors and love the person', which is easier said than done. Limitations may be consequent to unpleasant past experiences as well as karmic influences and also affected by social programming and belief systems, some of which may be outside of awareness and operate unconsciously.

The relinquishing of judgmentalism greatly increases the capacity of Love, as does surrendering the wanting of anything from others. Thus, people are not perceived according to what they have or do but by appreciation for what they are and have become.

Love is self-fulfilling and thus does not seek gain or to compensate for lack. Because it does not need to 'get', it is therefore free to peacefully 'be with' and appreciate. To Love, the world is more benign and its people appear more friendly and available. There is an increased feeling of safety and identification with mankind in general and concern for the welfare and happiness of others. The energy field is accompanied by a radiant aura that intrinsically has an effect on others who themselves then tend to become more benign as do their perceptions. This energy field has an influence on all life, which intuits the safety of Love through the field effect. Characteristic of this level are an unmistakable 'sweetness' of personality, speech, attitudes, and lifestyle that is inwardly nurturing

Transcending Consciousness Level 500

By consciousness level 500, Love is dominant as a persistent positive emotion and an influence in society, as well as a contributor to the elevation of the overall collective consciousness of mankind. To continue to advance requires surrendering the limitations of conditional love to unconditionality. This necessitates surrendering love as a positive attachment so that it can become an overall contextualization and potentiality to align life as a way of being in the world rather than as an exclusive emotion between separates. As a result, love becomes not a quantitative emotion but an expression of essence whereby loving becomes lovingness and, by identification, eventually becomes what one 'is'. Love as a mode of existence requires no 'others' as objects for fulfillment or expression. It is an independent quality with no subject, object, verb, or adjective and thus is nonlinear and unlimited.

The limitations of Love have to do with perceived qualities and differences. By inner self-honesty and examination, these areas of limitation are revealed, usually as residual judgments or as the impact from prior experience. A key to making Love unconditional is the willingness of forgiveness to undo past reservations, experiences, and viewing people as unlovable. By the willingness to forgive and surrender one's perceptions, they may be recontextualized and now seen simply as limited or influenced by programming as spiritually underprivileged and reflective of the ego's proclivity to be blind to falsity. By intention, awareness may be changed from the perceptual duality of good/bad to witnessing 'desirable' versus 'less desirable', or even just preferable or less preferable.

Forgiveness ensues from the willingness of humility to surrender the world and its events to God. The change in appearance that is the consequence of deep surrender is a focus of the well-known *A Course in Miracles*, where the miracle is the consequence of the recontextualization of the limitation by which the inner innocence and innate holiness of others and life are revealed. This is a subjective transformation that is not under volitional control. A transformative mechanism is the relinquishment of faith in the validity of one's ideas and thinkingness itself and seeing that they are only images from the past, with no current validity or reality.

By surrender, the request to the Holy Spirit for a miracle is thereby the willingness to surrender one's perceptual positionalities and their egoistic gain to the revelation of Truth. The phenomenon is often accompanied by a recontextualization of time, place, and intention, and it is a literal, experiential phenomenon that is transformative in itself.

The difficulties of this world appear to be the consequence of all different levels of evolutionary development being thrown together simultaneously, which results in social turbulence. Simultaneously, however, the availability of such a wide spectrum allows for the greatest opportunity for growth and the undoing of 'bad karma' and, by choice, accumulating the merit of 'good karma'. Thus, this domain is one of maximum spiritual opportunity with a great multitude of options and choices that provide maximum potential for the evolution of consciousness about which one can be grateful instead of resentful. As the Buddha taught, "Rare is it to be born a human being, rarer still to have heard of Enlightenment, and even rarer still to pursue it."

CHAPTER 15

Unconditional Love, Joy, and Ecstasy
(Calibration Level 540-599)

Introduction

As Love becomes increasingly unconditional, it begins to be experienced as inner Joy. This is not the sudden joy of a pleasurable turn of events but instead is a constant accompaniment to all activities. Joy arises from within each moment of existence rather than from any outer source. Level 540 is also the level of healing and of spiritually-based self-help groups.

From level 540 upward is the domain of saints, spiritual healers, and advanced spiritual students. Characteristic of this energy field is a capacity for enormous patience and the persistence of a positive attitude in the face of prolonged adversity. The hallmark of this state is compassion. People who have attained this level have a notable effect on others. They are capable of a prolonged, open visual gaze that induces a state of love and peace.

At the high 500's, the world one sees is illuminated by the exquisite beauty and perfection of creation. Everything happens effortlessly by synchronicity, and one sees the world and everything in it to be an expression of Love and Divinity. Individual will merges into Divine will. One feels the power of the Presence that facilitates phenomena outside conventional expectations of reality, termed 'miraculous' by the ordinary observer. These phenomena represent the power of the energy field, not of the individual.

One's sense of responsibility for others at this level is of a quality different from that shown at the lower levels. There is a desire to use one's state of consciousness for the benefit of life itself rather than for particular individuals. This capacity to love many people simultaneously is accompanied by the discovery that the more one loves, the more one can love. Near-death experiences, characteristically transformative in their effect, frequently have allowed people to experience the energy level between 540 and 600.

Discussion

Unconditional Love is the goal of the majority of spiritually-committed people and especially of serious spiritual devotees and aspirants. It is also the ideal of Christianity as well as other religions. In the world's overall population, level 540 is reached by 0.4 percent of the populace. However, Unconditional Love is a practical and reachable goal and not just an idealized, wishful condition for those who seriously choose it as an inspirational, devotional goal.

The consciousness calibration level is indicative of a stage along the scale of the evolution of consciousness that reflects not only the progress made in this lifetime but also the consequence of prior karma. From an overall spiritual viewpoint, this earthly life could be viewed as a transitory staging area that offers maximum karmic advantages, as noted by the Buddha.

In highly motivated, spiritually-disciplined groups, approximately fifty to fifty-five percent of the people in the group reach the goal of Unconditional Love (e.g., twelve-step groups, spiritual/religious ashram devotees, monastic renunciates, members of spiritual communities, such as Zen monasteries, etc.).

The occurrence of advanced states is also facilitated by closely following the teachings of a very advanced primary teacher or alignment with a great Avatar. The silent, nonverbal benefit of being in the actual presence of such a teacher is advantaged by the silent transmission of the high-frequency energy of the teacher's aura (the 'Silent Teaching', 'Transmission of No-Mind', 'Grace of the Teacher', or Benediction).

The serious spiritual student is also benefited by seeking literature and teachings of verifiably high calibrations and avoiding questionable diversions from the path, which are innately merely amusements of astral origin. It is also well to avoid fanciful spiritual claims that are actually fiction, and, despite their popularity, calibrate below 200.

The goal of Unconditional Love is reachable by very simple means, but to bring about results, they have to be lived continually on a daily basis. Unconditional Love is a condition and quality of being with oneself in the world that arises and emerges by virtue of serious commitment to the spiritual principles of willingness to surrender obstacles and all limitations or positionalities and their (often unconscious) pay-offs. By this level, those that are obvious have already been recognized (to be 'right', to gain, to win, to be admired, etc.). In place of these obvious limitations, more subtle ones appear, such as the mind's presumption of "I know," or "I know all that." To know about a thing is not the same as to 'be' it.

The advantage of experience with mature, genuine spiritual groups or companions is the value of examples, insights and information that is shared, and the inspiration that occurs by cross-fertilization. Rather high levels of consciousness are also exhibited by organizations that are not spiritually committed in a formal manner but act on the level of unconditional mercy, such as Doctors Without Borders (cal. 500) who minister without reference to which side of the conflict a soldier may have been on.

Ego Dynamics of Unconditional Love

By alignment with Love as a primary goal, along with spiritual dedication, the evolution of consciousness is supported and facilitated by an infusion of the powerful spiritual energy that emanates from the Self. The influx of this unique energy starts at calibration level 200 and progressively increases. Its observable effect is the change in brain physiology (as per the Brain Function chart) from dominance of the animalistic left brain to the benign, spiritually-oriented right brain.

Acceleration of spiritual energy is facilitated by the relinquishment of narcissistic, egoistic self-interests, such as the seeking of personal gain. The energy is facilitated by the intention and alignment of humility, mercy, compassion, and dedication to the relief of suffering of others in the forms of benevolence, mercy, and kindness.

The spiritual energy catalyzes the transformation of linear positional perception to the greater context of the nonlinear inclusiveness that transcends the limitations of time, space, sequence, or the limitation of the perception and belief in the operant principle of cause and effect. Thus, the revelations that ensue are aptly described as 'miraculous' and transformational.

The source of joy stems from the inner subjective experience of the innate source of one's existence itself, unimpeded by the limitation of presuming the personal self to be a causal or primary agent. By humility and surrender, the imaginary control is relinquished to God and Divine Will. This frequently results in what the world denotes as saintly (cal. 555) and selfless attitudes and behaviors.

As consciousness continues to advance, the innate perfection and stunning beauty of all that exists shine forth like a luminous radiance. All of life becomes more beautiful as innate illumination reveals the Divinity of the Creator. The subjective experience of the flow of the spiritual energy is felt as an exquisite sweetness. It feels as though it flows up the back and into the brain itself, as well as flowing out through the heart region, where it may spontaneously flow externally and even for some distance to influence external events. The energy also influences the subjective state of others who are enveloped by the field, which has an uplifting effect (the traditional Grace of the Teacher).

Spiritual energy ('kundalini') potentiates the transformation from perception to vision, and from the limited linear to the unlimited nonlinear nature of existence. This is an expression of the basic reality that all comes into existence by virtue of potentiality's becoming actuality when conditions (including karma) are favorable. This confirmation is also facilitated by intention and spiritual alignment. Thus, no 'person' performs miracles; they are the impersonal consequence of the spiritual energy field itself that acts like a catalyst, as does the energy radiating from the auras of advanced teachers that catalyzes the spiritual intentions of the spiritual student.

While functioning in the world efficiently is still possible, the high 500s may require leaving the ordinary world of endeavor and commerce and abandoning one's social world and prior occupation. By persistent spiritual alignment and practice, the spiritual energy may continue to flow and increase to the level of Ecstasy (cal. 575), which becomes incapacitating to ordinary worldly function and thereby requires retreat from the customary world of endeavor. It is best to be prepared for the fact that the world has little or no understanding of such a state or the actual necessity for such a transition that others may even resent or find unsettling.

Unlike the calm tranquility that returns again at level 600, subjectively, the state of Ecstasy is one of very high energy and tireless capacity. The beauty of Creation is radiantly exquisite, and the innate Divinity and perfection of all Creation shine forth with a brilliant and overwhelming intensity. Its power is subjectively experienced, and thus the energy and strength of motor performance becomes inexhaustible. No tiredness occurs, nor does one have to stop to eat or even perform basic physiological functions. Instead, for instance, one can dance nonstop for endless hours without food, rest, or respite. Without consciousness calibration, the world would not know whether the state is pathological or one of 'Divine Intoxication'.

(The differential diagnosis of spiritual states from pathological states is included for reference.)

Authentic Spiritual State	Pathological State
Samadhi	Catatonic
Religious ecstasy	Mania (bipolar hyper-religiosity)
Illumination	Grandiosity
Enlightenment	Religious delusion
Piety	Scrupulosity
Inspiration	Imagination
Visions	Hallucinations
Authentic spiritual teacher	False guru, imposter, spiritual con artist
Devotion	Zealotry, hyper-religiosity
Committed	Obsessed, brainwashed by cult, victimized
Dark night of the soul	Pathologic depression
Detachment	Withdrawal, indifference
Nonattachment, acceptance	Passivity
Transcendent state	Mutism
Trusting	Naïve
Advanced state	Psychosis, egomania
Beatific	Euphoria
Humility	Low self-esteem
Spiritual sharing	Proselytizing
Commitment	Religiosity
Inspired	Messianic
God shock	Schizophrenic disorganization
Spiritual ecstasy	Manic state, high on drugs
Genuine spiritual leader	Spiritual politician, cult leader
Free	Psychopathic
Teaching	Controlling

Although the state of ecstasy is recognized in spiritually-advanced communities and the subjective experience has been described by well-known mystics such as Ramakrishna, it is unknown to the world at large to which it is really incomprehensible.

Spiritual Phenomena: The Siddhis

From consciousness level 540 and up into the higher 500s, phenomena occur spontaneously that are inexplicable by reason, the customary conceptualization of logic, or cause and effect. They are an accompaniment to the progressive dominance of the spiritual energy (kundalini) and occur as a consequence of the contextual field rather than by volition. They are witnessed and seen to occur autonomously. These have been classically termed *siddhis* (Sanskrit) and denote 'supranatural' or 'miraculous/mystical powers', as they are not explicable by logic.

In the early stages of their appearance they may be sporadic, but as consciousness advances, they become frequent and sometimes continuous. They are unintended and arise of their own accord. These include faculties such as distant viewing, precognition, clairvoyance, clairaudience, extrasensory perception, psychometry, bilocation, and the occurrence of the miraculous, including spontaneous healings and transformations. There are also unique facilitations that are beyond expectation or possible explanation.

The capacities or phenomena are not within personal control; they are not the consequence of 'cause and effect'. Therefore, students are forewarned not to claim them as personal as they occur independently of the person's 'I', or self. Thus, as said previously, no 'person' performs miracles for they are solely a consequence of the Spirit. Inflation of the spiritual ego is precluded by honesty and humility, which results in temptation of exploitation for gain. The phenomena tend to emerge and become strong for variable durations of years. Some seem to fade away and become less predominant, and others continue permanently.

The kundalini energy flow is itself extraordinary in that subjectively, the sensation can only be described as exquisite as it flows up the back and into the brain, emerges as though through the heart chakra, and then goes on out into the world where its presence facilitates the unfoldment of the truly wondrous. The occurrences are witnessed as happening without intention. It is as though Divine qualities are brought into manifestation via higher realms that transcend the mundane physical world.

Eventually, the apparent 'extraordinary' becomes a new reality as though one now lives in a different dimension in which the seemingly impossible manifests effortlessly as though orchestrated. The power of the field autonomously facilitates the emergence of karmic potentiality into a manifested actuality in a harmonious unfoldment. The dynamics are nonlinear and therefore incomprehensible to the intellect, which presumes the limitations of the linear Newtonian model of causality and is unable to conceptualize emergence, Divine Order, or Harmony.

Transcending Joy and Ecstasy
The surrendering of all limiting beliefs, positionalities, doubts, and attachments allows for the inflow of spiritual

energy, which is the concomitance of devotion (cal. 555). Persistent devotion to spiritual truth and love allows for the dissolution of resistances. Transcendence requires the relinquishment of all attachments, even those characterized by self and society as 'responsibilities'. Thus, relationships, positions, titles, and social roles are eventually abandoned to the commitment to realize the Self or reach the state of Enlightenment. The reluctant devotee who holds back clings to doubt and asks naïvely, But what about? The solution is to surrender all the 'but what about's' to God and Divine Providence.

A major transition also necessitates responsibility to others by making necessary and realistic adjustments and helping others to accept the required changes. This transition may therefore take considerable courage and patience as well as conviction, for it brings up residual doubts, attachments, guilt, and the like.

The eventuality of a major leap in consciousness is seldom taken into consideration as a serious possibility, much less a likelihood, among most aspirants who, unless forewarned, may not have made anticipatory plans. Therefore, serious students should be informed and also have spiritual alliances or relationships that are capable of recognizing advanced states of consciousness.

The inner state is progressively dominant as self diminishes by the eclipse of the Self. The consequent changes, both inner and outer, turn out to be more major than anticipated.

The emergence of progressively higher levels of consciousness requires periods of adjustment, such as that required by a new pair of glasses, and thus, worldly function may be impaired periodically due to shifts of orientation. In this reorientation, phenomena are discovered to be happening spontaneously of their own rather than via the usual presumed premise and perception of cause and effect. Pleasure is no longer something one acquires but is innate consequent to the power of the field rather than via some agency or personal decision. It is also progressively discovered that there is actually no 'doer' of actions, and one witnesses the autonomous unfoldment of karmic potentiality from a new paradigm of reality that is beyond the presumptive dualistic principle of causation. Thus, life becomes an endless series of revelations of intrinsic charm and delight that initially seem amazing. Then comes the realization that what appears to be miraculous is merely the constant unfolding of the potentiality of the evolution of Creation by which the subjective experience of time dissolves and is replaced by the knowingness of all Is-ness. Likewise, the perception of 'change' is replaced by the progressive emergence of the ongoingness of Creation as becoming the fulfillment of potentiality's actualizing into manifestation.

With neither past nor future, likewise, there is no 'now', and it is comprehended that the past, present, or future are all illusory contextualizations consequent to the limitation of a paradigm. With the surrendering of all belief systems and positionalities, the unfoldment of Creation is self-revealing. The unfolding process may bring up presentations, uncertainties, or transitory doubt that have to be surrendered to faith and devotion as there is very rarely a really advanced spiritual teacher available for consultation. At these points, the

Knowingness inherent as a vibratory frequency within the field of consciousness itself unfolds and reveals the reality of the emerging paradigm. By virtue of the Radiance of the Self, the revealing effulgences are silent. The world then becomes a revelation of Essence rather than an appearance.

The self-revelation becomes progressively recognized and identified by Knowingness as Divinity. The major shift of paradigm cannot be anticipated or even really imagined, and its onset is sometimes described cryptically as 'God shock'. The consequence is profound awe by which the mind goes silent in the presence of Divinity and disappears at level 600. Henceforth, all is merely as it is as a continuous unfoldment that reveals itself as neither beginnings nor endings nor divisions such as 'then', 'now', or the 'future'. Realization no longer occurs as a consequence of mentalization, thought, or by the agents of a personal self because it no longer exists.

Adherence to basic spiritual principles is requisite to major transformation, and of these, faith, devotion, and surrender are its primary modalities. It merely requires the surrendering of any and all belief systems and the understanding that all fear is illusion due merely to clinging to a positionality and its perceptions, including one's adherence and faith in the familiar, customary paradigm of 'reality'. Nothing is actually the way the ego has perceived it for the linear dimension is merely presumptive, and the nonlinear Absolute is a very different paradigm that operates on totally different principles that are self-revealing rather than sequential understandings or comprehension.

In Reality, 'existence' *is* its meaning and identical with it. There is no subject, predicate, or verb, and the understanding is beyond languaging. As can be best stated, the 'meaning' of a thing *is* what it 'is'. Identity *is* its meaning. It becomes apparent that all delineation and definition are dualistic abstractions and mentations that circuitously reify their original definition. Truth is autonomously self-evident by virtue of its existence as Allness. Without the artifact of the dualistic separation of presumed subject and object, the all-encompassing Oneness of Existence is its own definition and meaning. Thus, a cat 'knows' it is a cat by virtue of *being* a cat and therefore is not dualistically separated from its own reality. The knower and the known are one and the same identity.

The transcendence of spiritual ecstasy and joy depends on the willingness to surrender all to God, no matter what, including even the exquisite state of ecstasy, which is of a dimension beyond description. The state itself is now a temptation and can delay the evolution to the state of Enlightenment. At first, there is a reluctance and dismay to surrendering such a glorious condition to God, and yet, there arises a knowingness that even this wonderment, too, must be released. The anguish and hesitancy of having to take the step reveals that an attachment to the condition and its wonderment has already unwittingly taken place. Then, because of commitment and intention, there is conviction that yes, this, too, must be surrendered "to Thee, O Lord," and with its surrender, an infinite Peace prevails that is beyond all understanding or description at level 600. The condition reveals itself to be the actuality of the Peace of God.

Section Four

Calibration Levels 600-1,000
The Illumined, Enlightened States

Section Four – Overview

Transcendence

Illumination, Self-Realization, and Enlightenment denote the Divine states that have historically demonstrated the highest levels of consciousness. These conditions represent the transcendence of the limitations of the constraints of the linearity of the ego and the emergence of the Radiance of the Infinite Reality and source of Existence.

Technically, the enlightened states emerge at consciousness level 600, which is that of Infinite Peace and Bliss illuminated by the Light of the Radiant Self. The emergence of God Immanent as Self frequently precludes continuation of ordinary human activities and results in withdrawal from the world or may even result in physically departing from it, an option that is taken by fifty percent of those who reach it. The state of Bliss is total and characterized by the disappearance of all wants, needs, desires, or aversions, including that of physicality.

The levels from 700 to 850 are extremely rare and have been denoted as the states of Self-Realization that characterize very advanced teachers who often tend to stay at a given level for an entire lifetime. The uniqueness of these levels attracts followers and devotees who subsequently transcribe remembrance of teachings in abbreviated form for the generations to follow.

The states of very advanced spiritual awareness have occurred intermittently in history in different religious cultures and civilizations. Although advanced states of consciousness (*satori*) may occur temporarily in highly-progressed spiritual devotees, it is rare for the state to become permanent and thus result in a fully ripened teacher. When this does occur, the teachings are of great value for centuries and are translated into many languages, thus denoting their recognized value to humanity.

Characteristically, accurate teachings calibrate at the same consciousness level as that of the teacher; therefore, misinterpretations or mistranslations are indicated by any deviance between the two. This is important since such misunderstandings are very common, and deviations and errors even predominate in some religions, which therefore calibrate lower than the original teaching.

Rarest of all throughout history are the occurrences of consciousness levels beyond 850, which represent the full realization of Divinity by whatever name. Here again, misinterpretations frequently occur, along with lack of comprehension of Truth, which thereby become misunderstood due to the limitations of the capacity of the ego/mind to understand the teaching. Therefore, of great value has been the validation of the highest teachings of great sages who themselves were of a very advanced state of consciousness.

Despite their rarity, illumined spiritual teachers throughout history have had a major impact on civilization, and their teachings have strongly influenced all levels of society, whether overtly acknowledged or not. For example, in the current world, a pattern has emerged of institutionalizing and absorbing the benefits of spiritual truth into the basic structures of society and then subsequently disowning or discarding acknowledgment of the sources of that inspiration through the process of secularization. Each person has to decide for themselves what they believe to be the ultimate truth by which to live. This is also demonstrated by even the ardent atheist. The differentiation of the illusory good from the real good in today's world can now be readily determined by the emergence of a science of consciousness that differentiates the ego's illusions and perceptions from the confirmable essence of truth, just as the emergence of metallurgy enabled the distinction between fool's gold and the genuine metal, and DNA testing enabled confirmation of identity. Even though the human mind itself is prone to error, it nevertheless values and pursues what it perceives to be the truth and the means of its discovery. The same road is demonstrated by the sincerity of the strictly materialistic scientist who is thereby devoted to the intellect as being the sole province of truth.

Besides teaching Truth itself, Enlightened Teachers emanate the powerful field of inspiration, devotion, and compassion, which is all inclusive and uplifting into the energy field of humankind. Without the emergence of this powerful Divine spiritual energy, the evolution of the consciousness of mankind would have stopped at level 200 and precluded further evolution of which the state of Enlightenment represents the ultimate possibility and realizable potentiality. Thus, Jesus Christ stated that he was simultaneously the "Son of Man" and the "Son of God" by virtue of the incarnation of Divinity. Krishna represented the truth of The

Supreme Teacher, and Buddha taught that the Ultimate State was beyond all nominalization.

These truths are confirmable in today's world by utilization of the calibration of consciousness levels, which affirms that Avatars at consciousness level 1,000 represent the highest level possible thus far in the human domain. Thus, veneration for the great teachers of history is based on confirmable fact and not just myth. Even the method of consciousness calibration itself emerged as a consequence of mankind's dedication to the pursuit of truth and provided a means of discernment beyond the capability of even the most educated intellects (e.g., Newton, Freud, and Einstein calibrated at 499).

CHAPTER 16

Peace, Bliss, and Illumination
(Calibration Level 600)

Introduction

The states of Enlightenment emerge at consciousness level 600 consequent to replacement of the linear by the nonlinear. This energy field is associated with the experience designated by such terms as Transcendence, Illumination, Bliss, and God-consciousness. When this state is reached, the distinction between subject and object disappears, and there is no specific focal point of perception. Frequently, individuals at this level leave the world because the state of bliss precludes ordinary activity. Some persist, however, and become spiritual teachers, and others work anonymously for the betterment of mankind. A few return to the world and become notable geniuses in their respective fields, making major contributions to society. Those who remain within a religion may eventually be officially designated as saints, although at this level, formal religion is commonly transcended and replaced by the pure spirituality out of which all religion originates. There are currently six people on the planet who calibrate at 600 or over (anonymous); three are between 600-700; one at 700-800; one at 800-900; and one at 900-1,000.

Action at the level of 600 and above is perceived as occurring in slow motion, suspended in time and space. All is alive, radiant, and continuously flowing, unfolding in an exquisitely coordinated evolutionary dance in which significance and Source are over-whelming. This awesome revelation takes place without thought or conception so that there is an infinite silence in the mind, which has stopped conceptualizing. That which is witnessing and that which is witnessed are the same identity. The observer dissolves and becomes equally the observation. Everything is connected to everything else and unified by the Presence whose power is infinite, yet exquisitely gentle.

Great works of art, music, and architecture that calibrate between 600 and 700 can transport us temporarily to higher levels of consciousness and are universally recognized as inspirational and timeless.

Discussion

Transcendence from the linear to the nonlinear 'domains' of consciousness results in a major shift of paradigm. At this level, there is no 'this' or separate 'person' witnessing the transition because it is Self-contained, such that the 'Knower' and the 'Known' are the same. There is the condition of an infinite Peace that is unmistakable as the Presence of God, which is of a different dimension than emotional or psychological peace or tranquility.

In the stillness, all occurs of its own accord, autonomously and spontaneously. Sound has no effect on the silence that persists even within the sound. The state is traditionally and historically referred to as *sat-chit-ananda* (silent bliss). Physiological functions can come to a halt. There is no desire to move or speak, and the inner Silence is mute as though suspended in timelessness.

Whether the body continues on and survives or not is uninteresting and actually without meaning. It is a matter of no interest and up to the Universe to direct. If the karmic propensities are aligned with physical continuation, the body survives. If not, the body is simply abandoned, for it came from the earth and returns to the earth when it has served the purpose of the spirit.

Approximately fifty percent of the time, when this level of consciousness is realized, the body will be relinquished. If not, then physical continuation is in accord with the response of the world, which may urge the necessity of eating or drinking. From within, there is no inclination one way or the other, nor is there a need to communicate or speak.

The Presence is self-fulfilling and complete, uniquely exquisitely soft and simultaneously powerful. Its essence pervades all manifestation as the Source of Existence. All is seen to arise from the unmanifest's becoming Manifest as Creation from a source that is innate, All Present, and beyond volition.

In Unity and Oneness, everything is simultaneously intrinsic to everything else, but not by virtue of being either the 'same' or 'else'. Within the infinite context of Allness, potentiality is activated by Divine Ordinance, commonly known as God's Will. The term 'Will' is, however, somewhat misleading in that it implies volition. Creation is witnessed as the unfolding and revelation of the emergence of infinite potentiality as Creation. Thus, there is no duality of a 'this' (Creator) creating a 'that' (Creation) for Creator and Creation are one and the same, and Creation is self-effulgent.

Everything that exists is perfect and complete. Creation does not move from imperfection to perfection, as is witnessed by the ego, but instead moves from perfection to perfection. The illusion of moving from imperfection to perfection is a mentalization. For example, a rosebud is not an imperfect rose but is a perfect rosebud. When half open, it is a perfect unfolding flower, and when completely opened, it is a perfect open flower. As it fades, it is a perfect faded flower and then becomes a perfect withered plant, which then becomes perfectly dormant. Each is therefore perfect at each expansion of its expression as the emergence and unfoldment of the evolution of Creation. Thus, the illusion of 'change' is replaced by the witnessing of the process of the manifestation of actuality from potentiality (transition, emergence, unfoldment, metamorphosis).

Without interference by mental interpretation, the perfection of All that Exists is evidenced by its intrinsic beauty, which is the transformed physical appearance of its perfection. Without the editing and classification that emanates solely from the linear mind, everything is seen to be equally exquisite. What the world ignores as a weed is of beauty equal to that of the flower. The living-sculpture design of all nature is equal, without classification, and everything is realized to be of the same merit or worth. All is an expression of Divinity as Creation—all is equally sacred and holy.

Equal to anything else, the body is also autonomous and moves about on its own. In the level of the 600s, there is no volitional causal locus, such as a personal self, a 'me', or an 'I' that is imagined to be a causal agent or a 'decider' of action.

Dynamics of Peace and Illumination

In ordinary life, the ego claims to be the author of action. This egoistic claim, which is experienced as an inner reality, is a delusion based on the unrecognized function of the ego, that of instant editing. This phenomenon happens 1/10,000th of a second after a phenomenon has actually occurred. The best analogy to this function of the ego, as mentioned previously, is that of the tape-monitor function of a tape recorder. As sound is recorded on the tape, the tape-monitor function allows one to hear what has just been recorded a split second ago. Therefore, one is not experiencing the source but that of a recording with a split-second delay. This delay is intrinsic to all ego experiencing of ordinary life by which the mind does not experience reality but its delayed instant playback through the screen of perception. At level 600, this delay disappears and with it the delusion of a 'this' or a 'that', for without the processing delay, the 'this' and the 'that' are joined in a unity that is not artificially separated. Without the inner position of the ego's screening device, phenomena are experienced directly and not via the illusion of a spectator.

To be at one with phenomena instead of separate from them results in experiencing the aliveness and Allness of the Presence expressed as All that Exists. All that has existence is not just passively 'there' but instead seemingly presents itself to awareness as a quality of its existence rather than as a volitional intention. Thus, the universe appears to be a gift of exquisite beauty and perfection that shines forth with the intrinsic Radiance of Divinity.

Phenomenonally, the witnessing could be described as entrancing as all movement is witnessed as if in slow motion.

Phenomena, movement, and action, which have been previously ascribed to the ego/self, are now seen to be autonomous, with no specific focus of origination, much less that of an independent 'I' or 'me'. Instead, the sense of 'I-ness' expands and is all inclusive to a level that is more primordial, all encompassing, and innate as Essence rather than as separate identities. As a consequence, this perception of relationship also disappears because it is a mental construction relating to the perception of separation, which is replaced by the awareness of nonlinear inclusiveness. Thus, without perceived separateness to be explained, the notion of relationship becomes meaningless and inapplicable. The Self does not have a 'relationship' with the world because Existence is its indivisible Essence. (Analogously, science has discovered that there is no identifiable 'center' to the universe.)

Although the data bank of memory continues to be available, its value is the capacity for descriptive recognition that allows for the continuation of bodily function if that is the karmic option. The body then seems to operate on a principle roughly comparable to momentum. As described in prior works, it is like a 'karmic wind-up toy' that runs its course all by itself.

The transformation at level 600 and over is consequent to the dissolution of the narcissistic core of the ego, which delusionally presumes itself to be sovereign and therefore a primal causal agent and the author of volition. This inference is included in the meaning of the term 'egocentric'. Thus, the core of the ego is its basic presumption by which it identifies itself as the primary source of existence, action, and decision, and thus usurps the sovereignty of Divinity. This primitive presumption is openly displayed in the pathological state termed 'malignant messianic narcissism' in which the core of the ego is actually worshipped. Throughout history, this self-deification has been overtly expressed from the time of the Roman emperors when they declared themselves literally to be God, up to present world leaders who exhibit grandiose, omnipotent ego inflation. (The syndrome, *malignant messianic narcissism* [cal. 30], is described in detail in Chapter 15 of *Truth vs. Falsehood*.)

Transcending Level 600

To ordinary conceptualization and education, it would seem that the state of Bliss would be the ultimate state. Looking at it from the viewpoint of the ego itself, it is precisely that. Gone are anxiety, anticipation, regret, attraction, or longing. Gone also are rules, objectives, goals, processes, and conditions to be fulfilled or completed or roles yet to be played. At this level, there is no person, self, or others to contend with. All occurs effortlessly and spontaneously and merely presents itself starkly as what it is. Similarly, 'qualities', which are descriptive perceptions, disappear. Everything simply is as it is, without adjectives. The mind is still because, without a subject or an object and with no actor of a 'this' doing a 'that', there is no necessity for verbs. Without qualification, there is no need for adjectives. In addition, there is the disappearance of volition as there are no decisions to be made, and all evolves spontaneously and autonomously as the expression of the evolution of Creation. What remains after the dissolution of these ego functions is awareness/witnessing, but actually without a witness; it is consciousness itself that remains. As such, there is no necessity for processing since options are no longer separated by superimposed linear qualities. Thus, there is no necessity to choose or to weigh pros or cons. Operationally, information is sufficient unto itself and thereby action is autonomous. Decision-making is no longer necessary because concordance replaces relationship or options. Also, with no 'doer', nothing 'happens', the experience of which would require the projection of a limited point of view and accompanying mentation.

With cessation of the experience of time, sequence disappears; thus, there is no 'before' or 'after'. The harmony of the Unity of Concordance is evolutionary as potentiality's expressing itself as manifestation but void of intentionality. The best analogy would be the movements of the universe that are harmoniously concordant with the totality. Thus, gravity is intrinsic to Creation and its field is 'concomitant' rather than 'causal' or 'consequential', which are terms that represent mental exploratory hypothetical constructs. Concordance is an expression of Divine Unity and Harmony, which becomes apparent with the transcendence of Descartes' dualistic split of *res interna (cogitans)* and *res externa/extensa* (the world as it is). In the Unity of Oneness, there is no separate 'this' causing a separate 'that'.

To transcend level 600 requires dropping identification with the witnessing/observing qualities, which are actually autonomous qualities inherent to consciousness itself. With deep meditation, it is discovered that these qualities have unconsciously been identified with, which requires the surrender of the illusion or pay-off of being the witness or the observer.

The primary block to moving on to even more advanced levels of Enlightenment is the satisfaction, pleasure, and unwitting attachment to the state of Bliss itself. In addition, it is experienced as completion and totality. Then arises the knowingness that even this, too, as exquisite as it may be, is to be surrendered to God. With its surrender arises an as yet unimagined, even more expansive paradigm.

For Reference

Calibration Levels of Some Teachers and Writings in the 600s

Teachers		Writings	
Abhinavagupta	655	Abhinavagupta	655
Aurobindo	605	*A Course in Miracles*	
Karmapa	630	(workbook)	600
Kasyapa	695	Aggadah	645
Magdeburg	640	Genesis (Lamsa Bible)	660
Muktananda	655	Gospel of St. Luke	699
Satchidananda	605	Gospel of St. Thomas	660
Towles, J.	640	Kabbalah	605
Tzu, Lao	610	Teachings of Lao Tzu	610
Vivekananda	610	Midrash	665
		Mishneh	665
		New Testament	
		(King James)	640
		Psalms (Lamsa Bible)	650
		Vijnana Bhairava	635

CHAPTER 17

Self-Realization
(Calibration Level 700-849)

Introduction

This is the level of sages, the Great Teachers of *Advaita or Vedanta* who described the spiritual realities of Self-realization. It is the level of powerful inspiration as these Enlightened Sages set attractor energy fields in place that influence all of mankind. At this level there is no longer the experience of an individual personal self separate from others; rather, there is an identification of Self with consciousness and Divinity. Divinity Immanent is realized as Self beyond mind. This is near the peak of the evolution of consciousness in the human realm.

Great teachings uplift the masses and raise the level of awareness of all humanity. To have such vision is called Grace, and the gift it brings is infinite Peace that is ineffable and beyond words. At this level of realization, the sense of one's existence transcends all time and all individuality. There is no longer any identification with the physical body as 'me', and therefore, its fate is of no concern. The body is seen as merely a tool of consciousness through the intervention of mind, with its prime value being that of communication. The self merges back into the Self. This is the level of non-duality, or complete Oneness. There is no localization of consciousness; awareness is equally present everywhere.

Great works of art depicting individuals who have reached the level of Enlightenment often show the teacher with a specific hand position, called a *mudra*, wherein the palm of the hand symbolically radiates benediction. This is the act of the transmission of this energy field to the consciousness of mankind, which is also depicted by a halo. This is the level of Divine Grace, which can potentially evolve up to 1,000, the highest level attained by any persons who have lived in recorded history, such as the Great Avatars for whom the title 'Lord' is appropriate: Lord Krishna, Lord Buddha, Lord Jesus Christ, and Zoroaster.

Discussion

Beyond Bliss are the levels of the great mystics whereby Knowingness is the consequence of the Presence of Divinity as Self (God Immanent). The distinction of God as immanent versus transcendent is a theological, intellectual, conceptual distinction. The Presence of Self constitutes the classic *perusha*, or Radiance of Self as Source. Self 'knows' by virtue of identity with Divinity itself. It thereby is its own Awareness, and by its Presence it thereby makes itself 'known' as the 'Knower'. Thus, it does not know 'about' but is the Completion of its own Essence.

The transcendence of Bliss may allow for the resumption of limited function by which some reentry into the world is again possible. This is now, however, an emergence within the nonlinear domain rather than a decision, although to external appearance, it is mistakenly perceived to be volitional. Actually, there is no 'decider' to 'decide', nor are there 'options' that would necessitate choice or decision. Life becomes phenomenologically autonomous as an expression of the evolution of Creation and the omnipresent field of consciousness itself, which is also innately versatile by virtue of the quality of its Essence.

Consciousness levels 600 and up are classically termed 'no mind' because sequential thinkingness stops and in its place is the nonlinear awareness of consciousness itself, which is often referred to as Mind in the world's literature. By virtue of Divinity, the Unmanifest as potentiality becomes Manifest as actualization. The Enlightened Mystic becomes the translator for the explanation of the Innate to the expressed description by which it becomes known to the world. Subjectively, the Presence is that of consciousness itself whose quality is that of Truth as an expression of Love and, reciprocally, of Love as the effulgence of Truth.

The consciousness levels of the 700s are historically classified as the levels of Self-Realization or of advanced mystics, such as those represented in recent times as Ramana Maharshi, Nisargadatta Maharaj, Sri Aurobindo, Mahatma Gandhi, and Patanjali. Familiar writings at these levels are the Zen teachings of Bodhidharma; the Cloud of Unknowing; the Diamond, Heart, and Lotus Sutras; the Koran; the New Testament (without Revelations); and the Yoga Sutras of Patanjali, as well as the *Rig Veda*. (For convenience, a representative list is included at the end of the chapter.)

Notable is that several of the best-known teachers are relatively recent. Some have been accorded recognition by society at large. Their impact on society is on two levels in that they have expressed specific teachings and simultaneously silently radiated an energy field from their auras into the collective consciousness of mankind. The effect of that radiation is two-fold: the first is to counterbalance the negativity in the world, and the second is to contribute to an upliftment of the overall evolution of consciousness of mankind in general and devotees in particular.

As mentioned previously, the mass consciousness level was 90 at the time of the birth of the Buddha, at 100 by the time of Jesus Christ, and then it rose to 190, where it stayed for many centuries. In the late 1980s, it suddenly jumped to 205 and advanced again in November 2003 to its current level of 207.

In traditional spiritual literature, there are descriptions and classifications of various advanced levels of consciousness described as states of *Samadhi*. Often these are descriptively associated with states of meditation consequent to transcending the limitations of the ego. Some of these are transitory, such as the various states termed as satori, or awakenings. These are often dependent on the meditative state itself. In the beginning, the satori state necessitates remaining still, with the eyes closed. As it develops, it continues, even with the eyes open. As it advances further, it remains, even with the eyes open, and one walks about, resuming activity. As the famous Zen ox-herding pictures, originating in the 1500s, depict, the progression is to first locate and identify the ego (the ox), then tame it, then transcend it, then leave the world, then the world disappears, and then, as a seasoned sage, return to the world. At this point, the world is depicted as merely a reflection on the water (of consciousness itself).

It appears that as consciousness evolves, it seems to remain at a given level for variable periods of time that are described as periods of 'ripening', realignment, and readjustment through the more advanced energy field. There is a necessary realignment with the functioning and location of the body and the resumption of physiological functions, as well as the capacity to speak and communicate. For example, Ramana Maharshi, after a sudden, unexpected Enlightenment, was mute for two years until encouraged to speak. He took no care of the body at all. Nisargadatta Maharaj wandered off on foot to the Himalayas and had to be taken back to Bombay.

The subjective experience of this return is that it is a spontaneous response to love, appeal, entreaty, or the influence of others in the environment. From within, the mind is silent and there is no 'personal' inclination to speak or need to communicate, nor is there even any necessity to continue on in the life of the body itself.

Intrinsically, each advanced level of consciousness is complete within itself. Most sages have stayed at a given level for a lifetime; others have managed to return to functioning in the world in limited areas. To return to functioning in the world requires readjustments that are difficult to describe. The people in the world consider the sage to be an individual person. Initially, this is rather surprising because there is no individual person present to be spoken to. What evolves is the development of an interface with the world, best described as a 'persona'. It is not the inner reality but it meets the world's expectations that perceive the Self to be located as a separate individual body and a separate identity (the 'personality'). In a manner of speaking, these expectations of the world are somewhat humored by at least approximations in order to dispel comment, for the interchanges are of a greater dimension than the world perceives.

Another difficulty that requires adjustment is understanding the verbal communication of others. Although they are heard auditorily, there is a slight delay whereby some process of inner translation reveals what the speaker intends by the words. Thus, the persona seems to serve as a translative interface, and its development is autonomous. There may be a delay of even years before such a phenomenon occurs. Some sages never did leave their original locations. Ramana Maharshi stayed at Aranachula Mountain all of his life. After his death, the ashram remained active and is still there. Nisargadatta Maharaj, after being brought back from wandering off to the Himalayas, stayed in his attic room in Bombay over the bidi shop. These lifestyles also reflected an interface with cultural traditions.

The truly enlightened sage has no interest in developing a 'following', controlling the lives of followers, the building of edifices, theatrical displays, or worldly possessions. There are no needs or desires to be met, much less the desire to control others. Also, the teacher's remarks may be viewed as cryptic because they are brief, precisely to the point with nothing more needing to be said.

The term 'transcendence' is really a style of languaging, for in the nonlinear domain, there are progressive dimensions rather than actual levels. Instead, the transition could be more correctly likened to the sunlight that emerges consequent to the evaporation of the clouds. On these levels, the condition or state of consciousness may or may not evolve farther during this lifetime, depending on karmic potentiality and Divine will. The surrender of identification with each state releases it, including letting go of any attachment to its familiarity. Consciousness evolves as though attracted to return to its Source. Each advance expands the paradigm of awareness that, transitionally, has a certain sense of 'home'.

Many sages, once they reach the level of the 700s, remain at that level for the remainder of their lives. Occasionally, however, the process continues spontaneously when allowed to do so. Each level represents the completion of the evolution that precedes it, but it is also the doorway to the next. Subjectively, transition is more like an emergence or an unfolding, which is the province of awareness itself, about which there is no mentalization because these are the states of 'no mind' (paradoxically also labeled as 'Mind').

From level 700 on up, resistances that reside in the collective consciousness of mankind have to be transcended within the teacher. This is physically subjectively comfortable until it reaches the consciousness level of approximately 800, at which time painful physical symptoms arise and the nervous system feels like it is carrying too much electricity, resulting in a burning feeling. Each time something comes up from the collective consciousness, it has to be processed. (Jesus Christ sweat blood, and the Buddha remarked that his bones felt like they were being broken. Numerous symptoms have been reported in these previous writings and by various mystics throughout history.)

Unlike ordinary physical symptoms or pains that can be handled by nonresistance, these burning electric sensations persist until the specific error in the collective unconscious is identified and voluntarily surrendered and cleared. While functioning in the 700s is theoretically possible (e.g., Mother Teresa), there are delays at this level to handle the internally arising phenomena. To facilitate this transition, it is helpful to have knowledge of the chakra systems and the various Jungian archetypes in the collective unconscious. These are represented by various social/cultural subgroups and their endemic attitudes and positionalities that can be intuited or diagnosed by the consciousness calibration technique.

Surrender at ever-increasing depth becomes invitational to the progression of consciousness/awareness, and this occurs at a level beyond the intention because the process is self-evolving.

The invitational attitude of surrender could be likened to a very 'Yin' consciousness posture, which could also be physically likened to a *mudra* (classic hand position). Thus, the overall posture of consciousness is one of 'allowance' (to receive) rather than the contrasting 'Yang' attitude of intentionality (to get). By alignment with surrender to being a channel of God's will, one's life thereby becomes transformed into a prayer by which one *is* that prayer.

For Reference

Calibration Levels of Some Teachers and Writings in the 700s

Teachers		Writings	
Bodhidharma	795	Bodhidharma,	
Charya, Adi Sankara	740	Zen Teachings	795
de Leon, Moses,		Cloud of Unknowing	705
of Granada	720	Diamond Sutra	700
Dogen	740	Heart Sutra	780
Eckhart, Meister	705	Koran	700
Gandhi, Mahatma	760	Lotus Sutra	780
Maharaj, Nisargadatta	720	New Testament (King	
Maharshi, Ramana	720	James, minus Revelation)	790
Patanjali	715	Rig Veda	705
Plotinus	730	Yoga Sutras, Patanjali	740
Shankara	710	Ramayana	810
Teresa, St. of Avila	715	Teresa, Mother	710

(Note on Plotinus: His available writings, as listed in the *Great Books of The Western World*, calibrate at 503. Plotinus himself in later life calibrated at 730.)

CHAPTER 18

Full Enlightenment

(Calibration Level 850+)

Introduction

While consciousness levels over 600 are statistically very rare, those above 850 are rarer still. During the last 1,000 years, for fifty percent of the time, there has been no one at level 850, and for twenty percent of that time, there has been no one over calibration level 600. The very high energy frequencies of Enlightenment transmit a vibration to the collective consciousness field of mankind in general and become inscribed in the auric fields (etheric spiritual energy bodies) of spiritually aligned people by 'silent transmission'. The frequency vibration of this energy remains within the spiritual etheric body for very long periods of time and (confirmed by consciousness calibration research) can last for as long as twenty-five incarnations or up to even one thousand years, where it lies in wait to be claimed.

The unique power of the field of extremely high levels also counterbalances the negative energies that prevail in the majority of the world's population, of whom, as previously cited, seventy-eight percent are currently below calibration level 200 (forty-nine percent in the United States). The other service that advanced levels of consciousness provides is information that is of transformative value and usually transmitted down through the centuries for the benefit of spiritual students (as per lists at end of chapters). Many teachings of this high calibration were originally of very ancient origin and were promulgated via the ancient *Vedas*, such as the *Upanishads* and the *Bhagavad-Gita*, as well as the *New Testament*, the *Zohar*, and others. In some cases, the actual authors are unknown but the teachings are from Divinity or the Great Avatars who calibrate at 1,000 (Christ, Buddha, Krishna, Zoroaster).

The Great Teachers themselves primarily taught Truth only at the highest levels. The various world religions were established much later by followers, sometimes many centuries later, which inadvertently allowed for error, as is well known to Biblical scholars. The calibrated teachings of religions themselves per se are therefore less than that of the original founders. It is historically unusual and rare for Great Teachers to be the actual authors of the texts of their teachings. At times, the disparity and error are very great, such as the inclusion of the Book of Revelation (cal. 70) in the New Testament. When it is removed, the calibration of the New Testament moves up from 640 to 880 (Lamsa Bible translation).

Enlightened sages were primarily Self-realized mystics or recipients of Divine Incarnation, such as Jesus Christ. The oldest sources of the highest spiritual truth historically came down from the great Aryan sages of ancient India (i.e., the *Vedas*, the *Upanishads*). These originated in approximately 5,000 B.C. (The Buddha lived approximately 563 B.C.). The sages who reached level 850 or over became primary influential teachers, and their teachings form the core of important schools and revered spiritual traditions. Thus, a major teaching retains its intrinsic value over many centuries. The authenticity and validity of teachers and their teachings are now validatable by the emergence of the science of consciousness and its capacity to calibrate confirmable levels of truth.

While the actual numbers of very advanced, enlightened sages that influence mankind have been limited down through the centuries, their teachings have been essentially the same, even though they arose independently in different parts of the world, in different cultures, and in different millennia. Thus, it can be said that truth is always true because there is only one truth to be discovered. The great teachers and their teachings emanate extremely powerful high-frequency energy fields into the collective consciousness of mankind, without which it probably would have exterminated itself (calibrates as 'true').

Dynamics of Enlightenment

At very high levels, the subjective experiencing of existence is no longer limited by the narcissistic ego or the psychological blocks of the positionalities. This condition is the consequence of progressive surrendering at great depth of all limitations and belief systems. The requirement is the persistent 'one-pointedness of mind' processing-out of emotional/mental residuals of lower consciousness levels and surrendering of all self-identities and mental belief systems. This process is assisted and supported by the unimpeded inflow of the spiritual kundalini energy to the higher etheric spiritual bodies above the crown chakra.

The flow of the kundalini energy is a response to

surrendering the personal will directly to the Divine Teacher, Avatar, Sage, or Divinity by whatever name invoked (e.g., as per the Ninety-first Psalm, or the words of Krishna, or Jesus Christ that "All who call on me by whatever name are Mine and dear to Me").

The love of God by worship, devotion, commitment, declaration, or selfless service is the catalyst and the formal invitation for the intercession of Divinity via the power of the nonlinear field of consciousness itself, which is omniscient, omnipresent, and omnipotent. By surrender of all resistances, this powerful nonlinear field becomes progressively dominant and eventually an all-encompassing Presence.

Transcending Level 850

From the viewpoint of the intellect, the problematic duality encountered at consciousness level 850 may seem somewhat academic and therefore the province of metaphysics, theology, or ontology, but when the level is reached experientially, it is far more than that. It is a very major step with very major differences in the outcome because spiritual devotees who reach this level have often been influenced by misinterpretations of the teachings of the Buddha that misidentify the meaning of 'Void' and believe that the Nothingness/Void is the ultimate state, which it decidedly is *not*, as determined by both consciousness calibration research and subjective experience.

In traditional spiritual languaging, each of these advanced levels is 'guarded' by the 'dragons' of a duality. This is especially true at level 850 where the presenting limitation to be transcended is the conundrum of the seeming opposites/alternatives of whether the ultimate Reality is Allness versus Nothingness, or is Existence versus Nonexistence.

The void of Nothingness calibrates at 850 and is the end point of the pathway of negation that denies the reality of every*thing* or any*thing* (i.e., the linear form or 'thingness' as attachment). The error that follows is the presumption that the transcendence of all form is the sole condition of Buddhahood. This is an easy mistake to make because experientially, the condition of the Void is enormously impressive. As it unfolds, it is ineffable, infinite, timeless, Oneness, all encompassing, still, silent, unmoving, and strangely inclusive of the 'awareness of nonawareness' that precludes even beingness or existence. This state is definitely and experientially, without question, beyond duality. There is neither subject nor object; there is nothing left to surrender and no one left to surrender; thus, it indeed seems to be the ultimate state of Enlightenment itself. Another difficulty at that level is that there are no teachers with whom to consult, share, or reflect confirmation, much less instruction, for the state is indeed wondrous, and the need for such a direction would not seem to be necessary or present itself for confirmation.

If the state of Void (Nothingness) were the ultimate reality, it would be a permanent condition, and there would be no entity to report it. However, it is not, and therefore, sooner or later, one leaves the Void and returns to conscious existence. Next occurs the subjective experiential phenomenon of suddenly emerging into Existence from the oblivion of the

Void. (In this lifetime, the occurrence was at age three, as described elsewhere. Suddenly, out of Nothingness and nonawareness, there was the shock of not only Existence, but also the discovery of physicality and that a body accompanied the return from Nothingness to Beingness. Thus, in this lifetime, the dilemma at calibration level 850 was initially presented strongly in early life, and it recurred later, at which time it was rejected and transcended. (It took thirty-eight years to resolve.)

The Knowingness that is needed to transcend this level is that Divine Love is also nonlinear and without subject, object, form, conditionality, or location. The limitation (incompleteness) of the Void is reached as a consequence of intense dedication to the pathway of negation; however, missing is the realization that Love is a primary quality of Divinity and is also nonlinear, and that spiritual love is not an attachment. The error of the pathway of negation is to misidentify and refuse Love because, in its general, ordinary human experience, it is a limitation and an attachment (between a 'me' and a 'you' or an 'it').

In contrast, Divine Love is predominant, powerful, overwhelming, and the primary quality or essence of the Presence. It is profound and unconditional, with no subject or object. It is not an emotionality but a condition or a state that is liberating rather than limiting. The Void (cal. 850) is comparable to infinite, empty, conscious space. In contrast, the Presence of Divinity is like the heart of the sun. There is no mistaking it for the Love is realized as the very core and Source of one's primary Self.

Clarification of the Problems of The Void

Advantaged by the advent of consciousness calibration research plus subjective experience, the misunderstanding of the subject of the Void can be further clarified. The confusion arises from the pathway of negation as well as from the terminology ascribed to alleged statements by the Buddha (who advised to not use the term 'God' due to widespread misinformation about the true nature of Divinity). To assist understanding, the following calibrations are very useful:

	Calibration Level
Reality as witness/observer	600
Arhat	800
Seeing into one's 'self-nature'	845
Void	850
Oneness	850
Nothingness	850
Reality as Consciousness	850
Reality as Awareness	850
Omniscience	850
Omnipresence	850
Omnipotence	850
Allness	855
The Buddha	1,000
The Creator	Infinity
Divinity	Infinity
God	Infinity

As can be seen from the above, calibration level 850 denotes identification with attributes, qualities, or characteristics of Divinity but not Divinity itself. Thus,

Allness, Omnipresence, Nonlinearity, Oneness, etc., are qualities of Divinity but still lack the core identity, which is conscious awareness of *God* as *Divinity* and thus the Creator of the seen and unseen (the linear and the nonlinear) and the Source of Love and consciousness/awareness. The teachings of the Buddha were ostensibly worded to avoid preconceptions about the term 'God', but because the Buddha calibrated at 1,000, he therefore was indeed God Realized.

The transition from calibration level 850 to 1,000 is the consequence of rejection of the Void as the ultimate reality and affirmation of the Realization that the Source of the Enlightened states is *Divinity* as *God*, which is inclusive of all the attributes that calibrate at 850, *plus* God as Infinite *Love*. Full Enlightenment realizes the Presence as God and Divinity as the Source and Essence of Life, Creation, Consciousness/Awareness, and Existence. God is therefore descriptively omnipotent, omniscient, and omnipresent, and both Immanent and Transcendent, as well as Manifest and Unmanifest (the Godhead). Calibration level 1,000 is the ultimate state possible within the human domain (calibrates as 'true').

Transcending the Void

While spiritual students may consider that the problem inherent to the very advanced, extremely high-level problem of transcending the Void is not likely to be a challenge in this lifetime, they can be quite mistaken, for any student can suddenly find oneself at an extremely high level with no advance warning. Thus, all students should be instructed ahead of time as to how to handle very advanced states of consciousness. It is not just a catchy phrase that says that heaven and hell are only one-tenth of an inch apart. One can, in fact, go from the very depths of Hell to the most extremely advanced states (as described in the subjective experience of the author in previous works).

One reason for the seemingly endless delays on the way to Enlightenment is doubt, which should be surrendered as a resistance. It is important to know that it is actually extremely rare for a human to be committed to spiritual truth to the degree of seriously seeking Enlightenment, and those who do make the commitment do so because they are actually *destined* for Enlightenment.

At this time, spiritual evolution is proceeding at an ever-exhilarating pace, and spiritual information never before available is now readily accessible. The progress of a spiritual student of today is already accelerated and advantaged by access to spiritual information that in past times was limited to the very select few.

Spiritual progress does not follow in convenient, definable, progressive steps, as a description such as this on transcending the levels of consciousness might seem to imply. On the contrary, unexpected great leaps may very well occur at any time, and all students should be advantaged by having the necessary information of what to know at certain points along the way. The knowledge that is needed at 'the end' is essential right from the 'beginning'.

To know what is necessary to know in order to reach Divine states accelerates progress; otherwise, there is an unconscious resistance of fear due to ignorance. This fear is overcome by the acquisition of the necessary understanding; therefore, there is nothing left to fear, and all fear is an illusion—a knowingness that is also required at very advanced states. Any student who is serious about spiritual alignment and devotion to God, to Love, to Truth, to fellow humanity, or to the alleviation of human suffering or in all sentient beings, is already very far advanced.

Consistent application of any spiritual principle can unexpectedly result in a very major and sudden leap to unanticipated levels. At that point, memory may not even be available, and instead, the Knowingness of Spiritual Truth presents itself silently. Spiritual students should accept the reality that they are *already gifted*. A serious reader of a book such as this could hardly be otherwise. Divinity knows its own; therefore, to accept that truth is to already feel joy. To not experience joy by understanding this means that it is being resisted. This awareness is reinforced by understanding that, contrary to the dualistic Newtonian paradigm of reality, one is not just the consequence of the past. On the contrary, the present position is due to the attraction of potentiality, because both the past and the future are illusions. Therefore, commitment to Enlightenment now becomes like a magnet pulling one towards it, and the rate of evolution is up to the individual's willingness to surrender resistances.

Enlightenment is not a condition to be obtained; it is merely a certainty to be surrendered to, for the Self is already one's Reality. It is the Self that is attracting one to spiritual information.

The Final Surrender

At the previous levels of consciousness, the illusions of perception have been surrendered, as have interpretations of superimposed 'meaning', value, and significance. This leads to loss of identification with emotionality or linearity in the form of mentalizations and withdrawal of investment of interest in that which is transitory, including the physical body and worldly phenomena.

Eventually even the illusion of witnesses/observer/ watcher dissolves into awareness/consciousness itself, which is discovered to be nonpersonal and autonomous. There is no longer the limitation of 'cause and effect' or 'change'. The illusion of 'time' also dissolves into the Allness of Divine Concordance. There is neither attraction nor aversion to even existence itself for even the manifest is seen to be a consequence of discernment by consciousness as a concept.

All has been surrendered to God, and then the very last remnant of the self remains as the seeming source of life—the core of the ego itself, with the conviction that *it* is the author and primordial *source* of one's very life and existence. As this arises, so also does a knowingness that 'even this, too' must be surrendered to God. This last barrier is signaled by a sudden burst of the last remaining fear, which is very strong and intense—the very basic fear of death. Then arises a knowingness, which has been nascent in the spiritual aura, that 'all fear is an illusion' and 'death is not a possibility'. Then, as a consequence of faith and devotion, the last illusion is surrendered. Next emerges the literal, actual, feared sensation of dying—a brief but very intense agony because, unlike physical death, it has never been faced before. That is the only and final 'death' possible. As the agony dies away, there is an emergence into the Revelation of the Infinite Glory of Divinity. The last vestige of the ego/mind disappears into the Silence of the Presence. The stunning perfection and beauty of the Allness of Creation as Divinity radiates forth, and all is still, beyond all time. *Gloria in Excelsis Deo* is *the State itself.*

For Convenient Reference

Calibration Levels of Teachers and Writings at 850+

Bhagavad-Gita	910
Huang Po, Zen	850
Lamsa Bible (minus Revelation and Old Testament except Genesis, Psalms, Proverbs	880
Nicene Creed	895
Upanishads	970
Vedas	970
Zohar	905

Note: The Zen Teachings of Huang Po are problematic in that they describe the Pathway of Negation and mistakenly declare the Void State (cal. 850) as the Ultimate Condition of Buddhahood (cal. 1,000). Subsequent to his classical sermons about the Void, he himself transcended the limitation and eventually reached consciousness level 960 later in life. Therefore, negate only the linear but do not negate the nonlinear Reality of Love. Negate only special, limited personal attachment, which is a limiting emotionality. Divine Love is a universal quality and a nonlinear context that is innate as the Radiance of the overall context.

Section Five

Transcendence

Section Five – Overview

Spiritual Transformation

The progression of the evolution of consciousness is accelerated by the combination of intention plus attention. In worldly terms, the process is explicable as the Heisenberg principle, whereby the potentiality is activated to actuality by the introduction of consciousness and intention. This explanation applies to the mechanics of the phenomenon and is termed the 'collapse of the wave function', the consequence of which then appears as emergence. (In mathematics, the transition from the Schrödinger time-dependent and time-independent equations to their resolution as the Dirac equations.)

While the scientific model is very interesting, informative, and confirmative of the effect of consciousness, it does not take into account the relative power of the observer's level of consciousness or intention. Scientific objectivity calibrates in the 400s, whereas spiritual intention is far more powerful and calibrates from 500 on up. For instance, at highly-evolved levels of consciousness, merely holding an optimal resolution in mind tends to bring it into manifestation, as do affirmations (e.g., "My life is ruled by order and harmony.").

As demonstrated by the Map of Consciousness, the calibratable power increases logarithmically; thus, spiritual evolution is progressively facilitated by the higher levels of spiritual advancement as compared to the consciousness of the scientific observer, which characteristically calibrates in the mid-400s.

The influence of spiritual intention can therefore be over one thousand times stronger than ordinary intellectual effort (calibrates as 'true'). Thus, the spiritual devotee need not be an apologist to the skeptical materialist but instead merely explain that they are simply applying the Heisenberg principle for the benefit and betterment of self and the world.

When phenomena appear that are beyond the expectations of logic or reason, they tend to become described as 'mystical, ineffable, or miraculous' to denote the consequence of intention and the response of the contextual field that results in emergence. Therefore, to 'expect a miracle', or 'pray for the highest good' accelerates the resolution of a perceived problem. This is facilitated by surrendering judgmentalism or the desire to control outcomes. Thus, one is 'responsible for the effort and not the results' (a dictum of twelve-step spiritual groups).

Surrendering the control of outcomes is also beneficial in that it precludes either self-blame or pride about them. Whether a conclusion is seen as desirable or undesirable depends on the level of consciousness of the observer (i.e., positionalities).

Spiritual endeavor is fulfilling and self-propagating because of the inner satisfaction of subjectively experiencing the fulfillment of potential. Focus of attention in and of itself tends to support progress, which consequently becomes progressively effortless. Delays may be encountered due to strong resistances that may arise out of a long prior karmic history and therefore may take even years to overcome because of their recurrent reinforcement over long periods of time.

The Problem of Paradigm

Each person experiences, perceives, and interprets the world and its events in accordance with their own predominant level of consciousness. This is further reinforced by the mind's proclivity to explain via mentalization and interpretation of perceived data. Thus, each level tends to be self-reinforcing by the circuitry of reification. This process results in what is best described as 'paradigm allegiance', or the presumption that the perceived/experienced world represents 'reality'.

Because the mind, by virtue of its innate structure, is unable to differentiate perception from essence, or *res cogitans (interna)* from *res extensa (externa)*, it makes the naïve assumption that it experiences and therefore knows 'reality', and that other viewpoints must therefore be 'wrong'. This phenomenon constitutes illusion, which is the automatic consequence of the limitation resulting from the mental process.

For comfort and mental reinforcement, people tend to congregate with others who share the same paradigm. Paradigm is also alluded to as 'dimension', and more distinctly as 'context' or 'overall field'. The problem is addressed philosophically as 'metaphysics', which literally means beyond the physical by which the mind derives levels and categories of abstraction (e.g., species, class, genus, etc.) or common characteristics (living versus inert).

Context determines parameters with implied or stated qualifications or limits, as well as requirements and specifics that identify levels of abstraction that in turn modify or determine 'meaning' (hermeneutics) that is concordant with appraisals of value, significance, or worth.

Paradigm is also parallel to expectation and also intention, much as the search engine preselects the range of possible discoveries on the Internet. Paradigm thus predetermines the range of possible experiences or discoveries and is a factor about which ordinary consciousness is unaware. Paradigm is thus infrequently defined directly; most often it is merely presumed.

The importance of paradigm is markedly seen at consciousness level 200, and most clearly at the transition from the Newtonian paradigm to quantum mechanics, and then again at consciousness level 500, at the emergence of the subjectivity of Love. The next major jump (very rare) is at consciousness level 600, which marks transcendence of the linear domain and emergence of the nonlinear dimension. This also reflects the differentiation between content (linear) and context (nonlinear), as shown by the following classifications:

Below 200	200 to 499	500 to 600	Over 600
Linear content	Content plus context	Context plus content	Context
Literal, concrete	Objective	Subjective	Ephemeral
Materialistic	Moral	Loving	Compassion
Cause – Effect	Cause – Effect	Intentional	Unfoldment
Pedestrian, mundane	Sophisticated	Abstract	Awareness/witness
Left-brain physiology	Right-brain physiology	Etheric plus right brain	Etheric brain
Definable, describable	Identifiable	Experiential	Confirmable
Mechanical, simplistic	Multifactorial	Volitional	Emergent
'Animal'	'Human'	Spiritual	Enlightened
'Think'	Reason	Appreciate, value	Knowingness
Body	Mind	Spirit	Presence
Narcissistic	Self plus others	Selfless	Self

From the above, it is apparent that context profoundly affects experience, meaning, significance, importance, and value. Also affected is expectation, which, in and of itself, is unwittingly selective, coloring experience and even seeming perceptions.

The linear dimension is within the province of the objective 'provable', whereas, in contrast, the nonlinear is affirmable, demonstrable, and confirmable, but primarily subjective and experiential. The nonlinear is neither subject to nor definable or describable by the linear as they are different paradigms but not mutually exclusive. These contrasts are classically noted by the differentiation between academic (Newtonian) science and clinical science. The former is predictive of outcomes, whereas the latter is subject to numerous influences of context, such as intention, integrity of purpose, calibration level of participants, and many identifiable, but also many unknown, variables. Thus, the seasoned clinician uses all appropriate modalities that experience has shown to be beneficial (e.g., 'nontraditional' modalities).

Academics deal with predictables and statistics. The clinician deals with outcomes and results. Thus, to 'have a heart' is requisite for the clinician but is not a measurable in academics. The clinical experience of seasoned clinicians is often with people and situations that have not been responsive to academia.

While academic science fails to recognize the validity of 'unscientific' ideologies or methods, or even denigrates them, the clinician is more versatile, intellectually humble, and therefore interested in what works. Perhaps the best-known and universally recognized example is that of Alcoholics Anonymous by which literally millions of the most hopeless have dramatically recovered, including many high-profile persons, celebrities, and even presidents. Also included in the recoveries are many thousands of doctors and other professionals. AA is decidedly totally 'unscientific' and very purely, solely spiritual yet profoundly powerful and effective. Often an active alcoholic comes to AA only after having run the gamut of standard academic treatments. However, the primary requisite for recovery is 'unscientific' humility and surrender to a Higher Power.

Thus, the spiritual and scientific are two totally different paradigms, and each has its appropriate place in society. The fact that there is fraudulent science does not disprove good science anymore than pseudospirituality disproves true, authentic spirituality.

The capacity to comprehend spirituality does not appear in the evolution of consciousness until calibration level 200, concordant with a shift in the brain's physiology and information-processing circuits. Thus, the incapacity represents an evolutionary physiological limitation that is calibratable even at the time of birth, e.g., as per AA's well-known citation from Chapter 5: "There are unfortunates constitutionally incapable of being honest with themselves. They are not at fault. They seem to have been born that way, but even some of them recover if they have the willingness...."

Temptations

Spiritual evolution is a process of unfoldment, emergence, and purification as a consequence of what one has become rather than as a result of what one is doing or has been. Spiritual errors can be concluded by humility and caution as well as forewarning. Temptations occur along the pathway and have been alluded to in the discussion of the various levels. It is best to periodically review them so as to be on guard. Those temptations that represent levels below 200 are often suppressed and therefore may suddenly re-emerge unbidden at levels over 200.

For review:

Level	Temptation
Courage	Bravado, macho, risk taking
Neutrality	Indifference, withdrawal
Willingness	Overcommitment, overinvolvement
Acceptance	Failure to take appropriate action
Reason	Intellectualism, stuck in cause and effect, rationalization
Love	Seduction, exploitation, misidentified as personal
Joy / Ecstasy	Poor judgment

At any level, Pride can return, accompanied by the temptation to exploit spiritual titles or control over followers. Spiritual pride can lead to overestimation of self as Self and make claims, such as 'higher than Jesus', or 'a great leader', or acclaim oneself as a 'performer of miracles' or an 'avatar' and exhibit global ambitions.

To be spiritually gifted is by Grace, which results in the humility that acknowledges the state yet does not take credit for the condition that would result in ego inflation, grandiosity, and a misstatement of truth that could lead to wanting or exploiting control over others as well as glamorization and theatrical display or exploitation of the phenomena that are the consequence of the *siddhis*. Supernatural qualities or phenomena are not of the personal self but of the field. It is an error to claim personal credit or specialness.

Vulnerability to the temptations is a consequence of naïveté, unpreparedness, or denial, which is motivated by the desire for gain or pride. There is also the attraction of the spiritual ego to status, rank, and adulation by followers consequent to fame. Teachers are placed on pedestals, which can easily result in inflation of the spiritual ego of the teacher or a feeling of importance. Humility and gratitude for the gift of the Spirit needs to be reaffirmed. Spiritual energy can also exhibit the emergence of healings when karmic propensities are favorable. It is an error to claim personal credit or exploit these phenomena, which are witnessed rather than being 'caused' by the 'practitioner'. Therefore, psychic gifts are to be respected and used for the highest good rather than for personal gain.

Transcending the Temptations

Vulnerability persists as long as there are still desires for gain, pride, vanity, control, wealth, or sensual pleasure. With spiritual maturity, perception is replaced by vision that reflects essence and spiritual truth, resulting in the capacity to see through self-deceptions. Vision is associated with spiritual wisdom, which makes clear that exploitation leads to loss and descent rather than progressive ascendancy.

Spiritual purity is the consequence of self-honesty, which is a result of true devotion. To be a servant of God is to align with Divine Guidance that leads to looking to the Self rather than catering to self or the world.

A strong sense of karmic responsibility also gives strength and the safety of humility. It is mindful that numerous are the once 'greats' who have yielded to temptations and fallen into traps by the mechanisms of self-delusion and rationalization.

The world offers great opportunity for ascent, but also equally of descent, which occurs only as a consequence of an act of the will, and therefore, neither blame nor excuses precludes consequences. Doubt can also be resolved by the utilization of consciousness calibration techniques that are very simple, such as merely asking whether an action or a decision would serve the highest good.

The Spiritual Ego

Devotion and dedication sometimes lead to what is best termed 'overambition', overzealousness, or even fanaticism, which represent imbalance. A frequent error is to try to force the rise of the kundalini energy by artificial exercises and practices. The kundalini automatically rises to its own appropriate level in accord with the energy field of the prevailing level of consciousness. This occurs as a consequence of what one has 'become' and 'is'. To force the spiritual energy by manipulative means can result in serious disorders, imbalances, and even irrational mental states of confusion or delusion. This may result in grandiose states and self-claims to be a 'prophet', or even 'Jesus Christ' or a 'messiah'. (These were observed during the author's years as a consultant to many religious and spiritual groups.)

Some spiritual practices may also lead to altered

states of consciousness or autosuggestive states that are misidentified as spiritual. While mantras and certain repetitious practices have some value, depending on the calibrated level of their truth as well as the intention behind them, they can also become a substitute for the progressive realizations that underlie and substantiate true spiritual advance. The true state is reflected in what one has become rather than what one believes or does. Thus, occult practices or magical manipulations and gymnastics are better bypassed in favor of true, substantial spiritual growth. Progress is facilitated by the willingness to surrender ambition to God. Error can be precluded by being alert to the ego's desire to survive by taking over the spiritual process.

The Lure of the Siddhis

There are many supposedly 'spiritual' techniques and systems that are merchandised and promoted, complete with testimonials and celebrities. The overt commercialization reveals the overall intention, which is to profit rather than promote the actual spiritual evolution of the naïve seeker. While some of the techniques certainly have value, they can be obtained free of charge from any integrous textbook on spirituality. Of equal danger are the seduction and proselytization of a variety of cults that are based on glamorization of leaders, control of followers, well-known brainwashing techniques, financial and sexual expectations, and control over personal lives. All of these calibrate extremely low. There is considerable information available about them under 'cults'. These organizations also specialize in the techniques of entrapment, seduction, specialness, and the exploitation of innocence and naïveté. The spiritual ego sees progress as gain or status rather than as a gift and, therefore, responsibility. It will even parade pseudohumility and overpiety and can become quite sanctimonious. It is also impressed by rank, title, and the adulation of large numbers of followers, as well as by pompous display, theatrics, and the manipulation of paranormal phenomena. The peddling of paranormal phenomena is a serious warning as the appeal is obviously to the ego, which is easily glamorized by parapsychological events (teleportation, telekinesis, distant viewing, bilocation, levitation, materialization of objects, astral projection, and more, including even the Doppelganger phenomenon (doubling).

To desire a *siddhi* for its own sake is a warning that the spiritual ego is seeking specialness. The real phenomena are unintended, nonvolitional, spontaneous, and autonomously emergent. They are very definitely not the consequence of techniques, nor can they be learned or taught, much less for a price. Artful gymnastics that are taught for a fee calibrate below 200. To begin with, the intention is nonintegrous, although frequently due to naïveté. Learning a water-into-wine trick does not turn one into a Jesus Christ. These imitations have flourished for centuries in India and have re-emerged as commercialized ventures in the Western world. They are to be avoided by any spiritual aspirant who is devoted to reaching Enlightenment. 'Caveat emptor' applies to a serious degree. The siddhis are a gift of God; they are *not* a commercial, artificially acquired skill. Therefore, they definitely are not the consequence of a training or a practice.

The True Siddhis

The phenomena occur naturally and spontaneously at the consciousness level of approximately 540 as a consequence of the intrinsic power of the consciousness field itself. They are intriguing, interesting, and pleasing but not desired for their own sake. They are therefore akin to the pleasing surprise of a sudden rainbow (which may also actually be an occurrence). There is no intention involved. What is held in mind may well actualize or not. Most often, the phenomena are not anticipated, but after a while, their frequent recurrence leads to a likely expectation. The assiduous positioning of basic spiritual principles is what precedes the appearance of the seemingly miraculous (hence the title of the spiritual treatise, *A Course in Miracles* [cal. 600]).

The witnessed phenomena are also seen by others and therefore are not personal subjective observations. Any or all of the siddhis may occur, and all are spontaneous and outside contextualization as cause and effect. They are the actualization of potentiality when conditions are fortuitous, as in a high level of consciousness.

The way to witnessing the true siddhis is simple and free of monetary requirements, repetitious practices, training, or instructions by adepts:

1. Surrender all attraction or desire for the siddhis themselves. They are a glamour and a distraction.
2. Surrender every moment to God, including all

attractions, aversions, or desires for control or gain.

3. Choose to be unconditionally compassionate and forgiving to all of life in all its expressions.
4. Choose to see the beauty, perfection, and sacredness of all life.

Integrous Health Systems

In contrast to the artificially manipulated imitations of the siddhis, there are integrous exercises and energy-building health systems that are designed to improve health, happiness, and the level of functioning for which there is an appropriate fee as it requires teachers, classes, and trainers, etc. In contrast to those that are deleterious, such programs calibrate over 200 and are designed to improve physical fitness and one's sense of well-being ('a healthy mind is a healthy body'). Appreciation for life often starts with increased attention to its quality, including aesthetics.

CHAPTER 19

Limitations and Distractions

Introduction

Although the spiritual literature supplies an enormous amount of information about spiritual reality and the truths to be realized, there still seems to be a scarcity of some important details and necessary information for the student. There are many helpful things to know that do not appear in the traditional literature unless one searches for them or concludes that such events are primarily of historic interest rather than diversions that may have occurred to any seriously committed spiritual traveler. It is better to know such things well in advance because when they occur, there may be no one around with whom to consult. Therefore, some information is of practical value and prevents consternation or confusion.

Discussion

Most discussions of such matters start at the bottom of the Scale of Consciousness and move up to the top, but in this case, it is important to start from the top and move down because the top of the Scale of Consciousness is the actual destiny of every seriously committed spiritual student. Unexpected advanced states of consciousness can emerge unannounced. Therefore, Transcendence beyond level 850 may bring up some problems that may be important to know about before hand. These are concomitant to moving into very powerful high-energy fields of consciousness for which the human nervous system is not prepared due to the infrequency of its occurrence throughout the evolution of Homo sapiens. One can see that as the levels increase, power increases logarithmically to high-frequency energy levels. Thus, very major increases occur in not only the power of the energy itself but also in its vibratory frequency. An analogy would be to compare the capacity of an old-fashioned radio vacuum tube with that of a transistor, or a 110-volt-capacity wire's being required to handle a 6,000-volt current.

Subjectively, the body can intermittently feel as though the nerves themselves are overstressed. This can be experienced as an uncomfortable and generalized burning sensation, as though one's aura is on fire. This may be accompanied by stressful aches or pains, sudden feelings of weakness, or the inability to function. These vicissitudes are common in the history of mystics or in the stories of well-known sages of ancient times who shared the problems and sufferings they experienced.

The ability to do personal consciousness research using the muscle-test diagnostic technique can be very helpful at these stages, and with prayer, the source of the resistance can be intuited and made conscious. At very advanced levels, it is not the personal ego from which resistances and positionalities arise, but instead from the collective consciousness of mankind. Thus, to locate the source of conflict, it is not fruitful to look at one's personal consciousness but instead to look at the overall levels of consciousness of mankind in its major movements throughout time. For example, there can be the arising of judgmentalism, indignation, or even rage at the sufferings of mankind, even though one has personally overcome this duality.

Although the personal self may have transcended right versus wrong, good versus bad, and lovable versus unlovable, these perceptions and positionalities are not resolved in the deeper layers of the collective unconscious. With deep prayer and deep humility, the fate of the world can be surrendered to God at ever-deeper levels, for it becomes obvious that all that is witnessed is actually in accord with Divine Providence and Wisdom. Worldly life provides the maximum opportunities for the evolution of consciousness via the undoing of past negative karma and the accrual of positive karma on both an individual and group basis.

A quick review of past human history reveals that there is obviously a lot of 'negative karma' to be undone, to say the least. Whole generations have been in accord with the grossest forms of brutality, savagery, and barbaric behaviors that continue to this day. Thus, this world can be surrendered to serve the highest good as a workshop of maximum opportunity. As the Buddha said, rare it is and extremely fortunate indeed to be born a human. Rarer still is it to hear of the Truth, and even rarer yet is it to pursue the Truth (Enlightenment).

Another unsuspected alteration in the functioning capacity of very advanced states of consciousness is that prior 'left brain' (linear) types of capabilities and interests decline. The Self is nonlinear, and it takes considerable energy to process sequential linear information, especially in its details. Thus, the world of technology, with all its gadgets and multiple operational options, is very likely to be completely beyond one's capacity. Unless a device works merely with a simple on-off switch, it is likely to be totally neglected. On the other hand, there is no problem at all with concentration; in fact, on the contrary, suspended mental processing facilitates it.

There are also unanticipated periods in which the option to withdraw from the body itself appears, even at seemingly very odd moments. This summons up any residual attraction or aversion to worldly life, and the option to disengage from the body is attractive and has to be surrendered to God. This occurs at a different level than it did in working through prior levels of attachment, aversion, or identification with the physical body. When the option to leave appears, it is merely witnessed. The option is very clearly an open one; therefore, one merely witnesses whether the body will walk on or not, or whether it will breathe again or not. There is no personal will in the matter or choice to be made. The outcome is obviously up to Divinity vis-à-vis one's karmic inheritance.

A variety of other transitory alterations occurs that have to do with changes in balance and interpretation of the input from the senses. Unlike earlier life experience, communication is on a different level, and what people are talking about in their languaging seems unintelligible and actually meaningless. One can request by prayer that the Holy Spirit interpret and translate it into comprehension. This intentionality need not be restated, and it is noticed that there is a split-second delay between the speaking that is heard and its inner translation into what it means. It is like being partially deaf or having a learning problem, but one quickly learns to cover up the delay (due to the absence of the 'experiencer') and therefore frequently responds to conversations with "What?" By the time the communication has been translated and the meaning has become clear, it appears that the central point of a seemingly lengthy conversation can really be summarized in just a few words. This difficulty is due to the disparity of styles in processing from linear presentation to nonlinear awareness.

The significance of communication is that of essence rather than the details of form. Thus, the spiritual response of the inner Self may be quite brief and cryptic because it is precisely focused on the essence of the question. The questioner is expressing not only linearity and the presumption of sequence, but also the Newtonian forms of subject/object and cause/effect contextualization, as well as this/that. For a variable period of time, customary socializing and discourse are neither really welcome nor facile in their performance. In the meantime, the body goes about spontaneous action in accord with its karmic propensities wherever it is apparently serviceable to Divinity, and its whereabouts is not really a matter of concern.

The adjustment encountered from level 600 on up occurs because the mind is silent and no longer processes data in a sequential, linear style. Thus, the customary data bank of memory is not processed according to sequential logic and prioritized compartmentalization. For example, in ordinary life, a lost object is traced back through memory to prior movements in a time frame. By contrast, in the nonlinear condition without time or sequence, there is no longer a question to be asked, and as the situation presents itself, the answer instantly comes forth unprocessed out of silence.

At consciousness levels below 600, a comparable rapid process can also be accessed by use of the muscle-testing research technique. 'True' or 'false' is an instant response of consciousness, which encompasses enormous data beyond mentalization, logic, or information processing. While numerical designation is suitable for consciousness research projects, it is not necessary in daily practice when the great majority of questions can be answered in the form of a simple 'yes' or 'no'. To provide the equivalent of what can be accessed via the muscle-testing techniques or the spontaneous functioning of the silent, nonlinear Self would require a great multiplicity of computers that even then would not be able to process the necessary evaluations of quality, importance, desirability, appeal, value, integrity, etc. For example, to fully evaluate a job offer would necessitate integrating close to a million factors, any one of which could spell success or failure. The options of a job venture include an enormous complexity of factors, such as the suitability of ambiance, congeniality, excellence of fit, and karmic appropriateness, as well as the likelihood of an enormous number of economic and social factors. Even if the processing of all that data were possible, it would still end up as only the best-educated guess.

In contrast, the field of consciousness itself, by virtue of its omnipresence and omniscience, automatically translates the infinite number of factors into a singularity such as a 'yes' or a 'no'. This occurrence automatically includes both conscious and unconscious factors, including unasked questions. All of this is correlated with suitability to the consciousness level of the questioner. Also to be considered is the disparity between the world view of the ego and that of the Self, so that what may appear to the ego to be a loss is actually a victory for the spirit (e.g., the paying off of a karmic debt to clear the field so that consciousness can continue to evolve). Thus, the ego/self might feel that it is losing at the same time the spirit is gaining.

The Impact of Spiritual Commitment

Naïvely, early spiritual students often expect that 'becoming spiritual' will bring about a magical kind of childlike happiness by which they will be transported to a stress-free, heavenly condition of better quality and pleasure for self and others. This is certainly true if the transition is from below consciousness level 200 to above level 200 where the rate of happiness does indeed rise very rapidly.

To continue to evolve requires development of courage, determination, and the alignment of priorities as a consequence of intention and, eventually, commitment. If vicissitudes along the way are understood to be normal, they will not result in dismay. Although each level of consciousness has its intrinsic attractions and aversions to be bypassed, from consciousness level 200 on up, there is facilitation and assistance from the power of spiritual energy that is lacking at the lower levels. The spiritual engine develops more horsepower as it travels the route. Obstacles that seem difficult or even impossible to overcome at a lower level are bypassed fairly easily at higher levels, and by the power of intention, they frequently disappear spontaneously as a consequence of merely becoming aware of them. Thus, the evolution and progression become a consequence of the power of the field itself rather than of the personal will or effort.

Making the transition from below 200 to above 200 may require the support and wisdom of spiritual groups, such as faith-based, religious, or specific spiritual study groups.

Spiritual intention and commitment, especially when accompanied by prayer, declaration, invocation, and devotion, change the predominant influential consciousness energy field, which is coordinated by its powerful 'attractor field' of energy. Thus, spiritual declaration and intention, inadvertently and often beyond awareness, change the rules by which one lives, and seemingly disparate life situations, including emotions, are now orchestrated from a different level that is frequently disparate with the customary expectations of the personal ego and society. These may result in transitory conflict in emotional or personal situations because the goals of the Spirit/Self are not those of the ego/self.

Forgiveness is an extremely important major tool, especially when it is combined with the willingness of humility and acceptance of human fallibility and susceptibility to error. From spiritual intention, the surrendering of egoistic options may seem like a sacrifice, but when recontextualized, they are revealed to be a hidden gift.

By analogy, it could be said that spiritual commitment brings up a whole new radar screen on one's spiritual computer. From a condensed viewpoint, it amounts to an entire educational system specifically designed for the devotee, taking into consideration an enormous multiplicity of factors beyond comprehension. It can be confirmed by the consciousness calibration technique that spiritual commitment does indeed bring up an entire spiritual program specifically and precisely autonomously designed that takes into consideration the appropriate inclusion of an enormous multiplicity of factors, including karmic details. The successful transcendence through this personal spiritual schooling is not possible for the ego but is made possible by the gift of Grace.

It may be dismaying at times to discover that surrender to the Self for one's salvation and spiritual evolution is in conflict with the ego's devious machinations to maintain control. One can be sure that the narcissistic core of the ego is certainly not going to welcome humility or the fact that the ordinary mind, unaided, is intrinsically not even capable of knowing the difference between truth and falsehood.

It is also well to know in advance that all suffering is not intrinsic to spiritual gain but strictly due to resistance to it. Suffering is due to dragging one's spiritual feet and the ego's insistence on having its own way. Abandoning the ego as God and turning to Divinity is what serves the evolution of consciousness.

If all life experiences are surrendered as they occur, they become transformed by gratitude into the miraculous and seen as gifts. This transformation is not within the province of the human will but is a gift of the Grace of God. To turn over one's life to be a servant of God, to grow spiritually, and to commit to the service of Divinity are very powerful acts of the human will. Faith is reinforced by remembering the promises of the Ninety-first Psalm and Upanishads that "all who call upon Me by whatever name are Mine and dear to Me." Faith in the infinite benevolence of Divine Love is itself transformative. At times, that is the only thing to which one clings in times of desperation.

The Tool of Simplicity

Another delay on the way to Enlightenment is the supposition that one has to master and assimilate a vast amount of spiritual information in order to achieve spiritual success. Spiritual libraries usually contain hundreds of books, in addition to which are endless workshops, training groups, and diversions that may lead to an intense study of theology, metaphysics, philosophers, religious histories, and the like. While valuable information does arise along the way, it often ends up being more of an interference than a help because the accumulated erudition reinforces spiritual pride and the self-delusion of "I know."

To cut through the complexity, it is really only necessary to know and apply a few simple spiritual tools, the efficacy of which is enormously empowered by the consistency of their practice and continuous application to everything, no matter what, with no exceptions. To be serviceable and useful, the tool has to be simple and brief, perhaps consisting of only a single concept. To be remembered is that spiritual evolution is not the consequence of knowing about the Truth, but the willingness to become that truth. To learn about spiritual reality is interesting and has some benefit. It is best to choose by intuition and attraction a spiritual teacher and teachings or a school to which one feels aligned and the validity of which has been verified by consciousness calibration techniques.

Simple Tools of Great Value

One can pick a primary tool, plus a few others, but many are not needed. Simple tools consistently applied will result in the revelation of spiritual truths that do not have to be acquired intellectually because they present themselves with great clarity. In addition, they only present themselves when suitable and serviceable, and because they are not an acquisition of the mind, they do not end up as spiritual vanity.

Some tried-and-true basic tools that have brought about tremendous results over the centuries are as follows:

1. Be kind to everything and everyone, including oneself, all the time, with no exception.
2. Revere all of life in all its expressions, no matter what, even if one does not understand it.
3. Presume no actual reliable knowledge of anything at all. Ask God to reveal its meaning.
4. Intend to see the hidden beauty of all that exists—it then reveals itself.
5. Forgive everything that is witnessed and experienced, no matter what. Remember Christ, Buddha, and Krishna all said that all error is due to ignorance. Socrates said all men can choose

only what they *believe* to be the good.

6. Approach all of life with humility and be willing to surrender all positionalities and mental/emotional arguments or gain.

7. Be willing to forgo all perceptions of gain, desire, or profit and thereby be willing to be of selfless service to life in all of its expressions.

8. Make one's life a living prayer by intention, alignment, humility, and surrender. True spiritual reality is actually a way of being in the world.

9. By verification, confirm the levels of consciousness and spiritual truth of all teachers, teachings, spiritual groups, and literature with which one intends to be aligned or a student.

10. Accept that by spiritual declaration, commitment, and surrender, Knowingness arises that provides support, information, and all that is needed for the entire journey.

The most powerful tool that is in the province of the will is devotion. Thus, it is not just spiritual truth but the degree of one's devotion to it that empowers it to become transformative. A great classic that demonstrates the efficacy of simplicity and devotion is that of Brother Lawrence's *The Practice of the Presence of God* (1692), which emphasizes the importance of constancy.

CHAPTER 20

Passing Through the Gates

General Guidelines

Spiritual progress is energized by intention that reinforces dedication and commitment as well as alignment with spiritual principles and practices. This results in dedication and willingness to focus effort, determination, and patience that require overall goodwill towards oneself and the process of spiritual endeavor. The above could be subsumed as a devotional attitude that transcends any specific linear definition. Goals automatically prioritize value and meaning, which thereby tend to provide the necessary energy for spiritual effort.

While it is usual to set aside some time specifically for spiritual practices such as formal meditation, it is generally more practical to incorporate spiritual principles into one's everyday life and lifestyle because special compartmentalized periods may lapse in the struggle of daily life and end up being abandoned altogether. In contrast, a contemplative lifestyle tends not to be dismissed as easily as do specifically set-aside periods of time that require a special, quiet environment. Isolated practice periods also tend to be compartmentalized and may become mentally isolated from daily life as something that one 'does' rather than being incorporated by the personality into what one 'is'.

Practically, it works well to select the spiritual principle and then make it one's inner rule of life to be applied consistently and relentlessly, 'no matter what'.

It is of great value to select a basic dictum to live by, such as the decision to be kind and of good will towards all life in all its expressions. This would, by inference, result in a willingness to forgive seeming negatives, observations, or mental constructs. The commitment to living according to basic spiritual dictums is strongly reinforced by prayer, supplication, and the decision to be a servant of God rather than the ego. It is also beneficial to ask God directly to be able to see things differently and to ask for guidance, information, and direction.

The Patterns

Spiritual commitment, alignment, and dedication initiate a nonlinear process in which phenomena and situations, both within and without, are now attracted by one's inner energy fields that also include karmic propensities and components. Life unfolds henceforth in different layers and altered presentations than would have occurred otherwise. Spiritual intention influences perceptions, memories, and interpretation of values that differ from previously prioritized egoistic goals and drives. Priority is now programmed by the Spirit in accord with intrinsic spiritual value and service to spiritual evolution. The evolution of consciousness is progressive and is an entire 'learning program' initiated by resolve that summons up the power of the spiritual will. Subsequently, all experience becomes valuable to the unfolding and developing of spiritual awareness. Thereby, 'mistakes' or 'successes' are of equal value in contrast to the ego's prior preferences.

As is well known, dedication to spiritual values and the purification process has a tendency to pull up their seeming 'opposites' by which karmic dualities are presented that require discernment of the positionalities from which they arise. One of the earliest persistent dilemmas that will almost certainly arise is the duality of good/bad, which is a very fruitful field for investigation. By observation, one will see that the good/bad dichotomy is merely the reflection of an overall contextualization based on unexamined presumptions. With deep humility, one will soon realize that unaided, the mind is really unauthorized, unequipped, and incapable of making such judgmental discernment. It can make this discovery by just beginning to ask for whom is it good, for whom is it bad, when, and under what circumstances. This eventually leads to examining one's overall contextualization of the significance and meaning of human life itself as a transitional learning experience.

Even a superficial, quick look at the human experience reveals that it is, first of all, mortal, temporary, and transitional, and the mind, unaided, cannot even tell from whence it arose or where it goes. It is also incapable on its own of telling truth from falsehood due to its inner structure. By what authority would it even be able to discern 'good' from 'bad'? This leads to the discovery that 'thinking' is not a very dependable method of arriving at spiritual truth or advancement, and that the mind, on its own, tends to merely pull up more thoughts rather than surrender them to a nonlinear, comprehensive understanding that would resolve the question altogether. Spiritual realization does not easily occur in a linear, logical mentalization but instead is a more diffuse, intuitive aura of comprehension and understanding that includes overall context and not just linear content.

Selecting a basic spiritual dictum to live by operationally becomes a set of attitudes that change perception. It is a style of positioning oneself and relating to life rather than a set of linear belief systems. Attitudes tend to generalize as discernment rather than as definable perception. This spiritual discernment tends to be open ended and invitational to an expansion of understanding. One therefore becomes aware that instead of saying "I think so-and-so," one says, "It seems to be such-and-such," or "It sounds like such-and such," or "It looks like such-and-such," or "It feels like such-and-such." These are the provisional sense-related proclivities for processing information rather than the limitation of definition and declarative statements saying, "He's all wrong, because...." With a shift of focus, experiencing becomes less linear, less defined, and less verbalized. As a result, one 'gets' what a situation is all about, much as one 'gets' the totality of a beautiful sunset without having to mentalize and say something like, "Isn't that beautiful?" or describe its colors, shapes, clouds, etc.

With this orientation, processing of information becomes increasingly more contextual and general rather than particular, and there is less mental vocalization and languaging. This evolves into the capacity to 'realize' and 'know', without thinkingness. The subjective experiential quality of holding a purring cat or encountering a dog's wagging tail does not require thinking or mentalization at all. Instead, one just 'gets' what the whole situation is about because of the progressive capacity for the discernment of essence rather than mentalized perception. By this process, it eventually becomes quite clear that everything 'just *is* as it *is*', and *what* it is, *is* its 'meaning', which reveals acceptance that requires no comment, content, or the staking out of a linguistic dualistic position, such as opinion. This style is akin to the time-honored 'Wu Wei' of the way of the Tao, whereby one effortlessly flows with life and abandons willfulness and judgment to God. Nonresistance leads to nonattachment rather than *de*tachment, which can be a form of avoidance.

Nonresistance does not mean to ignore or deny but instead to witness, observe, and be aware, which, as an experiential style, moves one from being the imaginary actor in the movie of life to being the witness/observer who is thereby emotionally uninvolved yet capable of participation. This attitude diminishes the temptation to invest in positionalities or outcomes. Thereby, personal will surrenders and Divine Will take its place where Creation is continuous, evolutionary, and subserves the unfolding of awareness.

In the above transformational process, it can be discerned that the underlying quality that activates experiencing is awareness itself. There is no 'who' witnessing, experiencing, or observing; rather, it is an innate quality that is operating effortlessly without the drain of the energy of intention to modify the process. All of life merely becomes a 'given', and awareness of the essence of subjectivity diminishes the sense of a personal 'I' or 'me' to the innate presence of the Self that is beyond thinkingness of content, but instead encompasses it. This awareness is the 'Light' by which we 'see' mentally and emotionally. By this awareness, focus now turns inward to the source of the Light instead of to the details of what is illuminated. It is solely by this Light that one can even be aware of the content of mind, or else how would one even know what one is experiencing or thinking about?

Distractions and Attractions

The animal energy of the ego results in focus by which psychic energy is directed and thereby emotionalized. The emotionalized mental content then attracts attention and becomes self-propagating. The result is attractions and aversions, as well as diversions, that eventually lead to entrapment as routine behaviors that, by the cathexis of energy and interest, gain importance and eventual levels of dominant behaviors, feelings, and thinking. These eventuate as energy fields of consciousness that align with and become entrained with the overall impersonal attractor fields of human consciousness. Thus, by selection of options, the individual 'tunes in' like a receiving set does with radio or television frequencies. Thus, to fear or hate attunes to frequencies completely different from those of forgiveness or acceptance. Each consciousness level influences perception, associated attitudes, and their concomitant positionalities.

Addiction to the ego's proclivities is like intoxication where pleasure is derived from the emotional payoff of negativity. Thus, negative positionalities tend to be self-perpetuating habits akin to addiction, based on presumptions and the inner seductive lure of the gratification of basic animal instincts. By repetition, they eventually gain dominance and control, which is the innate purpose of the narcissistic ego in the first place.

In spiritual work, these are termed 'temptations', and it is then presumed that sacrifice is necessary to give them up because one is relinquishing the pleasure of the emotional 'juice' of 'being right', 'getting even', feeling sorry for oneself, etc. A Pavlovian type of conditioning takes place as a self-reinforcing reward system that then becomes autonomous. Subsequent to that, interference with these surreptitious gratifications results in an unpleasant feeling of frustration and deprivation. Thus, it can be commonly observed that the ego's emotional mind clings to negativity and slavish bondage, and it mightily resists letting go and moving on to higher levels of functioning and coping mechanisms. As an example, the pit of resentment/blame/self-pity/victim is commonly a circuitous trap that quickly seeks validation by social encouragement and the pseudoimportance of self-inflating positionalities.

It is not uncommon for people to spend an entire lifetime nursing a grudge with elaborate justifications, retrospective falsification of memory, and deceptions. This commonly observed psychological complex is composed of a circuitous mix of all the consciousness levels below 200. It becomes highly defended and stubbornly immune to any challenge, much less the willingness to let go or surrender. As a result, forgiveness, acceptance, reason, and love are seen as antithetical to the ego's secret inner purposes.

It is not uncommon for people to destroy their entire lives in defense of nonintegrous fallacies that are carefully nurtured and clung to about them- .

selves, others, and the world. Self-deception is an innate defect of the emotional ego/mind, which, without the light of spiritual truth, is self-reinforcing, resulting in destructive consequences that preclude actual happiness. The victim is unable to discern pleasure (derived from the negativity) from actual happiness, which is really unknown by such people. This pathological complex is so strongly defended that people actually choose to die rather than give it up or even question its self-defeating premises. Fortuitously, this vicious cycle is sometimes interrupted by a confrontational life crisis that ends up being a blessing in disguise.

Escape to Freedom from the Emotional Ego/Body/Mind

The levels below calibration level 200 tend to be self-propagating because of the seductive emotional pleasure of the ego's animal-instinct pay-off. The only way out is by integrous self-honesty, which, unfortunately, is not even possible to accomplish when one is dominated and captured by this negative emotional complex. Because this complex consists of the animal energies of force, it is only the more powerful energies of truth that have any capacity to bring forth recovery. Due to the nature of Divinity, intervention is by invitation since Love is power and does not operate by instruments of force. Compassion arises from realizing that seventy-eight percent of the world's population calibrates below the level of Truth at 200, and this figure rises close to one-hundred percent in some subcultures and regions of the world that survive primarily by virtue of only animal instincts.

A Simple Two-Step Escape from the Negativity of the Ego: The Mechanism of Truth

To transcend all these limitations and cut through the complexity, it is only necessary to accept two ideas:

1. Negativity is based on an energetic *force* (animal origin) that can be overcome only by *power,* which is solely of Divine origin. Therefore, it is operationally necessary to request and invoke God's help by whatever means available.

2. Disidentify with the body/emotions/mind as 'me'. Be truthful and admit that they are *yours* but not *you.* While this may seem artificial, strange, foreign, and unnatural in the beginning, the basic reality is that it is a truth of higher order, which makes it a very powerful and formidable tool. The mind will try to deny this reality as well as truth (that is what it is 'supposed to do') because Truth is intuited as its nemesis.

Millions of people over the ages and in current life have been willing to actually die rather than acknowledge these two simple premises. People are willing to blow up themselves and others rather than admit they could be mistaken. Realize that the ego will happily lead you to your death and kill you rather than humbly admit that it made a mistake or could even be oh, that most horrible of all words: "Wrong."

Better than death and a hellish life is it to grow up and admit that the mind is misleading, cunning, ruthless, and not one's friend! The core of the ego is narcissistic pride, and secretly, it thinks that it *is* God. Without undue strain, it can be caught in its secret, inflationary, dualistic presumptions, which are undone by simple humility. This is the doorway to freedom and the experience of happiness.

One discovers the true nature of the mind when one tries to escape its clutches. When analyzed, the mind is seen to be a complexity of the presumption of 'my' thoughts plus a collection of observed factual data. Data is useful; in contrast, thoughts and views about that data are unreliable and, of necessity, distorted by the supposition of their being 'mine', with all the attendant positionalities.

Once thoughts or feelings are labeled as 'mine', they become magically imbued with presumptive omniscience and an assumed sovereign validity. These constitute what has classically been described in all spiritual literature as illusion, which frequently progresses to delusion. Unless stopped by integrous doubt and questioning, the rampant mind is on an endless siege to defeat reliable, verifiable truth, which would thereby challenge its presumptive sovereignty (i.e., the universal human proclivity to defend being 'right' against all evidence to the contrary).

The undoing of domination by the mind can be accomplished by one single step—humility—which is reinforced by simply recognizing that the mind is not sovereign, omniscient, or even capable of telling truth from falsehood. It has a utilitarian value when it comes to physical survival and the recognition of objects. Even when it comes to recognizing the physical world, the mind is incapable of understanding what the world means, just as it does not even recognize the ultrasimple observation that Evolution *is* Creation.

The mind is a useful tool within the protective confines and rules of logic and reason or intrinsic operational constraints and discipline. Thus, the mind is at its best when it operates as science, which does not allow for emotionality or the violation of logic. A friend once said, "I just realized that I don't have to have an opinion about everything—what a relief!" This discovery led to the enjoyment of greater freedom because opinions are imprisoning and restrictive, as well as routinely contentious and argumentative.

If thoughts or ideas are not really 'mine', then whence do they arise and who is their author? Actually, they don't have a 'who' of origin at all but instead merely arise from a 'what'. The content of a calibratable field of consciousness is like a thought bank regimented by a specific energy field of a level of the collective consciousness of mankind. Similar thoughts, concepts, and ideas congregate at various levels and are orchestrated under the influence of the attention of the central 'attractor field' that, like gravity, attracts ideas of similar gravity or density. The phenomenon is similar to the stratification of fishes and life forms at different depths of the sea. In human life, there are bottom feeders as well as those who leap above the surface of the water.

Certain types of thinking styles, belief systems, and *memes* (catchy phrases) are endemic to certain societies and subcultures that have been dominated by myths over the centuries. For example, there are major countries where integrity, honesty, and fairness are not even considered to be important in daily transactions. Instead, all interactions are based entirely on gain, and deception is a valued social technique and skill. In such a culture, morality is not only absent but also viewed as irrational, of no value, and indicative of weakness, as many naïve tourists discover when they return home with a supposedly priceless antiquity and discover it is actually worth only a few cents.

Clarification of the Ubiquitous Victim/Perpetrator Dualistic Fallacy

By spiritual endeavor, one discovers that it is *one-self* who has been a captive and a 'victim' ensnared by the clever deceptions of the ego. All of the ego's tricks can be observed in the evolution of the various species of the animal kingdom over great periods of time where entrapment, deception, rivalry, ego gain, self-servingness, camouflage, and force subserve survival. The evolution of the hominid eventuated as Homo sapiens, and concordantly, the prefrontal cortex emerged in front of the animal brain, which remained under the domination of animal instincts up to con-sciousness level 200. The animal instincts are totally directed to personal gain and continue to follow that path in conflict with the energy of spiritual power, truth, and especially love. The ego's deception is clever in that it deludes its victim and prisoner into believing that the perpetrators are 'out there', whereas they are actually innate and 'in here'.

What is the identity of the real perpetrator? Upon investigation, it will be found that there is no 'who' but just the energy field of a specific level of consciousness

that arose throughout evolutionary time and still prevails, and by which the majority of the world's population is dominated or still imprisoned. One can thereby
see the wisdom and truth of the Buddha's saying, "Rare
it is to be born a human being; rarer still to hear the
truth, and even rarer still, having heard the truth, to pursue it." The truth of the statement is verified by consciousness calibration, which identifies that only 0.4
percent of the world's population is capable of reaching the state of Unconditional Love.

Unconditional Love is a practical, reasonable, and
reachable goal in a human lifetime. From that level,
spiritual commitment and dedication evolve into states
of exquisite joy—even ecstasy—and eventually reach
the level of Peace at 600, which is the beginning level
of the mystic. The way of the mystic, in the true classical meaning of the term, can be defined as *Devotional
Nonduality*.

CHAPTER 21

Transcending The Mind

Introduction

In transcending the levels of consciousness, choices and options experientially tend to appear as seeming opposites or conflicting dualities. These are experienced as aversions or attractions that can seem difficult to dissolve unless they are disassembled. Attraction implies either surreptitious or overt pleasure, and aversion expresses expectations of displeasure or discomfort. Choices are also complicated by a moralistic sense of duty in the form of 'should' or 'ought to' and therefore may become resisted by inferences of subtle guilt and the temptation of avoidance. It is therefore best to eschew all presumptions, such as 'should'. A primary quality of spiritual evolution is freedom. Opportunities for change can be seen as invitations rather than as moral obligations, and these options really offer greater degrees of freedom and inner happiness. However, one is free at all times to hold them in abeyance, and then, at a different time in a different context, the choice or decision may come about more naturally.

The seeming obstacles along the path consist of two components: (1) a seemingly attractive pay-off or pleasure, and (2) fear of its presumptive alternative (i.e., lack of pleasure). Many of these conflicting pairs are innate to 'human nature' and were inherited along with human life itself as it evolved. These are to be expected as routine thresholds to be crossed by anyone seeking higher levels of consciousness. In actual experience, they are not as formidable as they may seem initially, and success with even a few of them brings confidence and realistic expectations of greater success as one progresses. The key elements are to spot the specific components of the conflict and to take advantage of the Spiritual Will, which is surprisingly powerful (cal. 850) and intervenes when one asks for God's help, followed by the willingness to surrender the pay-off and relinquish resisting the presumed aversion.

The common conflicting dualities can be generally grouped by similarities and can sometimes even be resolved as a class in one fell swoop.

Comparative Dualities

Anticipated Pleasure	The Fears
Control	Surrender
Familiarity, habit	Change, uncertainty, strangeness
Cling to the old	Fear of the unknown or the new
Easy way	Hard, effort
Ignore, deny, reject	Upset, look at, face
Refuse to own	Take responsibility, be accountable
'I can't'	The truth of 'I won't'
'Don't want to'	'Can't'
Rigidity, repetitious	Learn
Homeostasis, stability	Reprogram, shift, off-balance
The past as an excuse	The present as the change agent
'No will power'	Confront with lack of willingness
'Try', 'going to'	Do
'Tomorrow'	Now
Procrastinate	Failure
Pretend	Be honest
Unwilling, resistance	Acceptance

The above dualities are familiar to everyone as they generally apply to almost any endeavor to grow or evolve spiritually. Although conflicts may appear to be impossible to resolve, their resolution can actually be surprisingly simple through strict adherence to the proven tools of spiritual processing, i.e., the willingness to surrender to God at great depth and to let go of resistances by invoking the power of the Spiritual Will (cal. 850) subsequent to asking for Divine assistance. One can request help from the Holy Spirit, along with admission of the truth that "I, myself," (the ego) "am unable to accomplish this step alone." Operationally, this is actually a request to comprehend and contextualize the situation differently and thus dissolve apparent paradoxes.

The personal will operates only at the level of a person's calibrated level of consciousness at a given time in its evolution and is therefore frequently too weak to effect a desired change. Past efforts to change via the ego's mechanisms may result in doubt, a lack of self-confidence, and a refusal to face the issues out of defeatism. This is commonly expressed by the statement, "I tried," which is actually a fact—it is the small self that tried, which more often is a wish than a decisive action.

Good intentions flounder on the rocks of personal 'will power', which is frequently used as a moral club that evokes further guilt and self-blame. True, deep surrender to God cannot actually take place without surrendering the illusion of personal 'will power' and replacing it with a declarative *decision*. In everyday life, success is the consequence of dedication, persistence, and perseverance. This may seem to represent a personal sacrifice of short-term pleasures for long-term goals. In inner spiritual work, these same attributes may appear, not as a consequence of personal volition but as gifts from the Self as the answer from the Presence of God within.

A great resistance of the ego is the wish to control and derive pleasure from the ego's pay-offs. Therefore, the ego creates resistances in the form of fears, including expectations of discomfort, loss from change, or fear of failure. These, however, represent spiritual pride, which also needs to be surrendered. It is an egoistic vanity to presume that Divinity is either pleased, not pleased, or disappointed with human frailties and proclivities. Deep surrender therefore precludes programming God with presumptions and, by acceptance, surrendering to 'what will be will be', which is a more humble position. Resolution of conflicts is also a result of intention, degree of alignment, surrender of conditionalities, and the influence of karmic propensities.

Egoistic values find widespread social acceptance and rewards. In addition, these pay-offs are understood to be the consequences of cause and effect and a byproduct of doingness. With surrender of the perceived gain or loss, karmic possibilities actualize by assent and are an automatic consequence of what a person has become and not what they have or do.

As one evolves, what the world values can be seen as an encumbrance, and what the world sees as a loss can be viewed as spiritual gain or freedom. Inner peace results from surrender of either attractions or aversions. Perceived values are primarily projections of 'wants' and 'not wants'. The fewer the 'wants', the greater are the ease and satisfaction of life. Responsible stewardship of one's assets and gifts is integrous. Therefore, to avoid wealth or ostensibly to denigrate it are equally as fallacious as craving it. Pretentious poverty can also be a form of ostentation and spiritual pride. True asceticism is simply a matter of economy of effort. It is not possessions themselves but the presumed importance or value projected on them that is significant. Therefore, it is recommended that one 'wear the world like a loose garment'. Wealth, in and of itself, is of no real importance, as the capacity for inner happiness is not dependent on external factors once basic physical animal needs are met.

Egoistic attractions are reinforced by social values, cultural programming, and reward systems inflated by the media. These values are also the content of daydreams, wishful fantasies, and romanticizing. They also exhibit great variation within subcultures.

To find meaning, it is necessary to look beyond perception and appearance to discern essence. As Socrates said, everyone chooses what they perceive to be the 'good'. The problem is to discern appearance from essence in order to be able to differentiate the 'real' good from its illusory substitutes. Other than the basic requirements for physical survival and comfort, desirability is a projected value.

With discernment of essence, all that exists has an innate beauty, and its 'value' is that it is an expression of the evolution of Creation as it expresses the unmanifest's becoming Manifest. Worth is therefore innate to All that Exists by virtue of the Divine Source of Existence itself, which resides within the nonlinear and is therefore invisible to the limitations inherent to the mechanisms of perception.

Summary

Spiritual evolution is the automatic consequence of watching the mind and its proclivities as an 'it' from the general viewpoint of the paradigm of context rather than content. Instead of trying to force change, it is merely necessary to allow Divinity to do so by deeply surrendering all control, resistance, and illusions of gain or loss. It is not necessary to destroy or attack illusions but merely to allow them to fall away. It is not necessary or fruitful to use force by such mechanisms as guilt, nor is it necessary to try to pursue or propel spiritual evolution because it automatically evolves of its own accord when the obstacles and resistance of illusions are surrendered. The power of Truth itself is a quality of Divine Love that, in its infinite mercy, dissolves positionalities back into the Reality of the Self. It is also necessary to accept that timing is up to the Self, and not the self, because only the Self is capable of incorporating unknown karmic qualities.

The infinite, nonlinear field of consciousness is not only omnipresent and omniscient, but also omnipotent. Within the overall field, that which one has become automatically gravitates to its concordant level within the overall field, much like a cork rises in water as a consequence of the interaction of the cork, gravity, and the density of the water. The spirit is uplifted as the consequence of the quality of that which it has become by the consent of its own free will. Compassion for the self is an attribute of the Self. Thus, the last great resistance to be surrendered is the resistance to the ever-present Love of God.

CHAPTER 22

Becoming the Prayer

Introduction

Students often ask for practical advice on the 'how to' of pragmatically implementing spiritual truth subjectively and instituting spirituality as a way of being in the world that subserves spiritual progress and evolution. The educated student has usually already acquired a wealth of information about a multitude of spiritual practices and concepts. The transformation desired is to move from 'heard about' to 'know' to 'do' to 'be'. This progression is actually from the presumably known to the unknown, and from the familiar to the new. Thus, the actual application of spiritual information may still seem uncertain.

The mind itself becomes interested in evolution when it learns that there is a higher dimension of truth beyond customary mentation and the domains of reason and logic. The interest is then directed toward discovery and spiritual awakening.

Other students might become highly motivated by either inspiration or by fortuitous experiences that are transformative and initiate the process of consciously chosen spiritual progress and evolution. These may occur as sudden 'peak experiences' (Maslow, 1970) or even critical 'tipping point' shifts of context and perception (Gladwell, 2000). The inspired student then becomes attracted by potential, and focus of interest is on the practical application of spiritual processes in daily life.

The transition is characteristically to incorporate premises from the intellect to the experiential reality of subjectivity. Thus, the emphasis is on implementation and the actual 'doing' of spiritual practices and premises. By incorporation and practice, the new becomes habitual and the way one 'is', indicating that is what one has 'become'.

There is the emergence of actuality out of potentiality by virtue of propitious circumstances of which intention and volition are the fulcrum and activating energy. Fulfillment of potential has a positive feedback by which intention is reinforced, and the spiritual process gains momentum from the Self rather than the self.

Q: **It has been described that even only a single, very simple spiritual principle to live by is sufficient to making major progress, e.g., 'to be kind to all of life', or 'to forgive, no matter what', or 'to be of good will to all that exists', or to take a sentence or two from a favorite Psalm and reflect on it for days, weeks, or even months.**

A: That is the most effective way to begin. A single tool applied consistently and rigorously is more effective than reading all the books or having sporadic episodes of enthusiasm. Persistence is characteristic of 'one-pointedness of mind'. By analogy, by pulling on a single strand of yarn, a whole sweater unravels and becomes undone. Each step forward summons forth the appropriate, already-acquired information that amplifies and clarifies experiences. Thus, basic dictums become experiential and confirmative.

The learning phenomenon is not one of cause and effect, nor should rewarding experiences be considered as gains. By the practice of kindness, one becomes kind, for kindness itself is transformative. Thus, expectation needs to be put aside. By assent of the will, transformation occurs autonomously as a consequence of context, not just content.

To be friendly will not 'cause' others to reciprocate but it opens the nonlinear door to greater likelihood. Some people even recoil from kindness, generosity, or a friendly, benign approach that in people below 200 may trigger suspicion, embarrassment, or even guardedness or paranoia. It is useful as an experiment to just try smiling at the driver of another car next to your own that is stopped for a red light. Some drivers will return the friendliness; some will become stony faced and stare straight ahead; others will panic; and some will even pull away at great speed as soon as the light turns green. Thus, even a friendly smile has to be discrete.

Q: But how does a spiritual practice actually result in change? What are the psychological mechanisms? How can one change from a 'this' to a 'that'?

A: It is not a process of 'change', but of evolutionary emergence. The larva does not change into a butterfly but instead becomes the fulfillment of its potential as a product of the evolution of Creation. To repeat, Creation is evolution by virtue of the emergence of potentiality into actuality. Intention of the spiritual will is sufficient. The seemingly 'new' represents the unmanifest's becoming Manifest, just as unclenching the fist reveals the open hand.

Actualization is an option and a choice as an aspect of the will. Each positive choice increases the likelihood and probability of additional positive choices (which is also in accordance with quantum theory). Each positive choice moves one closer to a higher attractor field of consciousness. In the secular world where 'the rich get richer and the poor get poorer', it is equally true that by integrity and effort, the formerly poor can become rich, and the formerly rich, through error, can become bankrupt. Human life offers a great value as being the optimum opportunity for spiritual evolution. By choice, the 'iron filing' of the spirit is drawn to the various regions of the great omnipotent, omnipresent field of consciousness itself. This is analogous to the effect of a giant electromagnetic field of infinite power.

Q: But does not this definition of contextualization introduce the arguable concept of 'free will'?

A: The arguments about free will are usually spurious by virtue of inadequate contextualization and reliance on the hypothetical. They then end up as discursive, circuitous intellectualizations in which the unconscious hope is that free will will be negated as a possible reality, thus avoiding spiritual responsibility or accountability.

Options have parameters out of which arise responsibility as well as culpability. The range of options is the consequence of a great multiplicity of factors, both known and unknown, including what could be best termed karmic proclivities or momentum. These are further influenced by probability, including past rewards and failures, and also by intensity of effort, dedication, degree of integrity, etc. The hypothetical is not a reality, and the range of choices is a result of the distillation of complex factors, both linear and nonlinear. Thus, under different circumstances or prevailing conditions, quite different options may be available as well as chosen. Because of the nature of evolution/Creation, content and conscious context are transitory and descriptively, as well as experientially, ephemeral.

To surrender to God's Will and ask for Divine Guidance is so powerful that it alters the available options as well as their perceived values. From nonlinear dynamics also emerges the principle of 'iteration' by which a repeated choice or option progressively becomes a likelihood ('sensitive dependence on initial conditions').

Q: **What about major revelations or spiritual experiences that result in sudden major changes?**

A: It is by vibrational repetition that avalanches and other major natural phenomena occur. Egoistic positions become weakened by virtue of seemingly minor and insignificant steps. For example, even just saying "thank you" wherever possible can result in becoming a more grateful and generous person who, by attraction, now effortlessly sends forth benefits previously nonachievable by effort.

Major changes also occur as a consequence of release from negative karmic obligations. It is as though the unconscious mind is finally satisfied that a lesson has been learned or a debt has been settled by compensatory behaviors. In many ways, spiritual learning is also similar to new skills acquired by repetition and practice until they become natural, like one's second nature, and habitual. Learning is also facilitated by inspiration and identification with admired figures who display the desired attributes. We tend to become like those whom we admire.

Q: **What qualities are of major help to a devotee other than familiarity with advanced spiritual/consciousness information?**

A: Adopt the attitudes associated with Higher Mind (Overview, Section II) and select any of the virtues. Refuse or reject negative attitudes or positionalities. Act in a gracious manner in all circumstances towards oneself and others. Reject the violation of spiritual principles for short-term gain. Create an idealized image of oneself and practice it as if for a movie role.

Acting 'as if' brings to awareness the potentiality to actually become that which is admired. As a learning device, it is often surprisingly effective to 'pretend' to be the quality that is desired, and then, much to one's surprise, discover that it has been a nonactivated and latent aspect of one's own potentiality. Many people make self-improvement the number one priority in their lives and identify with admired figures instead of envying them.

As a practical exercise, before leaving the house, review how one would like oneself to be and decide to act that way. In so doing, note the response of others to one's being friendly, considerate, gracious, or loving. Decline seduction and temptation by that which is tawdry and sensational. Surrender the dubious pleasure of 'getting even' or 'getting the best of a deal' in emotional interchanges.

As a pleasant exercise, consciously and purposely allow other people to 'win' and thus discover one's own inner greatness and generosity. To be emotionally stingy creates emotional poverty. Every 'win' that one gives others paradoxically makes one richer, and by practice, one ends up emotionally wealthy.

Q: Is that not self-effacing or 'people pleasing'?

A: These are illusory attitudes consequent to spiritual poverty and low self-esteem. To act from spiritual Grace means being magnanimous because the source of Grace is Love, which is unlimited and nascent within. To act small and mean from stinginess supports spiritual poverty and closes the door to the Source of Infinite Grace that is already present as the Self.

The small self acts from limitation and sees itself as needy and insufficient. It is therefore defensive and watchful for gain. The small self is miserly, guarded, and greedy. It is experientially unaware that there is an alternative Self that merely awaits activation by invitation and assent. The small self is fearful and unwilling to trust the Self; therefore, transcendence requires both faith and courage.

Q: **By example, you often use humor during lectures and interpersonal interaction. People are often surprised because they have an image of a spiritual teacher as being serious and pious or as an orator of exhilarative, inspirational exhortation.**

A: The paradox is that humor is actually a quite serious approach to spiritual conflicts and dilemmas and is often far more effective than platitudinous homilies. Humor arises from abundance of good will. It offsets and precludes emotional pain and anxiety, and it transcends the negative by exposing unspoken fallacies that would otherwise be unapproachable.

By owning a fallacy as a hidden aspect of one's own personality, its absurdity is revealed. That is the mechanism of hyperbole that exposes invalid belief systems that are offered by rationalized distortions of truth. Humor bridges the gap between *res interna (cogitans)* and *res externa* (the world the way it is). Therefore, it forms a striking contrast between what the mind perceives or believes and the essence of the underlying reality. Humor thus exposes the ego's self-serving deceptions. Humor reveals alternative viewpoints and options and is therefore liberating and freeing. Clinically, it is also associated with improved health and even longevity. Humorists characteristically calibrate in the high 400s, are long-lived and beloved by everyone. Humor exposes the suppressed aspects of the human psyche so they can be identified and more easily acknowledged, owned, and thereby transcended by the transparency of their fallacy. One need not be defensive about human frailties and foibles if they are recognized, accepted, and owned. True spiritual awareness arises from recognition of essence.

Great humorists are beloved because their strength to own, face, and laugh at human weakness reveals the listeners' capacity to do the same. The effect of humor is therapeutic, and it also increases human bonding and compassion via mutual recognition. Humor reduces inner pain, shame, and guilt, thereby revealing more benign options.

Psychological denial stems from guilt, and when guilt is assuaged, inner honesty ensues. Humor is the antidote to emotional/psychological/spiritual poverty and its proclivity to smallness, meanness, and lack of stature.

Q: **Is humor therefore a palatable avenue by which to approach the painful downside of one's ego?**

A: Yes. It serves as the example of therapeutic/spiritual techniques that lead to inner freedom, honesty, and liberation. It is an antidote to shame, fear, and guilt. It subtly reveals the capacity of inner strength that allows the recognition of one's innate, nascent bigness. With humor, the unapproachable becomes available for recognition, ownership, and transcendence. Humor facilitates inner integrity. In contrast, the unmodified ego is humorless and grim.

Q: How does humor fit in with devotion? Are they not diverse?

A: Devotion is the dedication to Truth and Love by which humor becomes a handmaiden to assist in realizing the goal. It diminishes the value of fallacy by contrasting truth with falsehood by putting them into juxtaposition. The underlying intention of humor is actually quite serious and dedicated to liberation from illusion, fear, hatred, and guilt. It unmasks the ego, thereby decreasing its dominance. It leads away from the self to the Self.

Q: How does that come about?

A: The ego's programs are linear and are comprised and defined by the restriction of content. The spirit, or Self, is nonlinear and represents context. The restricted linear content of the ego is relinquished via exposure of the nonreality of its perceptions and positionalities. One can see that the ego's perceptions are aligned with conquest and gain. When the fallacies of its propositions are exposed to the daylight of awareness, the dominance of illusion fades away.

Realization of the Self is neither a gain nor an acquisition. It is the Realization that unfolds of its own when the obstructions are surrendered or removed. Efforting is merely the consequence of resistance that, in turn, is the product of illusion. As the clouds in the sky fade away, the sun shines forth of its own. The Presence within is to be welcomed, loved, and not feared for it is ultimately benign and reveals the transformative power of Love. The concept of God as fearful is actually the ultimate joke of the ego's theatre of the absurd.

Q: **How does devotion come to be a dominant quality?**
A: Accept that one is attracted by the destination rather than propelled by the past. The evolution of consciousness is one's karmic inheritance because it is a quality innate to human consciousness itself. Courage arises from commitment and integrity of alignment and dedication. A valuable characteristic of dedication is felicity, which eventually becomes empowered as a quiet but persistent inner fervor. The value of watchful witnessing is that even just awareness of an ego defect tends to undo it. By surrender and prayerful invocation, Divine Will facilitates transition from the lesser to the greater for the Self effortlessly supports and energizes intention. The Self is like a magnetic attraction by which the personal will is progressively surrendered and resistance is weakened. Thus, the pathway itself is self-fulfilling, gratifying, and reveals progressive rewards. Each step, no matter how seemingly small, is equally valuable.

Q: What about the effect of the Spiritual Teacher?

A: The consciousness level of the Teacher via silent transmission also facilitates transformation of information from the mental to a subjective experiential reality. The consciousness level and vibrational energy field of the aura of the Teacher is a product of the evolution of consciousness and is not personal. It activates nascent qualities in the student on a nonverbal level. By analogy, it could be termed the spiritual equivalent of the previously mentioned 'Roger Bannister effect'. It transmits as a high-frequency, high-energy field via the aura. Its quality derives from certainty that is based on experiential Reality. The same phenomenon is accepted by recovery groups in which the sponsor's power is derived from successful experience and, therefore, mastery of the presenting problem. Such spiritual groups radiate a high energy field that then benefits the newcomer by individual and group alignment maintained by self-honesty.

Each level of consciousness represents an attractor field that dominates a specific field of consciousness by virtue of its innate intrinsic power. In large groups of long standing, this is referred to literally as 'the Higher Power'. Often the word 'God' is avoided because it is prone to error of definition and multiple conflicting belief systems, including fear and guilt about anthropomorphic depictions of God.

To assist spiritual progress, choose verifiable teachers and teachings and avoid those that have something to gain by one's adherence to or align-

ment with them. Avoid groups or teachers that are
needy, acquisitive, or controlling. The Self is completely fulfilling and has no needs and nothing to
gain. The Teacher is a Servant of Truth and not its
originator. All serve God who strive for God.

Throughout the spiritual scriptures is the declaration, restated in different cultures and languages,
that Divinity is responsive to allegiance. It is usually
stated is some style such as "Those who acknowledge me are Mine." From these words, it is apparent
that it is not how far one is along the road that is
important but the fact that one is *on* the road.

*Gloria
in
Excelsis
Deo!*

Appendices

APPENDIX A

MAP OF THE SCALE OF CONSCIOUSNESS®

God-view	Life-view	Level		Log	Emotion	Process
Self	Is	Enlightenment	⇧	700-1000	Ineffable	Pure Consciousness
All-Being	Perfect	Peace	⇧	600	Bliss	Illumination
One	Complete	Joy	⇧	540	Serenity	Transfiguration
Loving	Benign	Love	⇧	500	Reverence	Revelation
Wise	Meaningful	Reason	⇧	400	Understanding	Abstraction
Merciful	Harmonious	Acceptance	⇧	350	Forgiveness	Transcendence
Inspiring	Hopeful	Willingness	⇧	310	Optimism	Intention
Enabling	Satisfactory	Neutrality	⇧	250	Trust	Release
Permitting	Feasible	Courage	⇕	200	Affirmation	Empowerment
Indifferent	Demanding	Pride	⇩	175	Scorn	Inflation
Vengeful	Antagonistic	Anger	⇩	150	Hate	Aggression
Denying	Disappointing	Desire	⇩	125	Craving	Enslavement
Punitive	Frightening	Fear	⇩	100	Anxiety	Withdrawal
Disdainful	Tragic	Grief	⇩	75	Regret	Despondency
Condemning	Hopeless	Apathy	⇩	50	Despair	Abdication
Vindictive	Evil	Guilt	⇩	30	Blame	Destruction
Despising	Miserable	Shame	⇩	20	Humiliation	Elimination

APPENDIX B

HOW TO CALIBRATE
THE LEVELS OF CONSCIOUSNESS

General Information

The energy field of consciousness is infinite in dimension. Specific levels correlate with human consciousness and have been calibrated from '1' to '1,000'. (See Appendix B: Map of the Scale of Consciousness.) These energy fields reflect and dominate human consciousness.

Everything in the universe radiates a specific frequency or minute energy field that remains in the field of consciousness permanently. Thus, every person or being that ever lived and anything about them, including any event, thought, deed, feeling, or attitude, is recorded forever and can be retrieved at any time in the present or the future.

Technique

The muscle-testing response is a simple "yes" or "not yes" (no) response to a specific stimulus. It is usually done by the subject holding out an extended arm and the tester pressing down on the wrist of the extended arm, using two fingers and light pressure. Usually the subject holds a substance to be tested over their solar plexus with the other hand. The tester says to the test subject, "Resist," and if the substance being tested is beneficial to the subject, the arm will be strong. If it is not beneficial or it has an adverse effect, the arm will go weak. The response is very quick and brief.

It is important to note that the intention, as well as both the tester and the one being tested, must calibrate over 200 in order to obtain accurate responses.

Experience from online discussion groups has shown that many students obtain inaccurate results. Further research shows that at calibration 200, there is still a thirty-percent chance of error. Additionally, less than twelve percent of the students have consistent accuracy, mainly due to unconsciously held positionalities (Jeffery and Colyer, 2007). The higher the levels of consciousness of the test team, the more accurate are the results. The best attitude is one of clinical detachment, posing a statement with the prefix statement, "In the name of the highest good, _____ calibrates as true. Over 100. Over 200," etc. The contextualization "in the highest good" increases accuracy because it transcends self-serving personal interest and motives.

For many years, the test was thought to be a local response of the body's acupuncture or immune system. Later research, however, has revealed that the response is not a local response to the body at all, but instead is a general response of consciousness itself to the energy of a substance or a statement. That which is true, beneficial, or pro-life gives a positive response that stems from the impersonal field of consciousness, which is present in everyone living. This positive response is indicated by the body's musculature going strong. There is also an associated pupillary response (the eyes dilate with falsity and constrict to truth) as well as alterations in brain function as revealed by magnetic imaging. (For convenience, the deltoid muscle is usually the one best used as an indicator muscle; however, any of the muscles of the body can be used.)

Before a question (in the form of a statement) is presented, it is necessary to qualify 'permission'; that is, state, "I have permission to ask about what I am holding in mind." (Yes/No) Or, "This calibration serves the highest good."

If a statement is false or a substance is injurious, the muscles go weak quickly in response to the command, "Resist." This indicates the stimulus is negative, untrue, anti-life, or the answer is "no." The response is fast and brief in duration. The body will then rapidly recover and return to normal muscle tension.

There are three ways of doing the testing. The one that is used in research and also most generally used requires two people: the tester and the test subject. A quiet setting is preferred, with no background music. The test subject closes their eyes. *The tester must phrase the 'question' to be asked in the form of a statement.* The statement can then be answered as "yes" or "no" by the muscle response. For instance, the *incorrect* form would be to ask, "Is this a healthy horse?" The correct form is to make the statement, "This horse is healthy," or its corollary, "This horse is sick."

After making the statement, the tester says "Resist" to the test subject who is holding the extended arm parallel to the ground. The tester presses down with two fingers on the wrist of the extended arm sharply, with mild force. The test subject's arm will either stay strong, indicating a "yes," or go weak, indicating a "not yes" (no). The response is short and immediate.

A second method is the 'O-ring' method, which can be done alone. The thumb and middle finger of the same hand are held tightly in an 'O' configuration, and the hooked forefinger of the opposite hand is used to try to pull them apart. There is a noticeable difference of the strength between a "yes" and a "no" response (Rose, 2001).

The third method is the simplest, yet, like the others, requires some practice. Simply lift a heavy object, such as a large dictionary or merely a couple of bricks, from a table about waist high. Hold in mind an image or true statement to be calibrated and then lift. Then, for contrast, hold in mind that which is known to be false. Note the ease of lifting when truth is held in mind and the greater effort necessary to lift the load when the issue is false (not true). The results can be verified using the other two methods.

Calibration of Specific Levels

The critical point between positive and negative, between true and false, or between that which is constructive or destructive, is at the calibrated level of 200 (see Map in Appendix B). Anything above 200, or true, makes the subject go strong; anything below 200, or false, allows the arm to go weak.

Anything past or present, including images or statements, historical events, or personages, can be tested. They need not be verbalized.

Numerical Calibration

Example: "Ramana Maharshi teachings calibrate over 700." (Y/N). Or, "Hitler calibrated over 200." (Y/N)

"When he was in his 20s." (Y/N) "His 30s." (Y/N) "His 40s." (Y/N) "At the time of his death." (Y/N)

Applications

The muscle test cannot be used to foretell the future; otherwise, there are no limits as to what can be asked. Consciousness has no limits in time or space; however, permission may be denied. All current or historical events are available for questioning. The answers are impersonal and do not depend on the belief systems of either the tester or the test subject. For example, protoplasm recoils from noxious stimuli and flesh bleeds. Those are the qualities of these test materials and are impersonal. Consciousness actually knows only truth because only truth has actual existence. It does not respond to falsehood because falsehood does not have existence in Reality. It will also not respond accurately to nonintegrous or egoistic questions.

Accurately speaking, the test response is either an 'on' response or merely a 'not on' response. Like the electrical switch, we say the electricity is "on," and when we use the term "off," we just mean that it is not there. In reality, there is no such thing as 'off-ness'. This is a subtle statement but crucial to the understanding of the nature of consciousness. Consciousness is capable of recognizing only Truth. It merely fails to respond to falsehood. Similarly, a mirror reflects an image only if there is an object to reflect. If no object is present to the mirror, there is no reflected image.

To Calibrate A Level

Calibrated levels are relative to a specific reference

scale. To arrive at the same figures as in the chart in Appendix B, reference must be made to that table or by a statement such as, "On a scale of human consciousness from 1 to 1,000, where 600 indicates Enlightenment, this _____ calibrates over _____ (a number)." Or, "On a scale of consciousness where 200 is the level of Truth and 500 is the level of Love, this statement calibrates over _____." (State a specific number.)

General Information
People generally want to determine truth from falsehood. Therefore, the statement has to be made very specifically. Avoid using general terms such as a 'good' job to apply for. 'Good' in what way? Pay scale? Working conditions? Promotional opportunities? Fairness of the boss?

Expertise
Familiarity with the test brings progressive expertise. The 'right' questions to ask begin to spring forth and can become almost uncannily accurate. If the same tester and test subject work together for a period of time, one or both of them will develop what can become an amazing accuracy and capability of pinpointing just what specific questions to ask, even though the subject is totally unknown by either one. For instance, the tester has lost an object and begins by saying, "I left it in my office." (Answer: No.) "I left it in the car." (Answer: No.) All of a sudden, the test subject almost 'sees' the object and says, "Ask, 'On the back of the bathroom door.'" The test subject says, "The object

is hanging on the back of the bathroom door." (Answer: Yes.) In this actual case, the test subject did not even know that the tester had stopped for gas and left a jacket in the restroom of a gasoline station.

Any information can be obtained about anything anywhere in current or past time or space, depending on receiving prior permission. (Sometimes one gets a "no," perhaps for karmic or other unknown reasons.) By cross-checking, accuracy can be easily confirmed. For anyone who learns the technique, more information is available instantaneously than can be held in all the computers and libraries of the world. The possibilities are therefore obviously unlimited, and the prospects breathtaking.

Limitations

The test is accurate only if the test subjects themselves calibrate over 200 and the intention for the use of the test is integrous and also calibrates over 200. The requirement is one of detached objectivity and alignment with truth rather than subjective opinion. Thus, to try to 'prove a point' negates accuracy. Sometimes married couples, for reasons as yet undiscovered, are unable to use each other as test subjects and may have to find a third person to be a test partner.

A suitable test subject is a person whose arm goes strong when a love object or person is held in mind, and it goes weak if that which is negative (fear, hate, guilt, etc.) is held in mind (e.g., Winston Churchill makes one go strong, and bin Laden makes one go weak).

Occasionally, a suitable test subject gives paradoxical responses. This can usually be cleared by doing the 'thymic thump'. (With a closed fist, thump three times over the upper breastbone, smile, and say "ha-ha-ha" with each thump and mentally picture someone or something that is loved.) The temporary imbalance will then clear up.

The imbalance may be the result of recently having been with negative people, listening to heavy-metal rock music, watching violent television programs, playing violent video games, etc. Negative music energy has a deleterious effect on the energy system of the body for up to one-half hour after it is turned off. Television commercials or background are also a common source of negative energy.

As previously noted, this method of discerning truth from falsehood and the calibrated levels of truth has strict requirements. Because of the limitations, calibrated levels are supplied for ready reference in prior books, and extensively in *Truth vs. Falsehood*.

Explanation

The muscle-strength test is independent of personal opinion or beliefs and is an impersonal response of the field of consciousness, just as protoplasm is impersonal in its responses. This can be demonstrated by the observation that the test responses are the same whether verbalized or held silently in mind. Thus, the test subject is not influenced by the question as they do not even know what it is. To demonstrate this, do the following exercise:

The tester holds in mind an image unknown to the test subject and states, "The image I am holding in mind is positive" (or "true," or "calibrates over 200," etc.). Upon direction, the test subject then resists the downward pressure on the wrist. If the tester holds a positive image in mind (e.g., Abraham Lincoln, Jesus, Mother Teresa, etc.), the test subject's arm muscle will go strong. If the tester holds a false statement or negative image in mind (e.g., bin Laden, Hitler, etc.), the arm will go weak. Inasmuch as the test subject does not know what the tester has in mind, the results are not influenced by personal beliefs.

Disqualification

Both skepticism (cal. 160) and cynicism, as well as atheism, calibrate below 200 because they reflect negative prejudgment. In contrast, true inquiry requires an open mind and honesty devoid of intellectual vanity. Negative studies of the testing methodology *all* calibrate below 200 (usually at 160), as do the investigators themselves.

That even famous professors can and do calibrate below 200 may seem surprising to the average person. Thus, negative studies are a consequence of negative bias. As an example, Francis Crick's research design that led to the discovery of the double helix pattern of DNA calibrated at 440. His last research design, which was intended to prove that consciousness was just a product of neuronal activity, calibrated at only 135. (He was an atheist.)

The failure of investigators who themselves, or by faulty research design, calibrate below 200 (all calibrate at approximately 160), confirms the truth of the very methodology they claim to disprove. They 'should' get negative results, and so they do, which paradoxically proves the accuracy of the test to detect the difference between unbiased integrity and nonintegrity.

Any new discovery may upset the apple cart and be viewed as a threat to the status quo of prevailing belief systems. That consciousness research validates spiritual Reality is, of course, going to precipitate resistance, as it is actually a direct confrontation to the dominion of the narcissistic core of the ego itself, which is innately presumptuous and opinionated.

Below consciousness level 200, comprehension is limited by the dominance of Lower Mind, which is capable of recognizing facts but not yet able to grasp what is meant by the term 'truth' (it confuses *res interna* with *res externa*), and that truth has physiological accompaniments that are different from falsehood. Additionally, truth is intuited as evidenced by the use of voice analysis, the study of body language, pupillary response, EEG changes in the brain, fluctuations in breathing and blood pressure, galvanic skin response, dowsing, and even the Huna technique of measuring the distance that the aura radiates from the body. Some people have a very simple technique that utilizes the standing body like a pendulum (fall forward with truth and backward with falsehood).

From a more advanced contextualization, the principles that prevail are that Truth cannot be disproved by falsehood any more than light can be disproved by darkness. The nonlinear is not subject to the limitations of the linear. Truth is of a different paradigm from logic and thus is not 'provable', as that which is provable calibrates only in the 400s. Consciousness research methodology operates at level 600, which is at the interface of the linear and the nonlinear dimensions.

Discrepancies
Differing calibrations may be obtained over time or by different investigators for a variety of reasons:
1. Situations, people, politics, policies, and attitudes change over time.
2. People tend to use different sensory modalities when they hold something in mind, i.e., visual, sensory, auditory, or feeling. 'Your mother' could therefore be how she looked, felt, sounded, etc., or Henry Ford could be calibrated as a father, as an industrialist, for his impact on America, his anti-Semitism, etc.
3. Accuracy increases with the level of consciousness. (The 400s and above are the most accurate.)
One can specify context and stick to a prevailing modality. The same team using the same technique will get results that are internally consistent. Expertise develops with practice. There are some people, however, who are incapable of a scientific, detached attitude and are unable to be objective, and for whom the testing method will therefore not be accurate. Dedication and intention to the truth has to be given priority over personal opinions and trying to prove them as being "right."

Note
While it was discovered that the technique does not work for people who calibrate at less than level 200, only quite recently was it further discovered that

the technique does not work if the persons doing the testing are atheists. This may be simply the consequence of the fact that atheism calibrates below level 200, and that negation of the truth or Divinity (omniscience) karmically disqualifies the negator just as hate negates love.

Also recently discovered was that the capacity for accuracy of consciousness calibration testing increases the higher the level of consciousness of the testers. People in the range of the high 400s and above get the most reliably accurate test results (Jeffrey and Colyer, 2007).

APPENDIX C

REFERENCES

A Course in Miracles. (1975) 1996. Mill Valley, Calif.: Foundation for Inner Peace.

Adler, J., V. Juarez, et al. (and editorial staff). 2005. "Spirituality in America." Special Report. *Newsweek,* August-September, 46-66.

Almeder, R. 1998. *Harmless Naturalism: The Limits of Science and the Nature of Philosophy.* Peru, Ill.: Open Court Publishing Co. (Limits of Scientism; expanding epistemology to account for the nonprovable subjective experience.)

American Psychiatric Assn. 2000. *Diagnostic and Statistical Manual of Mental Disorders* DSM-IV-TR, 4th ed. Arlington, Va.: American Psychiatric Assn.

Anderson, S., and P. Ray. 2000. *The Cultural Creatives: How 50 Million People Are Changing the World.* New York: Harmony Books.

Arehart-Treichal, J. 2005. "Witnessing Violence Makes Youth More Prone to Violence." *Psychiatric News,* 1 July.

―――. 2005. "Serotonin Gene Variant Linked to Anxiety and Depression." *Psychiatric News,* 18 March. (Overactive amygdala via 5-HT transporter gene.)

―――. 2004. "Gene Variant, Family Factors Raise Risk of Conduct Disorder." *Psychiatric News,* n.d.

―――. 2004. "Brain Receptor Abnormality Likened to Alcoholism Risk." *Psychiatric News,* 5 November. (Brain opiate system, NMDA receptor abnormality genetic.)

Bailey, A. 1950. *Glamour: A World Problem.* New York: Lucis Press.

Beauregard, M. (ed.) 2003. "Consciousness, Emotional Self-Regulation, and The Brain." *Advances in Consciousness Research 54.* New York: John Benjamins Publishing Co.

Begley, S. 2004. "Scans of Monks' Brains Show Meditation Alters Structure and Functioning." *Science Journal,* 5 November. (Proceedings of National Academy of Science.)

Benoit, H. [1955] 1990. *Zen and the Psychology of Transformation: The Supreme Doctrine.* Rochester, Vt.: Inner Traditions – Bear & Company.

Bogart, L. 2005. *Over the Edge: Hot Pursuit of Youth by Marketers and Media Has Changed American Culture*. Chicago: Ivan R. Dee, Publisher.

Brinkley, D. 1994. *Saved by the Light*. New York: Random House.

Bristow, D., et al. 2005. "Blinking suppresses the neural response to unchanging retinal stimulation." University College London, Institute of Neurology, as published in *Current Biology* 15, 1296-1300, 26 July. (Brain suppresses awareness of blinking.)

Bruce, T. 2003. *The Death of Right and Wrong: Exposing the Left's Assault on Our Culture and Values*. New York: Crown Three Rivers Press (Prima Lifestyles). (Social impact of narcissism.)

Canfield, J. 2005. *The Success Principles: How to Get from Where You Are to Where You Want to Be*. New York: HarperResource.

Cannon, W. B. [1929] 1989. *Bodily Changes in Hunger, Fear, and Rage: An Account of Recent Researches in the Function of Emotional Excitement*. Delran, NJ: Gryphon Editions, Classics of Psychiatry & Behavioral Sciences Library.

Carroll, L. 2000. *Alice's Adventures in Wonderland and Through the Looking-Glass*. New York: Signet Classics (reissue).

Chandler, S. 2000. *17 Lies That Are Holding You Back and the Truth That Will Set You Free*. Los Angeles: Renaissance Books.

Clayton, P. 2004. *Mind and Emergence: From Quantum to Consciousness*. Oxford, U.K.: Oxford University Press. (Duality, theology, and natural science: a synopsis.)

Chrichton, M. 2004. *State of Fear*. New York: HarperCollins. (The politicalization of science.)

Cohn, M. 2005. "Kamikaze Resurrection." *The Toronto Star*. 6 August. (Pilots now venerated for their noble sacrifice; establishment of Peace Museum for Kamikaze Pilots on Kyushu.)

Deickman, A.J. 1994. "The Role of Intention and Self as Determinants of Consciousness." *Toward A Scientific Basis for Consciousness*. Univ. of Arizona, April.

Descartes, R. 1952. *The Great Books of the Western World*, Vol. 31. Chicago: Encyclopedia Britannica.

Diamond, J. 1979. *Behavioral Kinesiology*. New York: Harper & Rowe.

———. 1979. *Your Body Doesn't Lie*. New York: Warner Books.

Dohrenwend, B., et al. 1992. "Socioeconomic Status and Psychiatric Disorders: Causation vs. Selection." *Science* 255 (5047), 946-952.

Duenwald, M. 2004. "Revenge: The Evidence Mounts." Science, 27 August. (Brain PET scans show activation of pleasure center when punishing perceived wrong doers.)

————. "Vital Signs: Update: Revenge: The Evidence Mounts." *New York Times*, 31 August (People seek revenge for the pleasure it brings. Study confirmed this by brain scans of striatum).

Evans, D., E. Foa, R. Gur, et al (Eds.) *Treating and Preventing Adolescent Mental Health Disorders:What We Know and What We Don't.* Oxford, U.K.: Oxford University Press. (An 800-page major encyclopedic reference.)

Few, B. 2005. "What We Know and What We Don't Know about Consciousness Science." *Journal of Consciousness Studies* 12:7, July, 74-87.

Flurry, G. 2005. "Did The Tsunami Shake Your Faith?" *Philadelphia Trumpet*, February.

Freud, A. 1971 *The Ego and Mechanisms of Defense.* (Rev.). Guilford, CT: International Universities Press.

Ginsberg, C. 2005. "First-Person Experiments." *Journal of Consciousness Studies* 12:2, February, 22-42. (Debate in intellectual/scientific circles about value or validity of subjectivity as a legitimate subject for study.)

Gladwell, M. 2005. *Blink: The Power of Thinking Without Thinking.* New York: Little, Brown and Co.

————. 2000. *The Tipping Point: How Little Things Can Make a Big Difference.* New York: Little, Brown and Co.

Godman, D., ed. 1985. *Be As You Are:The Teachings of Ramana Maharshi.* Boston:Arkana.

Goodheart, G. 1976. *Applied Kinesiology:* 12th ed. Detroit: Goodheart.

Gorner, P. 2005. "Animal Laughter Sheds Light On Emotional Problems in Humans." *Chicago Tribune*, n.d.

Hanson, M. 2005. "Spas Tapping Area's Spirituality." *Arizona Republic*, 6 July.

Harman, W. *The Mind in Matter.* (Video). Petaluma, Calif.: Institute of Noetic Sciences. (New directions in Psi research.) n.d.

Hawkins, D. 2005. *Truth vs. Falsehood: How to Tell the Difference.*Toronto: Axial Publishing Co.

————. 2005. Complete list of works by Dr. Hawkins: http://www. veritaspub.com

————. 2005. *Truth vs. Falsehood*. Chicago: Nightingale-Conant Corp. (Album-DVD+CDs).

————. 2005. "Consciousness Quantified." *Science of Mind* 78:6, June. 14-22.

————. 2005. "Devotional Nonduality" Lecture Series. Sedona, Ariz.: Veritas Publishing.

(Eleven 5-hour CD or DVD albums; video, audio cassettes.) *Vision* (Jan.); *Alignment* (April); *Intention* (May); *Transcending Barriers* (June); *Conviction* (July); *Serenity* (Aug.); *Transcending Obstacles* (Sept.); *Spiritual Traps* (Oct.); *Valid Teachers & Teachings* (Nov.); *God, Religion, & Spirituality* (Dec.)

————. 2004. "Transcending the Mind" Lecture Series. Sedona, Ariz.: Veritas Publishing. (Six 5-hour CD or DVD albums; video, audio cassettes.) *Thought and Ideation* (Feb.); *Emotions and Sensations* (April); *Perception and Positionality* (June); *Identification and Illusion* (August); *Witnessing and Observing* (Oct.); and, *The Ego and the Self* (Dec.).

————. 2004. *The Highest Level of Enlightenment*. Chicago: Nightingale-Conant Corp. (CD, Audiocassettes).

————. 2003. "Homo Spiritus" Lecture Series. Sedona, Ariz.: Veritas Publishing. (Six 5-hour CD or DVD albums; video or audio cassettes.) *Integration of Spirituality and Personal Life* (Feb.); *Spirituality and the World* (April); *Spiritual Community* (June); *Enlightenment* (August); *Realization of the Self as the "I"* (Nov.); and, *Dialogue, Questions and Answers* (Dec.).

————. 2002. "The Way to God" Lecture Series. Sedona, Ariz.: Veritas Publishing. (Twelve 5-hour CD or DVD albums; video or audio cassettes.) 1. *Causality: The Ego's Foundation*; 2. *Radical Subjectivity: The I of Self*; 3. *Levels of Consciousness: Subjective and Social Consequences*; 4. *Positionality and Duality: Transcending the Opposites*; 5. *Perception and Illusion: the Distortions of Reality*; 6. *Realizing the Root of Consciousness: Meditative and Contemplative Techniques*; 7. *The Nature of Divinity: Undoing Religious Fallacies*; 8. *Advaita: The Way to God Through Mind*; 9. *Devotion: The Way to God Through the Heart*; 10. *Karma and the Afterlife*; 11. *God Transcendent and Immanent*; and, 12. *Realization of the Self: The*

Final Moments.

―――. 2002. *Power versus Force: An Anatomy of Consciousness.* (Rev.). Carlsbad, Calif., Brighton-le-Sands, Australia: Hay House.

―――. 2001. *The Eye of the I: From Which Nothing Is Hidden.* Sedona, Ariz.: Veritas Publishing.

―――. 1995. *Power vs. Force: An Anatomy of Consciousness.* Sedona, Ariz.: Veritas Publishing.

―――. 1986. *Office Series: Stress; Health; Spiritual First Aid; Sexuality; The Aging Process; Handling Major Crisis; Worry, Fear and Anxiety; Pain and Suffering; Losing Weight; Depression; Illness and Self-Healing;* and *Alcoholism.* Sedona, Ariz.: Veritas Publishing. (Audio, videocassettes.)

Hodgson, D. 2005. "A Plain Person's Free Will." *Journal of Consciousness Studies* 10:1, January, 3-20.

Hutz, R. 2004. "Studies: Mind Makes and Breaks Its Misery." *Los Angeles Times,* 20 February.

James, W. [1902] 1987. *The Varieties of Religious Experience: A Study in Human Nature.* Reprint. Cambridge, Mass.: Harvard University Press.

Jung, C. J. 1979. *Collected Works.* Princeton, N.J.: Princeton University Press.

Kane, R. 2005. "Free Agency and Laws of Nature." *Journal of Consciousness Studies* 10:1, January, 46-53.

Lama, Dalai, and H. Cutler. 1998. *The Art of Happiness.* New York: Riverhead Hardcover (Penguin Putnam).

Lamsa, G. 1957. *Holy Bible from Ancient Eastern Manuscripts.* Philadelphia: A. J. Holmes Co.

Lawrence, Brother. [1692] 1982. *The Practice of the Presence of God.* New Kensington, Pa.: Whitaker House.

Lehman, C. 2004. "Young Brains Don't Distinguish Real from Televised Violence." *Psychiatric News,* 8 August.

Leiter, L.D. 2004. "Organized Skepticism Revisted." *Journal of Scientific Exploration* 18:4. (List of religious beliefs by disillusionment and membership of PLACT web site.)

Livingstone, I. 2005. "Stress and the Brain." *Physicians' Health Update.* Jan/Feb.

Mackay, C. [1841] 2003. *Extraordinary Popular Delusions & the Madness of Crowds*. Hampshire, U.K: Harriman House.

Maharaj, N. [1973] 1999. *I Am That: Talks with Sri Nisargadatta Maharaj*. (4th Rev. ed.) Bombay: Chetana Private, Ltd.

Maharshi, R. [1972] 2004. *The Spiritual Teaching of Ramana Maharshi*. Boulder, Col.: Shambhala

————. 1955. *Talks with Ramana Maharshi*. (3 vol.) Madras, India: T. N. Venkataraman.

Maslow, A. 1971. *The Farther Reaches of Human Nature*. New York: Viking Press.

————. 1970. "Religious Aspects of Peak-Experiences." *Personality and Religion*. Harper & Row: New York,

Mathew, R. J. 2001. *The True Path: Western Science and the Quest for Yoga*. New York: Perseus Publishing. (Neuroscience demonstrates positive effect on brain physiology to nondominant hemisphere of region, music, art, nature, and altruism.)

Mccain, J. 2005. *Character Is Destiny : Inspiring Stories Every Young Person Should Know and Every Adult Should Remember*. New York: Random House.

Miller, Z. 2005. *A Deficit of Decency*. Macon, Ga.: Stroud and Hall Publishers.

Monroe, R. 1992. *Journeys Out of the Body*. (Rev.) New York: Main Street Books.

Moran, M. 2004. "High Tech Reveals Secrets of the Social Brain." *Psychiatric News*, 2 July.

Oldham, J., D. Skodol, and D. Bander. 2005. *Textbook of Personality Disorders*. Arlington, Va.: American Psychiatry Association Publishing Co.

Partridge, C., Ed. 2003. *UFO Religions*. London: Routledge. (Critique of Unarius Science of Life, Aetherius, Heaven's Gate, Urantia, Nuwaubian Nation, Moors, Ministry of Universal Wisdom, Church of Scientology, Family of God, and others).

Pashler, H. 1999. *The Psychology of Attention*. Cambridge, Mass.: MIT Press. (Reprint ed.)

Person, E., A. Cooper, and G. Gabbard, eds. *The American Psychiatric Publishing Textbook of Psychoanalysis*. Arlington, Va.: American Psychiatric Association Publishing Co.

Paul, P. 2005. "The Power to Uplift." *Time*, 17 January. (Religion has across-the-board benefits including all areas of human life, including happiness.)

Po, Huang, 1958. *The Zen Teachings of Huang Po: On Transmission of Mind*. (J. Blofield, trans.) New York: Grove Press.

Poniewozik J. 2005. "The Art of Unhappiness." *Time*, 17 January. (Search for pleasure in externals of current society's marketing.)

Powell, R. 1999. *Discovering the Realm Beyond Appearance: Pointers to the Inexpressible*. San Diego: Blue Dove Press.

Reiss, S. 2005. "Human Individuality and The Gap Between Science and Religion." *Zygon* 4:1, March, 131-143. (Sixteen personality traits that influence attitudes regarding science and religion.)

Rose, G. 2001. *When You Reach the End of Your Rope...Let Go*. Los Angeles: Awareness Press. ("O-Ring" kinesiological test method.)

Ruell, D. 1980. "Strange Attractors." *Mathematical Intelligence* 2, 126-137 (Nonlinear dynamics, attractor fields.)

Sadlier, S. 2000. *Looking for God: A Seeker's Guide to Religious and Spiritual Groups of the World*. New York: Berkeley Publishing Group, Penguin Putnam.

Schwartz, B. 2005. *The Paradox of Choice: Why More is Less*. New York: Ecco/HarperCollins.

Searle, J. 2000. "Consciousness, Free Action, and The Brain." *Journal of Consciousness Studies* 7:10, 3-22.

Selye, H. 1978. *Stress of Life*. New York: McGraw-Hill.

Shear, K., et al. 2005. "A Treatment of Complicated Grief." *Journal of the American Medical Association* 293: 2601-08.

Sherwood, R. 2005. "Bullying victim boosts bill - UA professor wants to stop harassment." *Arizona Republic*, 20 January. (Bullied victim killed tormentor. Many years later, now a university Professor.)

Sommers, C., and S. Satel. 2005. *One Nation Under Therapy: How The Helping Culture is Eroding Self-Reliance*. New York: St. Martin's Press. (Commentary by resident scholars at American Enterprise Institute.)

Sowers, C. 2005. "Brawls and Kin Event An Issue." *Arizona Republic*. 20 January. (Fight energized by rap music.)

Spongg, J. S. 2005. *The Sins of Scripture: Exposing the Bible's Texts of Hate to Reveal the God of Love*. San Francisco: HarperSanFrancisco.

Stapp, H. 2005. *The Mindful Universe*. www-physics.lbl.gov/~stapp/MUA.pdf (Quantum mechanics, consciousness, attention, and decision making.)

———. 1999. "Attention, Intention, and Will in Quantum Physics." *Journal of Consciousness Studies* 6(8-9), 143-164.

Stein, M. B. 2004. "Anxiety and Depression," in Insights. *Psychological Times*. October Supplement.

Steindl-Rest, D. 2005. "Solving the God Problem." *Spirituality and Health*, June, 56-61.

Suzuki, D. T. 1991. *The Zen Doctrine of No-Mind: The Significance of the Sutra of Hui-Neng*. Boston: Weiser Books.

Szegedy-Maszak, M. 2005. "Mysteries of the Mind." *U.S. News and World Report*, 28 February, 53-61. (Role of the unconscious, which processes 95% of mental activity out of awareness.)

———. 2004. "Conquering Our Phobias." *U.S. News and World Report*, 6 December, 67-74. (NMDA receptor gene in amygdala responds to therapeutic doses of D-cycloserina.)

Tanner, L. 2005. "Parkinson's Disease Drug Linked to Gambling" (and also other addictions). Associated Press, from *Archives of Neurology*, July. (Mirapex. Reports some patients on drugs develop compulsions, such as sex, gambling, shopping, etc.)

Test, M., J. Greenberg, et al. 2005. "Construct Validity of A Measure of Subjective Satisfaction with Life of Adults with Serious Mental Illness." *Psychiatric Services*, March, 292-299.

Tiebout, H. 1999. Collected Writings. *Hazeldon Information and Educational Services*. http://silkworth.net/tiebout/tiebout_papers.html

———. 1949. "The Act of Surrender in the Therapeutic Process." *Quarterly Journal of Studies on Alcohol* 10, 48-58.

Tolson, J. 2005. "Divided We Stand." *US News & World Report*, 42-48. 8 August. (God and country.) *Twelve Steps and Twelve Traditions*. 1996. New York: Alcoholics Anonymous World Services.

Wallis, C. 2005. The New Science of Happiness." *Time*, 17 January, A1-A68. (Social, financial, psychological, religious, and marital aspects, plus brain chemistry.)

Walsh, M. 1991. *Butler's Lives of the Saints: Concise Edition, Revised and*

Updated. San Francisco: HarperSanFranciso.

Watt, D. 2004. "Consciousness, Emotional Self-Regulation with Brain." *Journal of Consciousness Studies* 11:9, 77-82. (Cognition is an evolutionary developmental extension of emotion.)

"Who Wrote the New Testament?" 2005. History Channel. 2 June.

Wilbur, K. 1989. "The Perennial Philosophy" in *The Essential Ken Wilbur*. Boston: Shambhala Publishers.

Wilson, Bill. 1992. *The Language Of The Heart: Bill W's Grapevine Writings*. Marion, Ohio: AA Grapevine, Inc.

ABOUT THE AUTHOR

Biographical and Autobiographical Notes

Dr. Hawkins is an internationally known spiritual teacher, author, and speaker on the subject of advanced spiritual states, consciousness research, and the Realization of the Presence of God as Self.

His published works, as well as recorded lectures, have been widely recognized as unique in that a very advanced state of spiritual awareness occurred in an individual with a scientific and clinical background who was later able to verbalize and explain the unusual phenomenon in a manner that is clear and comprehensible.

The transition from the normal ego-state of mind to its elimination by the Presence is described in the trilogy *Power vs. Force* (1995) which won praise even from Mother Teresa, *The Eye of the I* (2001), and *I: Reality and Subjectivity* (2003), which have been translated into the major languages of the world. *Truth vs. Falsehood: How to Tell the Difference* (2005), *Transcending the Levels of Consciousness* (2006) and *Discovery of the Presence of God: Devotional Nonduality* (2007) continue the exploration of the ego's expressions and inherent limitations and how to transcend them.

The trilogy was preceded by research on the Nature of Consciousness and published as the doctoral dissertation, *Qualitative and Quantitative Analysis and Calibration of the Levels of Human Consciousness* (1995), which correlated the seemingly disparate domains of science and spirituality. This was accomplished by the major discovery of a technique that, for the first time in human history, demonstrated a means to discern truth from falsehood.

The importance of the initial work was given recognition by its very favorable and extensive review in *Brain/Mind Bulletin* and at later presentations such as the International Conference on Science and Consciousness. Many presentations were given to a variety of organizations, spiritual conferences, church groups, nuns, and monks, both nationally and in foreign countries, including the Oxford Forum in England. In the Far East, Dr. Hawkins is a recognized "Teacher of the Way to Enlightenment" ("Tae Ryoung Sun Kak Dosa").

In response to his observation that much spiritual truth has been misunderstood over the ages due to lack of explanation, Dr. Hawkins has presented monthly seminars that provide detailed explanations which are too lengthy to describe in book format. Recordings are available that end with questions and answers, thus providing additional clarification.

The overall design of this lifetime work is to recontextualize the human experience in terms of the evolution of consciousness and to integrate a comprehension of both mind and spirit as expressions of the innate Divinity that is the substrate and ongoing source of life and Existence. This dedication is signified by the statement *"Gloria in Excelsis Deo!"* with which his published works begin and end.

Biographic Summary

Dr. Hawkins has practiced psychiatry since 1952 and is a life member of the American Psychiatric Association and numerous other professional organizations. His national television appearance schedule has included *The McNeil/Leher News Hour, The Barbara Walters Show, The Today Show*, science documentaries, and many others.

He is the author of numerous scientific and spiritual publications, books, CDs, DVDs, and lecture series. Nobelist Linus Pauling coauthored his landmark book, *Orthomolecular Psychiatry*. Dr. Hawkins was a consultant for many years to Episcopal and Catholic Dioceses, monastic orders, and other religions orders.

Dr. Hawkins has lectured widely, with appearances at Westminster Abbey, the Universities of Argentina, Notre Dame, and Michigan; Fordham University and Harvard University; and the Oxford Forum in England. He gave the annual Landsberg Lecture at the University of California Medical School at San Francisco. He is also a consultant to foreign governments on international diplomacy and was instrumental in resolving longstanding conflicts that were major threats to world peace.

In recognition of his contributions to humanity, in 1995, Dr. Hawkins became a knight of the Sovereign Order of the Hospitaliers of St. John of Jerusalem, which was founded in 1077.

Autobiographic Note

While the truths reported in this book were scientifically derived and objectively organized, like all truths, they were first experienced personally. A life-long sequence of intense states of awareness beginning at a young age first inspired and then gave direction to the process of subjective realization that has finally taken form in this series of books.

At age three, there occurred a sudden full consciousness of existence, a nonverbal but complete understanding of the meaning of "I Am," followed immediately by the frightening realization that "I" might not have come into existence at all. This was an instant awakening from oblivion into a conscious awareness, and in that moment, the personal self was born and the duality of "Is" and "Is Not" entered my subjective awareness.

Throughout childhood and early adolescence, the paradox of existence and the question of the reality of the self remained a repeated concern. The personal self would sometimes begin slipping back into a greater impersonal Self, and the initial fear of non-existence—the fundamental fear of nothingness—would recur.

In 1939, as a paperboy with a seventeen-mile bicycle route in rural Wisconsin, on a dark winter's night I was caught miles from home in a twenty-below-zero blizzard. The bicycle fell over on the ice and the fierce wind ripped the newspapers out of the handlebar basket, blowing them across the ice-covered, snowy field. There were tears of frustration and exhaustion and my clothes were frozen stiff. To get out of the wind, I broke through the icy crust of a high snow bank, dug out a space, and crawled into it. Soon the shivering stopped and there was a delicious warmth, and then a state of peace beyond all description. This was accompanied by a suffusion of light and a presence of infinite love that had no beginning and no end and was undifferentiated from my own essence. The physical body and surroundings faded as my awareness was fused with this all-present, illuminated state. The mind grew silent; all thought stopped. An infinite Presence was all that was or could be, beyond all time or description.

After that timelessness, there was suddenly an awareness of someone shaking my knee; then my father's anxious face appeared. There was great reluctance to return to the body and all that that entailed, but because of my father's love and anguish, the Spirit nurtured and reactivated the body. There was compassion for his fear of death, although, at the same time, the concept of death seemed absurd.

This subjective experience was not discussed with anyone since there was no context available from which to describe it. It was not common to hear of spiritual experiences other than those reported in the lives of the saints. But after this experience, the accepted reality of the world began to seem only provisional; traditional religious teachings lost significance and, paradoxically, I became an agnostic. Compared to the light of Divinity that had illuminated all existence, the god of traditional religion shone dully indeed; thus spirituality replaced religion.

During World War II, hazardous duty on a minesweeper often brought close brushes with death, but there was no fear of it. It was as though death had lost its authenticity. After the war, fascinated by the complexities of the mind and wanting to study psychiatry, I worked my way through medical school. My training psychoanalyst, a professor at Columbia University, was also an agnostic; we both took a dim view of religion. The analysis went well, as did my career, and success followed.

I did not, however, settle quietly into professional life. I fell ill with a progressive, fatal illness that did not respond to any treatments available. By age thirty-eight, I was *in extremis* and knew I was about to die. I didn't care about the body, but my spirit was in a state of extreme anguish and despair. As the final moment approached, the thought flashed through my mind, "What if there is a God?" So I called out in prayer, "If there is a God, I ask him to help me now." I surrendered to whatever God there might be and went into oblivion. When I awoke, a transformation of such enormity had taken place that I was struck dumb with awe.

The person I had been no longer existed. There was no personal self or ego, only an Infinite Presence of such unlimited power that it was all that was. This Presence had replaced what had been 'me', and the body and its actions were controlled solely by the Infinite Will of the Presence. The world was illuminated by the clarity of an Infinite Oneness that expressed itself as all things revealed in their infinite beauty and perfection.

As life went on, this stillness persisted. There was no personal will; the physical body went about its business under the direction of the infinitely powerful but exquisitely gentle Will of the Presence. In that state, there was no need to think about anything. All truth was self-evident and no conceptualization was necessary or even possible. At the same time, the physical nervous system felt extremely overtaxed, as though it were carrying far more energy than its circuits had been designed for.

It was not possible to function effectively in the world. All ordinary motivations had disappeared, along with all fear and anxiety. There was nothing to seek, as all was perfect. Fame, success, and money were meaningless. Friends urged the pragmatic return to clinical practice, but there was no ordinary motivation to do so.

There was now the ability to perceive the reality that underlay personalities: the origin of emotional sickness lay in people's belief that they *were* their personalities. And so, as though of its own, a clinical practice resumed and eventually became huge.

People came from all over the United States. The practice had two thousand outpatients, which required more than fifty therapists and other employees, a suite of twenty-five offices, and research and electroencephalic laboratories. There were a thousand new patients a year. In addition, there were appearances on radio and network television shows, as previously mentioned. In 1973, the clinical research was documented in a traditional format in the book, *Orthomolecular Psychiatry*. This work was ten years ahead of its time and created something of a stir.

The overall condition of the nervous system improved slowly, and then another phenomenon commenced. There was a sweet, delicious band of energy continuously flowing up the spine and into the brain where it created an intense sensation of continuous pleasure. Everything in life happened by synchronicity, evolving in perfect harmony; the miraculous was commonplace. The origin of what the world would call miracles was the Presence, not the personal self. What remained of the personal 'me' was only a witness to these phenomena. The greater 'I', deeper than my former self or thoughts, determined all that happened.

The states that were present had been reported by others throughout history and led to the investigation of spiritual teachings, including those of the Buddha, enlightened sages, Huang Po, and more recent teachers such as Ramana Maharshi and Nisargadatta Maharaj. It was thus confirmed that these experiences were not unique. The *Bhagavad-Gita* now made complete sense. At times, the same spiritual ecstasy reported by Sri Rama Krishna and the Christian saints occurred.

Everything and everyone in the world was luminous and exquisitely beautiful. All living beings became Radiant and expressed this Radiance in stillness and splendor. It was apparent that all mankind is actually motivated by inner love but has simply become unaware; most lives are lived as though by sleepers unawakened to the awareness of who they really are. People around me looked as though they were asleep and were incredibly beautiful. It was like being in love with everyone.

It was necessary to stop the habitual practice of meditating for an hour in the morning and then again before dinner because it would intensify the bliss to such an extent that it was not possible to function. An experience similar to the one that had occurred in the snow bank as a boy would recur, and it became increasingly difficult to leave that state and return to the world. The incredible beauty of all things shone forth in all their perfection, and where the world saw ugliness, there was only timeless beauty. This spiritual love suffused all perception, and all boundaries between here and there, or then and now, or separation disappeared.

During the years spent in inner silence, the strength of the Presence grew. Life was no longer personal; a personal will no longer existed. The personal 'I' had become an instrument of the Infinite Presence and went about and did as it was willed. People felt an extraordinary peace in the aura of that Presence. Seekers sought answers but as there was no longer any such individual as David, they were actually finessing answers from their own Self, which was not different from mine. From each person the same Self shone forth from their eyes.

The miraculous happened, beyond ordinary comprehension. Many chronic maladies from which the body had suffered for years disappeared; eyesight spontaneously normalized, and there was no longer a need for the lifetime bifocals.

Occasionally, an exquisitely blissful energy, an Infinite Love, would suddenly begin to radiate from the heart toward the scene of some calamity. Once, while driving on a highway, this exquisite energy began to beam out of the chest. As the car rounded a bend, there was an auto accident; the wheels of the overturned car were still spinning. The energy passed with great intensity into the occupants of the car and then stopped of its own accord. Another time, while I was walking on the streets of a strange city, the energy started to flow down the block ahead and arrived at the scene of an incipient gang fight. The combatants fell back and began to laugh, and again, the energy stopped.

Profound changes of perception came without warning in improbable circumstances. While dining alone at Rothman's on Long Island, the Presence suddenly intensified until every thing and every person, which had appeared as separate in ordinary perception, melted into a timeless universality and oneness. In the motionless Silence, it became obvious that there are no 'events' or 'things' and that nothing actually 'happens' because past, present, and future are merely artifacts of perception, as is the illusion of a separate 'I' being subject to birth and death. As the limited, false self dissolved into the universal Self of its true origin, there was an ineffable sense of having returned home to a state of absolute peace and relief from all suffering. It is only the illusion of individuality that is the origin of all suffering. When one realizes that one is the universe, complete and at one with All That Is, forever without end, then no further suffering is possible.

Patients came from every country in the world, and some were the most hopeless of the hopeless. Grotesque, writhing, wrapped in wet sheets for transport from far-away hospitals they came, hoping for treatment for advanced psychoses and grave, incurable mental disorders. Some were catatonic; many had been mute for years. But in each patient, beneath the crippled appearance, there was the shining essence of love and beauty, perhaps so obscured to ordinary vision that he or she had become totally unloved in this world.

One day a mute catatonic was brought into the hospital in a straitjacket. She had a severe neurological disorder and was unable to stand. Squirming on the floor, she went into spasms and her eyes rolled back in her head. Her hair was matted; she had torn all her clothes and uttered guttural sounds. Her family was fairly wealthy; as a result, over the years she had been seen by innumerable physicians and famous specialists from all over the world. Every treatment had been tried on her and she had been given up as hopeless by the medical profession.

A short, nonverbal question arose: "What do you want done with her, God?" Then came the realization that she just needed to be loved, that was all. Her inner self shone through her eyes and the Self connected with that loving essence. In that second, she was healed by her own recognition of who she really was; what happened to her mind or body didn't matter to her any longer.

This, in essence, occurred with countless patients. Some recovered in the eyes of the world and some did not, but whether a clinical recovery ensued didn't matter any longer to the patients. Their inner agony was over. As they felt loved and at peace within, their pain stopped. This phenomenon can only be explained by saying that the Compassion of the Presence recontextualized each patient's reality so that he or she experienced healing on a level that transcended the world and its appearances. The inner peace of the Self encompassed us beyond time and identity.

It was clear that all pain and suffering arises solely from the ego and not from God. This truth was silently communicated to the minds of the patients. This was the mental block in another mute catatonic who had not spoken in many years. The Self said to him through mind, "You're blaming God for what your ego has done to you." He jumped off the floor and began to speak, much to the shock of the nurse who witnessed the incident.

The work became increasingly taxing and eventually overwhelming. Patients were backed up, waiting for beds to open although the hospital had built an extra ward to house them. There was an enormous frustration in that the human suffering could be countered in only one patient at a time. It was like bailing out the sea. It seemed that there must be some other way to address the causes of the common malaise, the endless stream of spiritual distress and human suffering.

This led to the study of the physiological response (muscle testing), which revealed an amazing discovery. It was the 'wormhole' between two universes—the physical world and the world of the mind and spirit—an interface between dimensions. In a world full of sleepers lost from their source, here was a tool to recover, and demonstrate for all to see, that lost connection with the higher reality. This led to the testing of every substance, thought, and concept that could be brought to mind. The endeavor was aided by my students and research assistants. Then a major discovery was made: whereas all subjects went weak from negative stimuli, such as fluorescent lights, pesticides, and artificial sweeteners, students of spiritual disciplines who had advanced their levels of awareness did not go weak as did ordinary people. Something important and decisive had shifted in their consciousness. It apparently occurred as they realized they were not at the mercy of the world but rather affected only by what their minds believed. Perhaps the very process of progress toward enlightenment could be shown to increase man's ability to resist the vicissitudes of existence, including illness.

The Self had the capacity to change things in the world by merely envisioning them; Love changed the world each time it replaced non-love. The entire scheme of civilization could be profoundly altered by focusing this power of love at a very specific point. Whenever this happened, history bifurcated down new roads.

It now appeared that these crucial insights could not only be communicated with the world but also visibly and irrefutably demonstrated. It seemed that the great tragedy of human life had always been that the psyche is so easily deceived; discord and strife have been the inevitable consequence of mankind's inability to distinguish the false from the true. But here was an answer to this fundamental dilemma, a way to recontextualize the nature of consciousness itself and make explicable that which otherwise could only be inferred.

It was time to leave life in New York, with its city apartment and home on Long Island, for something more important. It was necessary to perfect 'myself' as an instrument. This necessitated leaving that world and everything in it, replacing it with a reclusive life in a small town where the next seven years were spent in meditation and study.

Overpowering states of bliss returned unsought,

and eventually, there was the need to learn how to be in the Divine Presence and still function in the world. The mind had lost track of what was happening in the world at large. In order to do research and writing, it was necessary to stop all spiritual practice and focus on the world of form. Reading the newspaper and watching television helped to catch up on the story of who was who, the major events, and the nature of the current social dialogue.

Exceptional subjective experiences of truth, which are the province of the mystic who affects all mankind by sending forth spiritual energy into the collective consciousness, are not understandable by the majority of mankind and are therefore of limited meaning except to other spiritual seekers. This led to an effort to be ordinary, because just being ordinary in itself is an expression of Divinity; the truth of one's real self can be discovered through the pathway of everyday life. To live with care and kindness is all that is necessary. The rest reveals itself in due time. The commonplace and God are not distinct.

And so, after a long circular journey of the spirit, there was a return to the most important work, which was to try to bring the Presence at least a little closer to the grasp of as many fellow beings as possible.

––––––

The Presence is silent and conveys a state of peace that is the space in which and by which all is and has its existence and experience. It is infinitely gentle and yet like a rock. With it, all fear disappears. Spiritual joy occurs on a quiet level of inexplicable ecstasy. Because the experience of time stops, there are no apprehension or regret, no pain or anticipation; the source of joy is unending and ever present. With no beginning or ending, there is no loss or grief or desire. Nothing needs to be done; everything is already perfect and complete.

When time stops, all problems disappear; they are merely artifacts of a point of perception. As the Presence prevails, there is no further identification with the body or mind. When the mind grows silent, the thought "I Am" also disappears, and Pure Awareness shines forth to illuminate what one is, was, and always will be, beyond all worlds and all universes, beyond time, and therefore without beginning or end.

People wonder, "How does one reach this state of awareness," but few follow the steps because they are so simple. First, the desire to reach that state was intense. Then began the discipline to act with constant and universal forgiveness and gentleness, without exception. One has to be compassionate towards everything, including one's own self and thoughts. Next came a willingness to hold desires in abeyance and surrender personal will at every moment. As each thought, feeling, desire, or deed was surrendered to God, the mind became progressively silent. At first, it released whole stories and paragraphs, then ideas and concepts. As one lets go of wanting to own these thoughts, they no longer reach such elaboration and begin to fragment while only half formed. Finally, it was possible to turn over the energy behind thought itself before it even became thought.

The task of constant and unrelenting fixity of focus, allowing not even a moment of distraction from meditation, continued while doing ordinary activities. At first, this seemed very difficult, but as time went on, it became habitual, automatic, requiring less and less effort, and finally, it was effortless. The process is like a rocket leaving the earth. At first, it requires enormous power, then less and less as it leaves the earth's gravitational field, and finally, it moves through space under its own momentum.

Suddenly, without warning, a shift in awareness occurred and the Presence was there, unmistakable and all encompassing. There were a few moments of apprehension as the self died, and then the absoluteness of the Presence inspired a flash of awe. This breakthrough was spectacular, more intense than anything before. It has no counterpart in ordinary experience. The profound shock was cushioned by the love that is with the Presence. Without the support and protection of that love, one would be annihilated.

There followed a moment of terror as the ego clung to its existence, fearing it would become nothingness. Instead, as it died, it was replaced by the Self as Everythingness, the All in which everything is known and obvious in its perfect expression of its own essence. With nonlocality came the awareness that one is all that ever was or can be. One is total and complete, beyond all identities, beyond all gender, beyond even humanness itself. One need never again fear suffering and death.

What happens to the body from this point is immaterial. At certain levels of spiritual awareness, ailments of the body heal or spontaneously disappear. But in the absolute state, such considerations are irrelevant. The body will run its predicted course and then return from whence it came. It is a matter of no importance; one is unaffected. The body appears as an 'it' rather than as a 'me' as another object, like the furniture in a room. It may seem comical that people still address the body as though it were the individual 'you', but there is no way to explain this state of awareness to the unaware. It is best to just go on about one's business and allow Providence to handle the social adjustment. However, as one reaches bliss, it is very difficult to conceal that state of intense ecstasy. The world may be dazzled, and people may come from far and wide to be in the accompanying aura. Spiritual seekers and the spiritually curious may be attracted, as may be the very ill who are seeking miracles. One may become a magnet and a source of joy to them. Commonly, there is a desire at this point to share this state with others and to use it for the benefit of all.

The ecstasy that accompanies this condition is not absolutely stable; there are also moments of great agony. The most intense occur when the state fluctuates and suddenly ceases for no apparent reason. These times bring on periods of intense despair and a fear that one has been forsaken by the Presence. These falls make the path arduous, and to surmount these reversals requires great will. It finally becomes obvious that one must transcend this level or constantly suffer excruciating 'descents from grace'. The glory of ecstasy, then, has to be relinquished as one enters upon the arduous task of transcending duality until one is beyond all oppositions and their conflicting pulls. But while it is one thing to happily give up the iron chains of the ego, it is quite another to abandon the golden chains of ecstatic joy. It feels as though one is giving up God, and a new level of fear arises, never before anticipated. This is the final terror of absolute aloneness.

To the ego, the fear of nonexistence was formidable, and it drew back from it repeatedly as it seemed to approach. The purpose of the agonies and the dark nights of the soul then became apparent. They are so intolerable that their exquisite pain spurs one on to the extreme effort required to surmount them. When vacillation between heaven and hell becomes unendurable, the desire for existence itself has to be surrendered. Only once this is done may one finally move beyond the duality of Allness versus Nothingness, beyond existence or nonexistence. This culmination of the inner work is the most difficult phase, the ultimate watershed, where one is starkly aware that the illusion of existence one here transcends is irrevocable. There is no returning from this step, and this specter of irreversibility makes this last barrier appear to be the most formidable choice of all.

But, in fact, in this final apocalypse of the self, the dissolution of the sole remaining duality of existence and nonexistence-identity itself-dissolves in Universal Divinity, and no individual consciousness is left to choose. The last step, then, is taken by God.

—*David R. Hawkins*

Hay House Titles of Related Interest

We hope you enjoyed this Hay House book. If you'd like to receive our online catalog featuring additional information on Hay House books and products, or if you'd like to find out more about the Hay Foundation, please contact:

Hay House, Inc., P.O. Box 5100, Carlsbad, CA 92018-5100
(760) 431-7695 or (800) 654-5126
(760) 431-6948 (fax) or (800) 650-5115 (fax)
www.hayhouse.com® • www.hayfoundation.org

———

Published in Australia by: Hay House Australia Pty. Ltd.,
18/36 Ralph St., Alexandria NSW 2015
Phone: 612-9669-4299 • *Fax:* 612-9669-4144
www.hayhouse.com.au

Published in the United Kingdom by: Hay House UK, Ltd.,
The Sixth Floor, Watson House, 54 Baker Street, London W1U 7BU
Phone: +44 (0)20 3927 7290 • *Fax:* +44 (0)20 3927 7291
www.hayhouse.co.uk

Published in India by: Hay House Publishers India,
Muskaan Complex, Plot No. 3, B-2, Vasant Kunj, New Delhi 110 070
Phone: 91-11-4176-1620 • *Fax:* 91-11-4176-1630
www.hayhouse.co.in

———

Access New Knowledge.
Anytime. Anywhere.

Learn and evolve at your own pace
with the world's leading experts.

www.hayhouseU.com